FRENCH TRAITS

FRENCH TRAITS

AN ESSAY IN COMPARATIVE CRITICISM

BY

W. C. BROWNELL

NEW YORK
CHARLES SCRIBNER'S SONS
1918

Copyright, 1888, 1889, by
CHARLES SCRIBNER'S SONS

Copyright, 1917, by
W. C. BROWNELL

TO RICHARD WHITEING

CONTENTS

I

THE SOCIAL INSTINCT

THE SOCIAL INSTINCT

THE apparent contrast between modern Frenchmen and the crusaders, between the " café-haunt-
ers " and the cathedral-builders, stimulates speculation as to whether the present interest of France is
commensurate with her historic importance. The
noblest monuments in the world attest the part she
once played in the drama of civilization. Were
Rheims and Amiens, Bourges and Beauvais, the embodied aspiration of the race whose activities one
observes along the Paris boulevards to-day? Are
there any signs in the actual Normandy of the spirit
which dotted the North coast with the stone temples
beside which their differentiation across the Channel
seems often flimsy and superficial? Or, at the other
end of France, as one descends the magnificent
thoroughfare which consoles the Marseillais for the
greater general splendor of Paris, does any linger-
ing reminiscence reach one of the instinct which
covered the Midi with the massive monuments of
Provençal Romanesque? As one observes the audience which listens to Guignol, it seems fabulous
that the Frank ever crossed the Rhine. As one
notes the gayety, the *bonhomie*, the bright gracious-

ness of a Parisian or provincial crowd, the Merovingian epoch seems a myth. Is there any traceable relationship between St. Remy at Rheims and St. Augustin at Paris, between St. Jean at Lyons and the Nouvel Opéra, between the Sainte Chapelle and the Panthéon? The difference is as vast as that between gloom and gayety, between the grandiose and the familiar, the mystic and the rational. From the Palace of the Popes at Avignon to the Marseilles Cannebière, from the Chartres sculpture to M. Falguière, from Plessis-les-Tours to the Tuileries, is a long way. The contrast seems not in epoch, but in character. In no other country is it marked in anything like the same degree. In England the same character is traceable in the London Law Courts and the ruins of Kenilworth ; Oxford Street and Piccadilly but deepen the impression of Chester and Warwick ; there is a subtle sympathy between Westminster and St. Paul's. One is sure that the ancestors of the shopmen in the Burlington Arcade and of the owners of the West End palaces fought side by side at Crécy and Poictiers, where they occupied pretty much the same reciprocal relations and entertained, *mutatis mutandis*, pretty much the same notions of life, art, and foreigners. In Germany it is not very different. The cavalrymen of 1870–71, who sabred the damask and stole the clocks of the French châteaux, were lineal descendants of the lanzknechts of the Rhine. Just as, no doubt, German "probity," directness, and simplicity remain what they were in the time of Luther—not to mention that of Arminius, whom even at this distance of time Professor Mommsen finds it difficult to refer to without emotion. Cologne Cathedral was finished within the decade, after the original designs. Bavaria goes wild to-day over the stories of the meister-singers. Even Dresden figurines and Saxon baroque in general are gothic in the last analysis— quite without the grace born of the Renaissance passion for the beautiful, and still as clumsy as perfected knowledge will permit. The succession to Winckelmann is certainly as little frivolous as Burgkmair and Schongauer, and German criticism is still metaphysical and scholastic. Italy, from the time of the Pisans down to the decline of the high Renaissance, and from the return of the popes to the French Revolution, visibly illustrates a natural evolution. The same may be said of Spain. And since the Revolution, whatever is distinctly modern in Italian or Spanish character and culture, any note of discordant modification, is to be attributed in no small degree to the French occupation. Only in France does there seem to be a break.

The times change, and the most acutely alive change most in them. Since the days of Louis le Gros, when the national unity began, France has most conspicuously of all nations changed with the epoch ; in those successive readjustments which we call progress she has almost invariably been in the lead. She was the star of the ages of faith as she is the light of the age of fellowship. The contrast between her actual self and her monuments is, therefore, most striking ; but at the same time it is superficial only and perfectly explicable. And its explanation gives the key to French character ; for there is one instinct of human nature, one aspiration of the mind, which France has incarnated with unbroken continuity from the first—since there was a France at all France has embodied the *social instinct*. It was this instinct which finally triumphed over the barbaric Frankish personality ; which during the panic and individualism of the Middle Ages took refuge in the only haven sympathetically disposed to harbor it and produced the finest monuments of Europe by the force of spiritual solidarity ; which, so soon as the time was ripe, extended itself temporally and created a civil organism that rescued the human spirit from servitude, and which, finally, in the great transformation of the Revolution, obtained the noblest victory over the forces of anarchy and unreason that history records. Thus in the days when the mediæval spirit of authority, of concentration, of asceticism, of individualism was almost all-powerful in Europe, the French social instinct triumphed in the only sphere in which exalted effort was productive ; and now that this instinct has been brought into harmony with the Time-Spirit, now that solidarity is not only secularized but popularized, France illustrates its new phases as perfectly as she did the old. There has really been no break in her historic continuity. The cathedrals are not feudal. They were the product of a spirit partly ecclesiastical, partly secular, but always social—the true Gallo-Roman spirit which, great as was the perfection attained by German feudalism in France, constantly struggled against and finally conquered its foreign Frankish foe. The cathedrals, in a word, are merely the bridge by which France clears the Middle Age. They are grandiose links in the chain which unites the Revolution to the twelfth century communal movement for *Bull !* equality. They mark a phase of the long struggle of solidarity with anarchic forces, as do the anti-ecclesiastical movement of Philippe-le-Bel, the national condensation of Louis XI., the Renaissance reversion to classic social as well as artistic ideals, and finally the burial at the Revolution of moral and material Byzantinism.

There is accordingly even a closer spiritual identity between the Nouvel Opéra and Notre Dame de Paris than there is, for example, between the English Cathedral and its perfunctory reproduction in the British Houses of Parliament—the identity of instinct differing only in phase. And this instinct is, as I said, the key to French character and the most conspicuous trait whereby French character differs from our own. French history is the history of this instinct. The fusion of Gallic characteristics with Roman institutions apparently developed a disposition of Athenian interdependence and solidarity, all of whose accomplishments were to be organically wrought, and whose failures were to come from the subordination of the individual member involved in the supremacy of the general structure. The Catholic Church came next and contributed an influence to the moulding of modern France which it is impossible not to recognize on every hand.

No one can pass from a Protestant to a Catholic country without being struck by the numerous characteristic differences which force themselves upon the sense and the mind. The two shores of the English Channel, of Lake Geneva, of the Hollandsch Diep, the two sides of the Vosges—wherever the two systems come into contact the contrast is marked. To a Protestant entering France the influence of Catholicism is especially striking, because in France, owing to French clearness and method, what elsewhere are only Latin tendencies become perfectly developed traits. It is indefinite at first, but very sensible nevertheless. Long familiarity deepens the impression. The absence of the individual spirit, the absence of the sense of personal responsibility, the social interdependence of people, the respect for public opinion, the consequent consideration for others, the free play of mind compatible only with a certain carelessness as to deductions, and a confidence that society in general will see to it that the world roll on even if one's own logic be imperfect—a dozen traits characteristic and cardinal one associates at once with the influence of the Catholic Church. The great work of the Reformation was to quicken the sense of personal responsibility by awakening the conscience. The predominant influence of the Catholic Church has been to enforce the sense of social interdependence among men, to destroy individualism by organizing and systematizing, and then itself assuming entire charge of the domain of the conscience. The conscience is, of course, the most important of the springs of human action. In proportion as the individual charges himself with soliciting and following its oracles his character is fortified and concentrated, his individuality intensified. In proportion as he resigns this charge into other hands, he places the true centre of his moral nature outside himself, his individuality becomes less marked, and his relations to others more sensible, more important. Is he not, indeed, vitally connected with something external which charges itself with the direction of the most powerful moral agent of his nature, and are not all his fellows thus connected also? The bond of union between men is thus infinitely stronger in Catholic communities than in Protestant, and in this way directly comes about, by gentle gradations of logical consistency, that considerateness, that deference, that sense of dependence upon others, that feeling that one's true centre is outside of one and in a safer place, so to speak, the respect for public opinion, the harmony with one's time and environment—all the fruits in fine of the social instinct re-enforced by religious system.

This is the direct, sensible influence of Catholicism, as on the other hand the direct, sensible influence of Protestantism has been to isolate and to individualize. But the indirect influence of each system for being less sensible is not the less real or important, and the indirect influence of Catholicism has tended to social expansion as potently as its direct influence to social concert. Renunciation and asceticism, ecstacy and elevation, the mediæval virtues, in fact, are often called especially Catholic virtues. They are, indeed, eminently virtues of the Catholic Church, but they have never been virtues of a Catholic society. Renunciation shines out beautifully and bountifully from the pages of the Legends of the Saints. History is full of instances of the divine self-forgetting of monks and nuns. Even Catholic fanaticism has always been marked by it. Ignatius had as much of it in his way as St. Theresa. But in Catholic societies themselves, the Catholic Church in this regard has always strictly separated itself from the world. It has been in them, but not of them. It has, so to speak, organized its renunciation, and its organized renunciation has sold indulgences to society in general. The result has been, of course, that society in general—that is to say, everyone with no clear vocation for thorough-going renunciation—improves its opportunity and uses its indulgences freely. That in France it never did, and certainly does not now, use these to their utmost limit is due to the native French talent for sobriety, but it is evident

that the instinct for social expansion has been fortified by Catholicism, as it has been repressed by
Protestantism, in the same way that one system has
quickened and the other lessened the sense of mutual interdependence among men. Just as, in contrast to the separatism of Protestantism, Catholicism
has tended to unify and nationalize, to render organic
the structure of society, so it has tended to develop
all those sides of man's nature which relate him to
the external world, and we have in France, as a result in great part of Catholic influences, not only a
people intensely organic and *solidaire*, but a people
possessed of the epicurean rather than the ascetic
ideal in morals, its unmoral nature harmoniously
evolved without restraint from a higher spiritual
law, its intelligence so highly cultivated as sometimes to supplant the soul in the sphere of sentiment, and its social and mutual activities carried to
an extent and refined in a degree of which we have
ordinarily a very inadequate idea.

The preponderance thus of unifying over controversial and separatist forces has rendered it the
most homogeneous in the world, and, accordingly,
if it be ever excusable to speak of a people in the
mass, it is excusable in the case of the French.
What one notes in the individual is more than anywhere else apt to be a national trait. There is, of
course, differentiation enough, but it begins further
along than with us, and is structural rather than
fortuitous. They vary by types rather than by

units.   The class only is specialized.   Their homogeneousness is not uniformity, but it is divided
rather in the details than in the grand construction.
The Parisians so bore each other often by force of
mutual sympathies and identical ideas, that *ennui*
itself has probably had a large share in the variety
of their political experimentation and in the evolution of their elaborate epicureanism.   They are
infinitely civilized.   Individuals are of less import
than the relations between them; hence manners
and art.   Character counts less than capacity; hence
the worship of the intelligence.   They have little or
none of our introspectiveness.   They understand
themselves thoroughly, but by instinct, and not as
the result of examination.   They are far more interested in you than in themselves, and contemplate
you much more closely.   This indeed they do very
narrowly, and an American who is himself enough
addicted to "taking notes" to remark the practice
under its skilful veil of interest and civility is apt to
find it irksome.   But even in your personality their
interest is never pushed to the extent of considering such of its complexities as arise from counter-
currents of mind and feeling and will—such as a
writer like George Eliot, for instance, or Hawthorne,
or Thomas Hardy, is so greatly attracted by.   They
seem always to fancy you a "plain case," and only
solicitous to learn what label to take from their
assortment (an assortment, by the way, far more
comprehensive than any other people's) with which

to ticket you. If your complexity is the chief thing
about you, they ticket you "fin" (for which our
word is "subtle"), and so pigeon-hole you without
further examination. It is humiliating to the American sense to note how often this is really all that
the case calls for; the suggestion is irresistible
that much of our personal "hair-splitting" is as
nebulously unprofitable as the refinements of Teutonic metaphysics. With the French, at all events,
the process of working out any social equation is
always marked by the use of the personal factor as
a known term. "X" is never you, but your capacities, your manifestations, what you, with your
Anglo-Saxon self-concentration, describe as your
mere "phenomena."

Idiosyncrasy, in a word, has little interest for
them. Until it has been embalmed in legend it is
rather resented than tolerated, even in its grandiose
manifestations. There is little hero-worship that is
either blind or vague. There is absolutely no
French sympathy with the notion that heroes are
made of essentially different stuff from the rest of
mankind. Great men are, if "nobler brothers,"
most of all "one in blood;" and it is by sufferance
only that they are permitted to "lord it o'er" their
fellows, in Sterling's phrase, by either "looks of
beauty" or "words of good." There is the Hugo,
the Millet, as there was the Napoleonic *légende*, but
their inspiration is mainly decorous and conformed
to the prevalent regard for the fitness of things

rather than emotionally sincere. "Cher maître" is a title borne by scores. M. Dumas *fils* is a "cher maître." And the popularity of this attitude is ascribable to the vanity which seeks association or identification with celebrity, not at all to the Germanic quality of admiration. Of Goethe's three kinds of reverence—for what is above us, for our equals, and for what is beneath us—the second only, that is to say what is more properly called deference, is commonly illustrated by Frenchmen. Such a book as Mr. Peter Bayne's "Lessons from my Masters" would be a solecism in France. The proceedings of the Browning Society would excite amazement. The spirit of the Molièristes and that of the Goethe adorers are in complete contrast. The intense emotion which led one of Carlyle's secretaries publicly to express a sense of spiritual indebtedness to him next after his "Lord and Saviour, Jesus Christ," would seem whimsically excessive. No Frenchman so surrenders himself to any personal influence; awe and abjectness are equally un-French. The anecdote of one contemporary English poet going, footstool in hand, to sit at the feet of another, indicates rather the French order of hero-worship, which if less cockney in its expression is characterized by the same sense of the importance of the impersonal function discharged in common by the hero and his worshipper.

Character, being thus less considered, develops less energy. "That which all things tend to educe

—which freedom, cultivation, intercourse, revolutions go to form and deliver—is character," says Emerson, with transcendental confidence. Yes! but not character as we understand it, not individual character independent of its environment. Freedom goes to form and deliver that, most assuredly, but not necessarily intercourse, cultivation, revolutions—of which the French have had far more than they have had of freedom. "Trust thyself!—every heart vibrates to that iron string." In France every heart thus vibrates only when the said string sounds a harmonious strain in concerted music. "The giants must live apart. The kings can have no company," says Thackeray. In France the giants are as rare as the pygmies. The social instinct is inimical to both. The great Frenchmen, it has been acidly remarked, are apt to be Italians, and in effect the way in which individual Italians and the entire French people have united, at various epochs in history, in the accomplishment of great works is exceedingly instructive as to the tendencies of either civilization. The great Frenchmen are generally great on their human and social sides, by distinction rather than by energy. They are never monsters. No ascetics are numbered among them. Their minds are lofty, but they are not self-gathered in them. Even the French heroes have less egoism than vanity ; it is Henry IV., not Napoleon, that is truly national. And, as history reminds us, they are not found isolated but in groups, whose members are mutually dependent and supporting. But for this, and for the general elevation of the subsidiary groups around them, the eminence of many of them would be more conspicuous than it is; many merely eminent names in French history would shine heroic and grandiose on the roll of almost any other nation, because of this difference in perspective. But the great accomplishments of France have, in general, been the work rather of the nation than of those heroes who "look at the stars with an answering ray." Wherever the task of progress has demanded intellectual inspiration or moral energy, it is the Spaniard, the Italian, the Englishman who excels, but it is the French people entire. The individual work of its exceptional volcanic spirits like Mirabeau, like Danton, is apt to be incomplete. Solider building is done by the nation organized—despotically under the Corsican Bonaparte, autonomously under the Genoese Gambetta. The Revolution, the conquering of Europe, the freeing of the human spirit, which the kings of the Continent and the aristocracy of England could only temporarily reimprison, in 1815, at Vienna, were Titanic works wrought by the social instinct of the most completely organic people in history.

In the familiar and every-day, as well as in the exceptional and heroic work of life, the power and importance of the social instinct show themselves in France in a way of which we have no experience.

The relations between individuals being exalted into a distinct social force, apart from the personalities therewith connected, these relations are regulated, utilized, and decorated to very noteworthy ends. They are used with us mainly for business purposes; it is chiefly, perhaps, the commercial traveller who exploits them. The rest of us enjoy them or neglect them as the case may be, but take no thought to organize and direct them. The social instinct, nevertheless, being native to man, even to man in our environment of riotous individualism, it incurs the risk of becoming depraved if it be not developed. This, indeed, is its very frequent fate in many of our communities, and the amount of positive debauchery due to a perversion of this instinct, which perversion is itself due to neglect, is very suggestive. And positive debauchery aside, the pathetic failure of genial but weak natures that in a truly social *milieu* would certainly have succeeded is still more significant because it is still more hopeless. In France social capacity is a principal part of the youth's equipment for his journey through life. In virtue of it young men rise in the world, obtain " protection," and acquire vantage ground. With us, hitherto, a turn for what is called society is fully as likely to be a bar as an aid to a young man's success, being accepted often as indicating frivolity, if not extravagance and dissipation, and, at all events, hostile to the industry and severe application which pass for credentials of

2

solidity. Success in an industrial society does not depend on the favor of women, and we are wont a little to contemn the large and interesting class of *petits jeunes gens* of which French society makes so much. On the other hand, we have many accentuated types wholly peculiar to ourselves and generated by the struggle of the ambitious and intensely concentrated individual with an amorphous and undeveloped society which he can in a measure mould as well as figure in, provided only his energy be sufficient to the task. Never was there such a field for the parvenu as that we furnish. Never was the parvenu so really estimable and distinguished a person. With energy and persistence, a man who only yesterday ate with his knife may to-morrow lay down rules of etiquette, a beneficiary dispense charity, a country merchant regulate a railway system—merely by the force through which strenuous personality imposes itself on a society whose solidarity is too feeble to protect it against assault from without and treachery from within. In most instances, indeed, our pretense of solidarity is pure snobbishness, and our parvenus really—as was said of Napoleon—*arrivés.*

The Frenchman's instincts and impulses receive, on the contrary, a social rather than an egoistic development. His position in the world, the esteem of his neighbors, everything, in fact, except looking for the resurrection of the dead, which prevents him from being of all men most miserable, are ob-

tained by a far more complex exercise of talent than
that ascetic concentration of effort known among us
as "looking out for Number One." Look out for
"Number One," the Frenchman certainly does in the
most unflinching and devoted manner ; but the process is with him adapted to gregarious rather than
insulated conditions. He easily spares more time
from business than we do from idling to expend in
the expansiveness necessary for elaborate social
development ; furthermore, social conditions with
him prevent time so expended from being, even in
an indirect sense, wasted, so that he is never more
profitably occupied than when he is, so to speak,
least concentrated. He conquers in love, war,
affairs, and society, not as with us, with the Germanic peoples generally, in virtue of strenuous
personality, but through many-sidedness, appreci-
ativeness, perception, sympathy—in a word, less by
energy than by intelligence. And this intelligence
itself is socially developed. The late M. Caro said
of the Abbé Roux that his genius, "formed in solitude, outside of all intellectual commerce, of all
expansion," is characterized by "an inner spring
and source of ideas in their native state, charged
with parasitical elements neither purged by essay nor
filtered by discussion ; by ignorance which aston-
ishes in connection with certain points of view truly
striking ; by faults of taste unavoidable in the absence of all exterior control and points of comparison ; by a certain awkwardness, sometimes a singular

want of discernment, and hence a defect of proportion and development between thoughts really new and those which seem so only to the eyes of the artist who believes himself to have discovered them." One could not better describe the traits which, in our life, as well as in our literature, our individualism throws into sharp relief in contrast with those of the French.

In his "Pensées d'un Solitaire" the Abbé Roux himself observes that "men of talent, so long as they have only intuitive experiences, are bound to commit follies," and the universal prevalence of this conviction in France secures great openness and spiritual reciprocity. There are no people whom it is "difficult to know," who are very "reserved" in the presence of strangers, who are particularly "reticent" about their own affairs, who have "secrets" and resent familiarity. A high development of the social instinct makes short work of these varieties of a type well known and rather highly esteemed among ourselves. It unmasks them at once as in some sort pretenders, as people who devote a large share of their attention, while the battle of life is raging, to keeping open the communications in their rear, either for opportunities of retreat or in order to execute some brilliant flank movement. In other words, either their self-distrust or their self-conceit is shown to be excessive. In France the battle of life is, socially speaking, nearly a pure figure of speech. The foe is at any rate impersonal.

No one's individual attitude is hostile or suspicious. There is none of the exciting competition which with us exists among friendly rivals even. Hence, beyond those matters which are essentially private, being nobody's business and rightfully appealing to nobody's interest, people generally have nothing to conceal. The *milieu* is not only friendly, but it is intelligent. Neither timidity nor strategy, of the kind we are familiar with, would avail much with it. It would be impossible to disguise them. The "reserve" of our young ladies, their true opinions on public questions, the secret they are thinking about, which young men are rewarded by being permitted gradually to discover as they become better and better acquainted, are, for example, peculiar to ourselves ; but in France, especially, they would be purposeless for the same reason that inquiries as to the secrets of freemasonry or the composition of patent medicines are—namely, not because they are undiscoverable, but because what is worth knowing about them can be divined. There is, of course, the contrast between the *bavard* and the *nature condensée*, but the latter is none the less a frank and not a secretive nature. There are no prigs.

Competition is a great word with us, but socially it implies a solecism. It means egoism, and the difference between our individualism and French social interdependence is very well shown in the correspondence of our egoism to French vanity.

How far egoism may be carried, what bleakness it may introduce into life, and how it may blight existence one may easily guess; but its baleful influence has never been so vividly shown as in that very remarkable book published a few years ago and entitled "The Story of a Country Town." A more important contribution to sociology has not been made within the decade. No one can have read it without being affected by its gloom, its moral squalor, its ashen tone. There is nothing more depressing in Russian fiction, and, like Russian fiction, it is wholly unfactitious. It is a picture entirely typical, and typical of one hesitates to say how many American communities. And no one can have read it attentively without perceiving that the secret of its dreariness is its picture of the excesses of individualism. Lack of sympathy with each other; a narrow and degrading struggle for "success;" a crying competition; a dull, leaden introspection; no community of interest, material or ideal, except of a grossly material religious ideality; duty ignorantly conceived; sacrifice needlessly made; generous impulses leading nowhither, and elevated effort clogged by the absence of worthy ends; the human spirit, in fine, thrown back on itself and operating, so to speak, *in vacuo*; and the partly tragic, chiefly vulgar, wholly sterile conclusion of all this Mr. Howe has painted for us with a master-hand. Beside his picture the wild orgies and bacchanalian frenzy of a society in decadence appear sane.

Beside it, at all events, French vanity seems anti-
septic. Vanity has its origin in approbativeness,
and to study to please is a safeguard against many
evils in morals as well as in manners. It is, to be
sure, mainly through their vanity that the French
show to us their weak side. It is a characteristic
that in excess causes character to atrophy. It
stimulates cowardice in the face of ridicule, and
leads infallibly to puerile confusions of shadow and
substance. And the French have far more of it
than any other people. Stendhal never tires of
reproaching his countrymen with it, and declares it
responsible for his exile in Italy. Only the other
day M. Albert Wolff, whose competence is conspicuous, declared it epidemic, affirming French society
entire to be *frappée par le fléau de la vanité*. But
vanity as the French possess it, and modified as it
is by their all-informing intelligence, is a not too
unpleasant, as it is an inevitable, concomitant of the
spirit of society. Its absence would mean, logically,
infinitely more loss than gain in social relations.
"Nothing," says Voltaire, "is so disagreeable as to
be obscurely hanged," and together with its obvious
vanity it is impossible not to see in the remark a
feeling of fraternity as well.

In France, indeed, fraternity is as it were in the
air. This sentiment, which is the poetic side of the
notion of equality, to which the French have been
so profoundly attached since the very beginnings of
modern society, during the break-up of the Middle

Ages, is to be read in the expression and demeanor
of everyone to be met with in the streets as unmistakably as it is stamped on all the buildings belonging to the state. Insensibly you find yourself setting out with the feeling that every stranger is ami-
cably disposed. Arriving from London, either at
Paris or at the smallest provincial town—Calais itself, say—the absence of individual competition, of
personal preoccupation, of all the varied inhospitality,
the stony, inaccessible self-absorption which depress
the stranger in London whenever he is out of hail
of an acquaintance, the conspicuous amenity everywhere, suffuse with a profoundly grateful warmth
the very cockles of the American's heart. At first
it seems as if all the world were really one's friends.
People with such an aspect and deportment would
be, certainly, in New York ; in New York you would
feel almost as if you could borrow money of them
without security. You look for the personal feeling,
the warmth, the glow which such evident amenity
stimulates in your own breast. You find no real
response. You feel somehow imposed upon and
resentful. Nothing is less agreeable to the Anglo-
Saxon heart than to discover that it has beaten with
unreasonable warmth, that the occasion really called
for no indulgence of sentiment. You understand
Thackeray's feeling toward the "distinguished foreigner" whom he met crossing the Channel, and
who "readily admitted the superiority of the Briton
on the seas or elsewhere," only to discover himself,

the voyage over, in his real character of a hotel-runner—or, as Thackeray puts it, "an impudent, sneaking, swindling French humbug." Nothing could be more unreasonable ; you are not in London or New York, transformed by the millennium, but in Paris—or Calais, as I said. The Apocalyptic thousand years' reign of absolute satisfactoriness is still in the distant future. Self-interest is still a motive, and if a cabman is less extortionate than in New York, or a policeman more specific and personal in his directions, or a fellow 'bus passenger more affably communicative, it is not to greater delicacy of moral fibre that it should be attributed, but to a universal feeling that mankind is a fraternity instead of a vast mass of armed neutrals, and that, *cœteris paribus*, there is greater pleasure to be got out of the lubrication than the friction of points of contact between individuals. This, elevated into a positive system, produces the amenity which is as clearly a boulevard as it is a *salon* characteristic in France.

Bonhomie is not necessarily *bonté*, but it is an extremely pleasant trait to find on every hand—in the promenade, in shopping, travelling, theatre-going, gallery-visiting, wherever, in fact, one encounters his fellow-men closely. It is pleasant not to be jostled and elbowed in crowds, to be greeted in entering a shop, to be spoken to civilly and copiously by a casual companion on a bench of the *Champs Élysées*, to be treated in every way, in fine, humanely and urbanely. Urbanity is a Latin word, and still retains its significance in Latin cities, notably in France; whereas with us it is in general "fine old country gentlemen" who chiefly illustrate the quality, and except in the interior of houses, urban and urbane are epithets of broadly differing significance. But charming as the urbanity of French out-door existence is, that other quality of *bonhomie*, of good-humor, with which it is in France so closely associated—and of which it is, indeed, more the outward expression than the twin trait even—is quite as charming. Urbane the *citadins* of Spain and Italy are, almost invariably; but their urbanity decorates a different quality—a high-bred chivalry, or, among the lower classes, a fine natural simplicity, Fernan Caballero's vaunted *naturalidad* in Spain; and in Italy a rich geniality which sometimes breaks quite through the urbanity and recalls our own Westerner. The French good-humor seems idiosyncratic.

It is not very deep. Often, in fact, it shows itself to be so shallow that very bad humor is easily perceived to lie in some cases disagreeably near the surface. There is a good deal of varied light and shade about the social instinct. Mr. Henry James permits the "roaring Yankee" of his "The Point of View" to speak of the Parisians in the mass as "little, fat, irritable people." In many respects Paris is not France, and probably nearly all the *genus irritabile* to be found in France is concentrated in the capital. At Paris you certainly hear, first and last, a good

deal of scolding. Your landlady is sure to scold
the servants from corridor to corridor, and these
latter—such is the spirit of fraternity—are sure to
scold back. More or less scolding is sure to force
itself upon your attention out of doors. The *cocher*
scolds his horse, the gendarme scolds the *cocher ;*
now and then you see groups actively engaged in
this kind of mutual remonstrance. It is to be borne
in mind that they never come to blows. "It costs
a lot to punch a Frenchman's head," I heard a compatriot remark one day—this condition of affairs
demonstrating a high state of civilization, or a decadence of manly spirit hedging cowardice about with
tyrannical regulations, as one chooses to consider it.
Certainly one might pass a lifetime in Paris without
witnessing anything similar to a scene of which in
London once I was an excited—until I observed
that a nearer policeman was a placid—spectator :
namely, a young man choking and cuffing a crying
young woman who exhibited every sign of pain and
anger, but no sense of outrage. Individualism fails
in various ways to decorate and render attractive
the daily life of a great city ; below a certain rank,
composed of the surviving fittest, moves an amorphous mass of units, specifically unattractive owing
to their profound lack of interest in themselves and
their conspicuous moral dejection, and—owing to
the prevalent individualism—destitute in the mass
of any organic or homogeneous interest. Even
where individualism has to contend against the kind

of fraternity with which it is not inconsistent—the
kind we illustrate in contrast with the English, the
kind born of large human sympathies exercised
under a democratic system and over a continent's
extent—even in New York I remember a characteristic incident which one could never expect to see
paralleled in Paris. Two friends had quarrelled in
a Bowery saloon, and having, in reporter's phrase,
"adjourned to the sidewalk," one was speedily on
top of the other, who, unarmed himself, clutched
desperately his foe's uplifted hand which held a
knife over him. A crowd quickly gathered and a
stalwart fellow rushed toward the struggling pair,
apparently to interfere, but drawing a clasp-knife
from his *poche américaine* (as it is called by French
tailors), he opened it and thrusting it into the hand
of the under-dog, exclaimed : "Here's a knife for
you, too, young fellow ! " A policeman supervened
and closed the incident. At Paris this would have
seemed savage to a " professional " assassin. In five
cases out of six the passion which produces in London and New York blows and pistol-shots, and in
Naples and Seville knife-thrusts, exhales itself in
vocables, and expends its force in gesticulation.
The French nature is frivolous and superficial, is
the explanation given in all the English books—the
books which, having none of our own, and knowing
no other language, we read exclusively ; querulousness takes the place of passion, bluster and storm-
ing the place of blows, adds the American observer

—the implication being the same; indeed, Mr. Henry James sums it up in so many words in one of his sketches of travel : " The French are a light, pleasure-loving people, and the longest study of life on the Boulevard des Italiens does not change the impression." Certainly not, in fair weather ; when the skies are clear and life is good there is no evidence of moping along this thoroughfare. But, seated at one of the innumerable little tables that fringe its gay terraces, the sentimental traveller may read in his Baedeker the suggestive statement that the asphalt beneath him was substituted by the crafty Napoleon III. for stone pavement because of the chronic disposition of the Parisians to transform the latter into barricades. *Cela donne à penser.* Readiness to get yourself killed upon slight provocation hardly attests frivolity, but seriousness in the English sense ; readiness to sacrifice one's life in defence of ideas witnesses the same quality in the French sense. A gradual and cumulative progress in every revolution of importance since the days of Divine Right, testifies to the seriousness of the Parisian people in every sense. Having regard simply to separate municipalities, that of Paris, in fact, seems the only serious one since the Middle Ages.

Nothing is more common with us, however, than to treat this same characteristic of the Parisian as not only marked evidence of his frivolity, but as merely the occasional exaggeration of his habitual querulousness. But nothing also is more superficial,

and one cannot live long in Paris without perceiving
that the querulousness which at first strikes one is
itself simply the defect of the quality of amenity,
which is, after all, universal if not profound; just
as blows and general brutality are the defect of the
estimable quality, so highly prized in Anglo-Saxon
communities, of absolute and profound personal
sincerity.   There is nothing absolute or profound
about French amenity.   Rightly apprehended the
nature of the quality excludes the notion of profundity.   It is rather a gloss, a veneer, a mere outward husk, but the veneer and husk of that very
solid feeling of fraternity which is so integral a
part of the French gospel.   In England, and among
the large and increasing class of anglicized Americans in this country, fraternity is still, of course, a
subject of philosophic controversy—the school of
Mill on one side, thinkers like Mill's implacable
critic, Sir James Fitzjames Stephen, on the other.
Sir James Stephen, for example, whose feeling comparison of the Comtist regard for humanity to "a
childless woman's love for a lap-dog" is a fair measure of his sympathetic quality, maintains that "the
French way of loving the human race is the one of
their many sins which it is most difficult to forgive,"
and that "it is not love that one wants from the
great mass of mankind, but respect and justice."
But the brutality of the Anglo-Indian is apt to be as
mistaken as it is brilliant.   Respect and justice are
precisely the qualities of French fraternity, and the

"love" with which Sir James Stephen objects to being "daubed" is quite foreign to it. The propagandism of the Revolution was rational, not sentimental. No doubt it and other manifestations of French feeling toward foreigners shine in friendliness and kindliness by contrast with the respect and justice accorded by Sir James Stephen's compatriots to their fellows in India and Ireland, but impatience with prejudice and tradition and an ardor for the rational and the real are their central characteristics. The Frenchman feels under no necessity of either disliking you or else becoming familiar by intruding his personality—which seems a not uncommon Anglo-Saxon affliction. We know best, perhaps, how to treat each other in intimacy ; Frenchmen, in the general situation. *Fraternité* has slight relations to "Friendship," as Thoreau rhapsodizes about it, and as the classic examples illustrate it. In friendship the individual element is intensified, in fraternity it is extenuated. Fraternity, in a word, is not a militant virtue ; it is simply the unfailing accompaniment of the social instinct, and in France, therefore, is universally accepted so much as a matter of course, as the necessary and natural basis of human relations, that its praise is become merely subject-matter for perorations, political and other, as the praise of freedom, for example, is with the English and with us. And when such a sentiment becomes a common-place, when such an idea comes popularly to be esteemed a platitude rather than a prin-

ciple, men no longer fall upon one another's necks
in illustration of its potency and in witness of their
personal adhesion to it.   All the same, it loses little
of its vitality.   The members of those large families
which, as an English writer astutely remarks, are
not apt to be very " civil-spoken things," certainly
do not act among us as if they had constantly in
mind the precepts of the 133d Psalm, with which,
nevertheless, they may be presumed to be in full
accord.   "A good father in conversation with his
children or wife is not perpetually embracing them,"
says Thackeray ; but the fact of relationship is none
the less potent as a pervasive influence on conduct
and demeanor.   And so the mutual activities of a
society which, like that of France, resembles very
closely a large family, are thus influenced in a very
delightful way, if not to an intense degree, by the
decorous and decorative virtue of fraternal kindliness and good feeling.   The home, the interior, may
mean less to Frenchmen than it does to us, but the
community means incontestably more, and the feeling for country easily becomes supreme.

Patriotism, in fact, takes the place of religion in
France.   In the service of *la patrie* the doing of
one's duty is elevated into the sphere of exalted
emotion.   To say that the French are more patriotic
than other peoples would be to say what is in its
nature incapable of substantiation.   But I think it
incontestable that, more than any other people, they
make patriotism the source and subject of their

profoundest emotional life. Only here do they lay aside reason and abandon intelligence to surrender themselves voluntarily to the sway of instinct and passion. Only in regard to *la France* do they permit themselves illusions. Only here does sentiment triumph freely and completely over calculation. Patriotism thus plays a far larger part in their national existence than in that of other peoples. None of its manifestations seem absurd to them. The classic remark regarding the charge of Balaclava, "C'est magnifique, mais ce n'est pas la guerre," is, to be sure, a protest against the excesses of corporalism. But such a sacrifice in direct illustration of patriotism would be regarded in France almost as an opportunity; it would be looked upon as the early Christians looked upon martyrdom.

Sir John Fortescue, exiled in France during the Wars of the Roses, writes: "It is cowardise and lack of hartes and corage that kepith the Frenchmen from rising, and not povertye : which corage no Frenche man hath like to the English man. It hath been often seen in Englond that three or four thefes for povertie hath set upon 8 true men and robbed them al. But it hath not been seen in Fraunce that vii or viij thefes have been hardy to robbe iii or iv true men. Wherefor it is right seld that Frenchmen be hanged for robberye for that they have no hertys to do so terrible an acte. There be therefor mo men hangyed in Englond in a yere

3

for robberye and manslaughter than there be
hangid in Fraunce for such crime in vij yers." Sir
John writes, you will observe, very much in the
spirit of modern English criticism of the French.
This is the feeling of which Thackeray, for example,
can never free himself, which inspires "Punch," which
all the Paris correspondents display, which underlies
every French allusion in our own anglicized journals.
In citing Sir John, however, M. Taine, who shame-
lessly records as current statistics "42 cases of high-
way robbery in France against 738 in England," explains, in a footnote, the reason for this lamentable
lack of "hertys" on the part of his countrymen.
"The English," he says, "always forget to be polite,
and miss the fine distinctions of things.   Understand here brutal courage, the disputatious and independent instinct.   The French race, and in general
the Gallic race, is perhaps among all the most prod-
igal of its life."

That is the difference, exactly.   The social and
the individual instinct operate here, we perceive,
each in its own way.   One has only to think of the
title of France to be called a military nation (even
Prussian military terminology is French), or of the
suggestions contained in the word "barricade" to
appreciate how reckless of everything men selfishly
prize in this world are all Frenchmen when patriotic
takes the place of personal feeling.   No country, it
is probable, except perhaps our own Southern States,
ever made such immense sacrifices of life and treas-

ure, after all reasonable hope was over, as France did between the fall of Metz and the Treaty of Frankfort. In no other country would such resistance to overwhelming force as that of Gambetta have proved a statesman's chief title to fame ; nowhere else would even the enemies of such a man so readily admit that to raise ill-armed, half-starved, under-aged, raw levies, and oppose them to disciplined troops of twice their numbers with a steadfastness that had outlived hope, was to save the honor of the country. The public opinion which thus magnifies patriotism into a religion is a force of which it is difficult to appreciate, and impossible to exaggerate the strength. A vivid illustration of it is given in an incident of one of the stories grouped by M. Ludovic Halévy under the title, " L'Invasion." A poor woman, whose husband and son had been taken by the last conscription, ejaculates, as the *mobiles* are leaving the village : " What cowards the French must be to let themselves be dragged to war like that ! " The utterance was a cry of individualism wrung from the egotism of a mother's heart, but M. Halévy chronicles it as extraordinary, and it only serves thus to emphasize the strength and universality of the feeling against which it protested, and of striking instances of which M. Halévy's little volume is full.

It is, indeed, a record of heroic self-sacrifice on the altar of country which in certain qualities it would be hard to match. The tone is low and

quiet, there is no exaggeration, and there is no disguise of the near proximity to gayety in which Gallic gravity always exists. I venture to translate the
following incident related in M. Halévy's words by
a nurse in the military hospital at Vendôme : "I
remember especially," says the *infirmier,* "a young
man, almost a child—he was eighteen years old. He
was brought to us, with a ball in the chest, Decem-
ber 16th. He had been wounded quite near Vendôme. He died three days afterward. He must
have suffered much, for his wound was very deep
indeed. He made no complaint, however. He told
us that he was an only son—that he had volunteered
in July, at the beginning of the war. His mother opposed his project, wept bitterly, and tried to retain
him. But he had done that as a duty. He had set
out in the Army of Sedan ; he had succeeded in escap-
ing through Belgium ; he had continued the campaign
in the Army of the Loire ; he had become a sergeant.
Before dying he confessed, and in the presence of
everybody he received the sacrament with a wonderful tranquillity. During the three days in which he
was dying—for we had seen at once that he was lost
—he gave way only when he spoke of his mother ;
then the tears stood in his eyes and he gazed long
at a photograph of her which he had taken with
him. He asked pardon of her for the grief his
death would cause her. He had asked us to lay
aside his tunic with his chevrons of sergeant to be
sent to his mother after the war. He died kissing

his little photograph. We were greatly embarrassed. We did not know whether we ought to keep this photograph for the mother or to put it in the coffin. It seemed to us better to put it with him in the bier, and that is what we did."

I think no one can fail to remark the admirable simplicity of this, quite unalloyed either with the solemn intensity that is undoubtedly Germanic or with the bravado we are ludicrously apt to fancy natural to the Frenchman. There is a distinct shade of elasticity of spirit noticeable in the moral attitude of this youth that is typically French. A contained exaltation quite unassociated with what we ordinarily mean by conscious renunciation seems to be his support or rather his stimulus. He is not a hero in any explicit way; his social side is uppermost. The same phenomenon is observable in death-bed scenes in which for the sacraments of the church the decoration of the state is substituted. And this discloses the real truth about this patriotism which is the religion of Frenchmen, in whose sphere calculation is lost in sentiment and interest is transmuted into self-sacrifice—namely, that it is the sublimation of the social instinct in a more eminent degree and more conspicuous manner than the patriotic sentiment of any other people in the world. All purely personal feeling is absorbed in it. Every personal aspiration is satisfied by it. To an American dying of a wound received in the defence of his country the presentation of a bit of red ribbon by the government of his country would undoubtedly seem a barren performance enough. His personal sense of duty discharged, of a supreme sacrifice unselfishly made, would in such an hour fill his mind to the exclusion of any demonstrations of a social order that the compatriots whom he was about to leave forever could make. Dying with us is a private affair ; the association with it of the paraphernalia of life is apt to jar upon our sense. "The world has been my country, to do good my religion," is a more consoling dying thought than the *dulce et decorum est* of Horace, even on the battle-field. We have been from our youth up so accustomed to personal concentration, so habituated to being in the world but not of it, so used to considering our environment hostile, that this feeling remains even if we have ceased to look upon heaven as our true home and the celestial hosts as our real family. Emerson's breezy lines,

> "Good-by, proud world, I'm going home,
>   Thou'rt not my friend, and I'm not thine,"

find an echo in all our hearts, but wherever one meets with anything of the kind in French literature the strain is factitious, the sentiment borders on bravado, and we feel instinctively that what disguises itself as longing is really lament.

Now, the moment we appreciate that in the character of the French people it is the social rather than the individual instinct which predominates, we can see how this is the secret of the French, how it accounts for the differences between them and us as individuals, and for our inveterate misconception of them; how they in distinction from ourselves live for the present world, are alive to actuality, desire passionately to please, are passionately pleased with admiration, have no talent for renunciation, but a very genius for expression and expansion; how practical and prosaic is their disregard for certain ideal qualities of the soul which are with us of a "sacred and secret" nature; how little personal life they have; how much more manners count with them than does character, beyond those points where both are tolerable. And we can see also how, nationally and organically, they have, since the communal revolution of the twelfth century, been not merely the chief but the only highly organized people which has succeeded to the civilizing work of the Roman Empire in itself essaying social experimentation, if not in the interest, at least to the profit, of mankind. "There are no questions," said Gambetta, superbly, "but *social* questions." The apothegm formulates the spiritual instinct of France since the days of her national beginnings. It formulates also, I think, the instinct of the future. That is why France is so inexhaustibly interesting —because in one way or another she, far more than any other *nation*, has always represented the aspirations of civilization, because she has always sought development in common, and because in this respect the ideal she has always followed is the ideal of the future. It is, at any rate, inseparable from the visions which a material age permits to the few idealists of to-day.

II

MORALITY

MORALITY

SINCE Professor Lounsbury's not too sympathetic but admirably thorough-going biography, it has become possible to cite Cooper again. In one of his sea-stories, a masterpiece in every way, but quite as remarkable for its "international" as for its purely dramatic and human interest, Cooper contrives a trifling incident which felicitously illustrates the habitual Anglo-Saxon attitude toward the French whenever there is any question of morality. The bluff, hearty, "thoroughly English" commander of a seventy-four during the wars against the first Republic has just succeeded, as he imagines, in burning the little French privateer Le Feu Follet, with all on board, after the fashion becoming a successor of Drake and Raleigh, and better adapted to the end of Britannia's ruling of the waves than reminiscent of the spirit which is supposed once to have animated what Mr. Frederic Harrison trenchantly calls "the rotten carcass of chivalry." As the fire-ship was bearing down on the French vessel, strains of music had reached the ears of the English. Ghita Caraccioli—a relative of the Prince whom Nelson was to hang the following day—was singing

to the strumming of her guitar on the Frenchman's
deck in the moonlight, her lover Raoul, the handsome young privateersman himself, by turns listening with delight and abstractedly reflecting on the
perverse piety which forbade his Italian mistress to
wed a confessed unbeliever—one of the prettiest and
most delicately touched love scenes to be found in
fiction.   The sincere and unsentimental Captain
Cuffe ends his report of his exploit to the Admi-
ral : "The lugger was filled with loose women ; our
people hearing them singing their philosophical and
irreligious songs as they approached with the fire-
vessel."

Cooper was very happy in this way.   A generation ago he furnished an excellent corrective to the
then popular notion of the *ex vi termini* baseness of
American Tories during the Revolutionary period ;
and his portraiture of American character includes
types which for intimately unflattering verisimili-
tude were a liberal education in catholic temper
and the faculty of seeing one's self as one really is.
At the present moment, while English influences
are permeating our political and social activities
from philosophy to fashion, we have certainly little
need of Cooper to persuade us that Englishmen
have the qualities of their defects.   But his treatment of French character, as in "Le Feu Follet,"
for example, and the slight stress he lays on it—as
if it were not at all a novel view that he was taking
—reminds one of an epoch in American feeling

when Franklin's reception in France and Lafayette's generous enthusiasm were more than memories; when the circumstance that "the streets of Paris rang with the name of Washington" was not ascribed to Versailles diplomacy, and when liberal spirits, at least, appreciated that even in such fundamental matters as morality, *la différence* need not—as Stendhal asserts that it does in fact—produce *la haine*.

Morality is indeed a fundamental matter, and French morality differs fundamentally from our own. But this is only all the more reason for replacing censoriousness by candor in any consideration of it. And the first admission which candor compels us to make is the unfairness of estimating the French moral fibre by what ours would be if subjected to the same standards and influenced by the same circumstances. Yet this is an error that we make continually. Consciously or unconsciously we conceive our manners and character as a constant quantity, and reflect on the fate which indisputably would overtake our morals if we should adopt French ethics. And by retaining our manners and character, and adopting their ethics, we should no more attain the French moral result than, to turn the case around a little, Sophocles, Solomon, Horace, Raphael, Goethe, would have attained their success had they committed their characteristic indiscretions amid the environment which produced Jonathan Edwards and Cotton Mather. The truth,

of course, is, that the French differ from us as much
in constitution and manners as in ethics. French
morality is a direct derivative of the social instinct.
Owing to the development of this instinct among
them morality is rather a social than an individual
force, and the key to its nature is to be found in
the substitution of honor for duty as a main-spring
of action and a regulator of conduct. The distinction is a very plain, a very real one. Between the
two there is all the difference that there is between
the inspiration, say, of Lovelace's fine lines :

> " I could not love thee, dear, so much
> Loved I not honor more,"

and that of Wordsworth's apostrophe,

> " Stern daughter of the voice of God ! "

Carlyle indicates very forcibly what seems to us
the inadequacy of the French ethical ideal in concluding one of the brilliant papers now buried for a
positive generation under the title " Past and Present." He says : " 'These poor, persecuted Scotch
Covenanters,' said I to my inquiring Frenchman, in
such stinted French as stood at command, '*ils en
appelaient*'—'*À la postérité,*' interrupted he, helping
me out. '*Ah! Monsieur, non, mille fois non!* They
appealed to the eternal God, not to posterity at all.
C'était différent!'" Every Anglo-Saxon reading
this instinctively agrees with Carlyle that it was
différent indeed. Any Frenchman, on the other

hand, would ascribe the distinction to the vague exaltation of fanaticism. To the French sense such a distinction indicates a lack of sanity, of that measure to which—if one may say so without paradox—the French are almost fanatically attached. "In all questions concerning the conscience," the Frenchman would say, "the important point is whether or no the conscience decides aright. The immense value Anglo-Saxons attach to its activity, its sensitiveness, becomes at once a misleading and fatal estimation whenever it decides wrongly ; in such instances the value attached to it only gives authority to error. Fanaticism, that most unpleasant and least useful condition of the mind, instantly ensues. The only real appeal in cases of disputed decision— cases like that of the Scotch Covenanters just mentioned—is to posterity, to time, to the universal conscience, the common consciousness of mankind. In any other sense than this—the sense in which *vox populi* and *vox Dei* are really identical—any talk about the arbitrament of the eternal God is too vague to be useful, and being vague too solemn not to be harmful. Even one of your writers who, as M. Challemel-Lacour has testified, seems to us to put an altogether exaggerated estimate upon conduct and morality, a writer who observes that a Methodist navvy 'deals successfully with nearly the whole of life,' while the 'dissolute, gifted, brilliant grandee,' whom he compares with him, 'is all abroad in it,' is nevertheless forced to say that with conscience one has ' done nothing until he has got to the bottom of conscience and made it tell him *right*.' "

One never talks with a Frenchman on these matters without perceiving that to be right, to be at the centre of things, not to be duped, is to his mind the *summum bonum*. It is the premise from which he invariably sets out; it is, in fact, a passion with him; of many Frenchmen it can even be said, as Taine said of Mérimée, that they are the dupes of their distrust. To rely implicitly upon one's conscience is, of course, a famous way of being profoundly duped. It is the infallible accompaniment of fanaticism; fanaticism is *bête ;* to be *bête* is impossible— the very notion of it insufferable. In this way the Frenchman comes naturally to think very little of conscience, to have very little to do with it. His reliance is upon an outward, not the inward monitor, the voice of society in general, the suggestions of culture, the dictates of science. His literature contains no analogue of Bunyan or of Johnson. To him the admonition, " the kingdom of God is within you," is addressed to the heart, the emotions, the soul—an aphorism consolatory and religious, but having less than nothing to do with the grand object of daily life, the great secret of success in this world—namely, the certainty that one's light is not darkness.

It is well known that our view, the Anglo-Saxon view, is just the reverse of this. We exalt the functions of conscience, and we are not concerned, so

long as we obey its behests, whether or no at some
future time it may not give us different counsel and
so, to a greater or less degree, stultify itself as a
guide. We admit its fallibility in advance, and it
surprises us that this should surprise the French
observer. Where is infallibility to be found, we
ask; it seems credulous and simple to seek it. The
important thing is to act up to the best light that
you have, in accordance with the first part of Bishop
Wilson's celebrated maxim; the other part will in
this way, we vaguely feel, gradually come to take
care of itself. We have no passion for pure reason.
We have, in fact, so little sympathy with mere cleverness, as we call it, with exclusive devotion to the
things of the mind, that it is difficult for us to appreciate how a society can be great and distinguished
which is, like France, wholly given over to them,
and which in matters of personal conduct, to us the
all-important concern of life, obeys not the inward
monitor of conscience but the outward constraint of
public opinion. This view the French themselves
invariably ascribe to Puritanism, which is not to be
wondered at, considering the substantial unanimity
with which the partisans of Puritanism among us
make the same ascription. But what is the origin
of Puritanism itself? The truth is that Puritanism
is merely the excess of the individual spirit manifested in the exaltation of conscience. It is itself an
effect. The intimate, personal view of morality is
held by peoples and persons who never came into

4

contact with Puritanism. It is as common in Norway as in New England, and is as firmly held where Luther re-enthroned the individual conscience as it is wherever the Shorter Catechism is expounded. Its only foes are the Catholic Church, which absorbs the devotion of the communities in which it reigns, and that extremely elaborate social development which the humanity of Catholicism indirectly fosters. Everywhere in Protestant and personal communities public opinion itself shares Owen Meredith's sentiment : "The Crowd-made Conscience is a Harlot bold "—a sentiment fairly swaggering with individual dignity.

M. Renan calls glory " the thing which, after all, has the best chance of being not altogether vanity." That would indeed be news to the Preacher, would it not? The Preacher's social instinct was far less developed than M. Renan's. How often have we not, all of us, ridiculed the French respect for *la gloire*, having ourselves an intimate conviction that in the entire catalogue of vanities there is none so hollow as this same extrinsic applause. No one would of course deny that there are individuals among us who care a great deal for this vanity, but it is, in fine, distinctly not our ideal, and we are saved in great measure from any danger of becoming openly enamoured of it by the abundance, the universality— and one might add the sincerity—of our cant upon the subject. But the French are unblushing about it, and probably incorrigible. It is another phase of their anxiety to be in the right—that is, to think rightly, without passion or personal prejudice, about any given matter—which leads them to place a high value upon extrinsic opinion, and to shun the eccentricity and whimsical fanaticism which are so often the concomitants of concentration and which, whatever the verdict of Carlyle's eternal God, they think posterity at all events will disapprove, even if current public opinion be mistaken. Thus by the operation of a natural law public opinion becomes in its turn much more worthy of being followed than it is where it occupies the subordinate place we assign it; its qualities increase in proportion to its dignity. It should be remembered that the pursuit of *la gloire* in France is a very different thing from the analogous seeking of the bubble reputation with us, and that in proportion as the prize becomes important, the effort to obtain it becomes laudable.

And the substitution of honor for duty as a moral standard has, generally, one immense advantage which, as the most superficial acquaintance with them discloses, the French unquestionably enjoy. Honor's dictates are plain. Those of duty are often obscure. Society knows what it esteems and what it despises. Conscience is often confused, often in need now of enlightenment now of quickening. The result is that in the moral sphere the French escape that vacillation so characteristic of ourselves. All is plain-sailing before them ; their chart is distinct and they mean to follow it. Morally speaking

we illustrate Mr. Lincoln's caution, on the other hand,
and never " cross Fox River before we come to it."
The difference is that between a written and unwritten political constitution ; we have an immense
amount of common-law morality, so to speak.
Many of our conscientious people do things which
other conscientious persons would not do ; the largest publisher of one of our cities publishes Zola
for all America ; the largest bookseller of the same
city will not vend Zola ; yet he, again, sells freely the
"Memoirs of Cora Pearl." You feel that we cannot
all of us be hitting the mark. Many of us do things
at one moment that we would not at another ; many
of us justify in ourselves to-day conduct of which
yesterday we disapproved. Our standard wavers
because it is upheld by a grace that is intermittent.
The conscience, finding itself deceived by some false
alarm, relaxes its vigilance in some parallel instance
with unhappy results. Our temptations vary. Our
moral life becomes a struggle, in comparison with
which the Frenchman's is serene. We may say, I
think, that the prayer " lead us not into temptation "
is rarely on his lips or in his heart. His attitude
toward temptation is not one of timorousness. He
believes rather with La Bruyère that " everything is
temptation to him who fears temptation." He does
not seek to fortify himself against it by acquiring
the habit of self-denial. He does not contemplate
the notion of yielding in spite of himself, of being
assailed by the tempter in an unguarded moment,

of the necessity of always having one's armor on.
Neither does he comprehend the relaxation and
relief all of us know so well of those moments during which we put this armor off for the nonce, when
we are sure temptation cannot assail us; nor our
occasional excesses when we find ourselves in error
as to this security. Discipline in this direction he
does not practise. He substitutes philosophy for it.
His philosophy may now and then be stoic, but it is
not ascetic. He does not strive to obey his higher
and control his lower nature. He appears, in fact,
to have no higher nature—and no lower ; to have,
morally speaking, a nature that is simple and single.

The result is twofold. He yields to temptation
more frequently and more easily, but his yielding is
of far less consequence. He does not suffer the
abasement involved in "sinning against light," as
the phrase is. His taking temptation so lightly as
he does prevents his attaching the same value to a
surrender to it that we do ; his fall is specific, tempo-
rary, and trivial, so to speak, and does not have the
general lowering effect on the whole nature which
succumbing after a resistance in which the whole
nature has been intensely interested does not fail to
have. It does not leave the same scar. The man is
morally on his feet again much sooner. Often, indeed, he has not fallen at all, only tripped. Society
in consequence takes moral errors much more lightly
than it does with us, as those who have not observed
it in French life cannot have escaped noticing in

French literature. That favorite incident in modern romance round which the story of "Adam Bede" centres, for example, is (minus the infanticide, of course, which would be foreign to either) in French literature and French life almost never taken grimly, but gently, not tragically but simply, not as a monstrous but as a natural error; in fine, it is still in France considered as remediable as it was in Galilee "twenty ages since." Similarly with other yieldings to temptation. The main consideration is to have the heart right; until that is corrupt nothing occurs which can be called irreparable; that is the French feeling. And it is a wonderful simplifier. Moral complexity beyond a certain point, the point at which the influence of jarring interests and clashing temptations ceases, is accepted in France as curiously factitious. The air is too clear, the sky too bright. George Eliot could never have written there.

On the other hand, an impartial observer would notice that yielding to temptation is apt to be pretty strictly proportioned to the strength rather of the temptation than of the tempted. When this presents itself in attractive form there is often scarcely a pretence of resistance. In fact, in this matter of resistance, the French strike us as having a certain curious helplessness, born doubtless of inexperience. They seem like the militia of the army of morality, not its regular soldiers. They show the lack of drill—at least in skirmishes and recon-

noissances if not in pitched battles where courage
and general intelligence are more serviceable. As
to these it will, of course, be understood that I am
here speaking mainly of peccadilloes and not
crimes; of those offences which their own society
cordially condemns, Frenchmen commit as few, it
need not be said, as any other people. But I should
say, for example, there were vastly more white lies
told in France than in America. There is a whimsical felicity in the circumstance that the scene of
Charles Reade's novel of that name is laid there.
The white lie is tremendously convenient, and is, I
think, destined to greater popularity with us than
it at present enjoys. In France its abolition would
revolutionize society. Society there owes to it
much of the smoothness with which its machinery
moves. The white lie of causing yourself to be declared at your door "not at home," it does not require a seared conscience to commit even among
ourselves. We say it is mere civility, it prevents
friction, and it deceives no one. It is in the same
tone of whiteness as certain customary forms of
signing letters. The same principle and practice
are merely carried much further in France. They
are carried, to be sure, to the $n+1$th power, but
their identity is not lost. The excess is chargeable
to the approbativeness characteristic of extreme
social development. Candor and courtesy, the desire to please and perfect openness, are mutually
inimical. French approbativeness is hostile to that

frankness which impels the truthful Earl of Elles-
mere, for example, to notify visitors to his galleries
by an announcement, printed at the head of his
catalogue, that, notwithstanding an absurd rumor to
the contrary, he is not legally obliged to have them
there at all—that frankness, in fact, which makes of
the average Englishman everywhere so concrete a
personality.

The result, however, is a noticeable difference in
the relations between people. A certain scepticism
takes the place of confidence. A person is believed
in trivial statements just in so far as he is obviously
disinterested in making them. The *gobe-mouche*
abounds ; a sense of the prevailing scepticism and
his consequent irresponsibility develop him rapidly.
No subject is too grave to secure immunity from
him. By way of compensation he is rewarded with
sympathetic attention or artistic interest instead of
with credence. Much the same views and gossip
about the French Republic are to be found in the
"Figaro" or the "Gaulois," and in the English and
American papers, but the latter only impose upon
their readers. In private a Frenchman expects his
neighbor to be courteous, companionable, sincere
in essentials, frank and open with him, but he does
not expect him to tell him the exact truth on matters of no moment if he has any motive for concealing it. The truth to him is not a fetich. It is not
only not to be spoken at all times, but it is now and
then to be perverted ; the great thing is to have

sufficient tact to know when, and sufficient elasticity
to do it with *aplomb*. He can thus venture audaci-
ties from which we are debarred, and enjoy an immunity from impertinence to which we are strangers.
His quick wit spares him the embarrassment of
blushing on many occasions, and his philosophy
saves him from the discomfort of remorse. You
quite envy him, at times, for the moment, but you
are sure to end by preferring your own way. I
shall always recall with a certain ridiculous pang a
small, unobtrusive, but morally brilliant white lie
once told me by a charming Frenchwoman with
the sole motive of sparing my feelings. But to
have betrayed how much more acutely they were
piqued by the discovery that I had been the victim
of this kind of considerateness would have been an
immense indiscretion.

It is certainly not calumniating the French to affirm that they have no genius for renouncement.
Renouncement is in France, for the most part, confined to the religious orders. It is opposed to the
French ideal of expansion. He that taketh a city is
decidedly more esteemed than he that ruleth his
spirit—unless the ruling be to the end of city-taking
or some such specific accomplishment. His success
or failure in life when "divine, everlasting Night, with
her star-diadems, with her silence and her veraci-
ties" is come, is measured rather by the career he has
run than by the character he has carved for himself.
To be *worthy* instead of to have been fortunate, in-

stead of to have hit some definite mark or other, is
to him an ambition of vague significance ; it is not an
aim of the social instinct. "Worthy of what?" one's
French friend always rejoins; "of eternal life, no
doubt : *c'est subtil.*" Scott's dying injunction to
Lockhart could hardly be translated into his tongue,
without the risk of appearing insipid. "Est-ce que
tous les honnêtes gens ne sont pas *good* alors?"
Certain individualities, with us comparatively frequent, whose main object in life seems to be to efface themselves most completely in order to be of
service to others, with whom the proffer of those an-
cillary attentions so exasperating to their victims is
relentlessly systematic, in whose eyes one can perceive the gleam of triumph when a coarse nature is
imposing upon their goodness—like the legendary
martyr's smile of beatification as the flames mount
higher—this kind of person is unknown in the three
parts of all Gaul. The nearest French analogue is
a *bonasse* person, a person weakly amiable by disposition, not by system, a person of a radically different moral fibre and far more infrequent. Self-sacrifice to the general end of spiritual perfection, which
however little it may be practised among us is nevertheless a principle in which we profoundly believe,
and which affects profoundly our judgment of ourselves and others, is not at all so esteemed by the
French. They have no instinctive confidence in
its salutariness. They believe it, on the contrary,
misleading, narrowing, retarding—a sort of burial

of one's talent in a napkin—unless it be strictly presided over and efficiently directed by the intelligence, by tact, by the sense of measure, of relative importance.

And not only does their estimation of the discipline of character differ from ours, but we have different conceptions of character itself, of what constitutes character. We mean by character, integrity; we mean what the New York "Sun" means when it affirms that character and brains are necessary to a newspaper's success. In France temperament, disposition, is what is meant. When we say of such and such a man that he has a great deal of character, we generally mean that he has disciplined his temperament, his disposition, into strict obedience to the behests of duty; that he has clear and peremptory ideas about right and wrong; in short, we think of his honesty rather than of his energy. On the other hand, it is his energy, his will, his *volonté*, that is meant when the Frenchman attributes *du caractère* to a person. Napoleon, for example, was a man of prodigious character in the French view, and making "his way to empire over broken oaths and through a sea of blood" only the more clearly illustrates it. In fact the French and ourselves see each his own side in the same man. Michelet, for example, speaks of Turgot's *férocité*: Mr. Matthew Arnold, having to compare Turgot to Butler in just this respect, says he should rather call the quality "*sœva indignatio*." Nothing could better indicate the two points of view—the scientific and impersonal, and the moral and sympathetic. The French attitude is critical, descriptive. M. Scherer calls M. Halévy *cruel.* M. Taine applies the same epithet to Thackeray. In each instance the word is used, wholly without reference to its moral significance, to characterize the fidelity with which baseness is portrayed. *Bon, méchant, d'un mauvais caractère*—a dozen epithets are used in this sense, more as we would apply them to children or the domestic animals than to persons supposably responsible themselves for their characters. Balzac's conception of Christianity, which he advocates with *naïf* ardor, is of a social police system. On the other hand, we not only bring everything moral at once into the ethical sphere, but we are apt to bring ethics themselves immediately into the sphere of religion, of emotion, of poetry—that is to say, our consideration of them is practically as far as possible removed from the scientific.

Where a people has thus the virtues not of discipline but of disposition, it at least partially atones for some of its shortcomings by avoiding the defect apparently inseparable from that personal morality which sets so much store by character as we conceive it—the defect of cant, of hypocrisy. The French disesteem for cant is as great as is ours for falsehood. Courage, candor, lack of vanity, egotism, contemptuousness, are all characteristics favorable to truthfulness, but they are the natural prey of hypocrisy. The constant danger of attaching extraordinary value to character, to conscientiousness, is the danger of misconceiving one's own. Innate optimism and self-respect contribute powerfully to prevent us from actual realization in many instances and on many occasions. Only rarely, for example, does such a journal as the conservative London "Morning Post" avow that "there is more licentious effrontery in a single London thoroughfare than in the whole of Paris." What you are most anxious not to do you are extremely slow to admit, even to yourself, that you have actually done. French *cafardise* is quite a different trait from cant. It is hypocrisy of a gross, colossal order that never takes in any one, least of all that inevitable victim of cant, the hypocrite himself. The tribe of Tartuffe is almost professional in its *cafardise*, which is, like the false humility of the Hebrew of literature, a special, a cultivated, not an integral and general quality. The French frankness in intimacy about falsehood of the "harmless" sort seems to us cynical only because we forget they have no cant. They are astonishingly sincere, amazingly unpretending, in point of character. The Orleanist's jeer at the Bonapartes, conveyed in the boast that of the family *he* served "all the men were brave and all the women virtuous," was taken as a *mot* rather than as an affront— a *mot plein d'esprit, et plein de malice,* nothing to make any one's blood boil except that of Plon-Plon, which was abnormally cool. How many of us are

in the habit of protesting, as the French continually
do, that we are no better nor worse than our fellows?
Are not the worst of us apt to cherish a faint hope
that we are a trifle better than the average, not to
say the majority—have a little finer feeling, a little
more scrupulousness, or if not that, at any rate a
little less Pharisaism? And these psychological con-
volutions, his frankness with himself and with others,
spares the Frenchman. In crises which really touch
him he shows a great deal of self-abnegation; gene-
rosity, charity, are French virtues. If he does not
willingly "lose" his life, if, on the other hand, his
ideal is to sell it as dearly as possible, he at least
sells it. And he sells it without any pretence, without any braggart sentimentality and self-deception,
but with an intellectual and often even an artistic
consciousness of what he is doing that is almost as
refreshing to the moral sense as it is to the intelligence. The soul may remain unsatisfied; but his
social, business, and public virtues may well, in his
esteem, be set over against our private ones.

Lack of personal discipline, however, means yielding to one's instincts, whether one mean by this
being in harmony with nature or really running
counter to her steadfast undertakings. The first
and finest of our instincts, setting aside the supernatural, is undoubtedly love, and it is in his abandonment to this instinct that the Frenchman is usually believed by us to be less successful in morality
than elsewhere. Certainly more distinctly and uni-

versally than anywhere else is it felt in France that love *vincit omnia*—that it is, as Thackeray affirms, "immeasurably above ambition, more precious than wealth, more noble than name," and that "he knows not life who knows not that." I say this feeling is more distinct and universal in France than among us, because there love not only conquers all things but one may almost say excuses everything. It is the passion of youth and eld, men and women. The young girl looks forward to an experience of its divine grace with an emotion excited in the breast of her American sister only by the supernatural. Of all the activities of his prime the old man regrets most the abandonment, the enthusiasm, the absence of calculation, the spiritual exaltation of the least egoistic of human impulses. Never to have made the voyage to Cythera is to have lived in vain. "Love is a thing too young to know what conscience is," says Shakespeare, and the sacrifices made to avoid thus missing the end of one's emotional existence are often very great; sometimes they are grotesque; now and then they are tragic to the last degree, and the misery and demoralization resulting from mistaking the factitious for the genuine in this momentous matter, colder temperaments may well congratulate themselves upon avoiding. But these mistakes are often the defects of a generous ideality, and we are prone to exaggerate their number and gravity; the nature that passes its life in resisting temptation is indisposed to judge fairly those who evade the struggle. We keep forgetting that our manners are different from French manners, and our natures constitutionally unlike. The French ideal is not that of St. Francis, of Thoreau. Mr. Arnold cites Paley to show how especially and organically corrupting is any swerving from Hippolytan pudicity. Undoubtedly for all dispositions to whom Paley is a sympathetic moralist. But the whole problem is different in the country of Stendhal, who finds in Paley the last refuge of moral and intellectual mediocrity. Sainte-Beuve, of whom Mr. Arnold never spoke without something akin to reverence, for example, says quite frankly of himself, when his integrity was attacked—like Hamilton's—: "J'ai mes faiblesses. J'ai pu regretter sentir quelquefois que j'y éteignais ma flamme, mais jamais je n'y ai perverti mon cœur." A society which substitutes personal, or at most domestic, for social virtues, where women are free from pursuit because men are indifferent, whose manners permit flirtation and prohibit gallantry, whose only *demi-monde* is a dissipated and defiant bachelordom, runs far more risk of perversion if it allows itself any relaxation in this regard than a society like that of France, whose qualities tend to humanize everything short of vice itself. What would be vice among us remains in France social irregularity induced by sentiment. The distinction is, I think, the most important of all that can be observed in any judgment of France by Americans. The irregularity may be very great and the sentiment very dilute, but between these and such vice as social irregularity of the kind generally means with us the distance is very great and the distinction very radical. To avoid misjudgments in this matter, to avoid talking of the French being "given over to the worship of their Goddess Lubricity," for instance, it is necessary constantly to remind one's self of this. When Madame de Chevreuse complains of Anne of Austria's austerity, and says she had all the trouble in the world to awaken in her some taste for the glory of being loved, when La Rochefoucauld affirms that "there are few honest women who are not sick of their trade," when M. Sarcey exclaims that the rejection of a suitor because he has had a mistress is a solecism, when Mr. Henry James recounts the tavern raillery of a Languedoc dinner-table, speculating in the presence of the blushing and good-natured servant herself as to whether or no she is *sage*, when, in short, either in French books or French life one encounters suggestion of the sensual triumph over correctness, it is to be remembered that the error has almost always an element of ideality. As to actual and recognized vice, international comparisons are very sterile as well as very odious.

Institutions have nowhere more influence than in France, and, given the French belief in the divine instinct of love, the lengths to which it may lead are easily seen to depend much upon marriage and divorce laws. We at all events find no difficulty,

5

in self-reproachful moments, in admitting the important influence of divorce upon national morals. Marriage being what it is, monogamy being so eminent a witness of the race's development and such an integral part of its highest attainment, the compromise in this respect of any society's ideal is easily seen to be inexpressibly vulgarizing. Easy divorce, at any rate, is express and legalized abandonment of one of the most precious conquests we have won from original anarchy. But I think our recognition of this, emphasized *a posteriori* as with us such recognition is, prevents us from conceiving readily the enormous effect which the complete absence of divorce has upon a Catholic society. A Catholic society is, as I have already said, far less self-concentrated, far more expansive and natural than a Protestant, and yet in regard to one of the most artificial of institutions—which in the sense of later development monogamy certainly is—it permits no elasticity whatever. Be the tension never so great it is never formally recognized. The result is inevitably that informally its rupture is too readily excused. It is, to be sure, possible to say to a Frenchman, who objects that he only does illegally what, were he an American, he would have abundant warrant of law for, and what neither the church nor the world would reprove in him, that offences against pure legality, unjustified by the compulsion of a higher law, are sin ; that if he does not instinctively feel this, reflection will prove it to him, and that his worthiness,

not his happiness, is the important matter for him
and his people. You may even add commiseration
at his misfortune in not being an American, so that
he might be happy and worthy at the same time.
He will be certain to esteem you a pedant. And,
in fact, between easy divorce and no divorce there
is not, morally speaking, anything like the abyss
that closet philosophy is apt to imagine. In the
effect upon society at large there is far more difference between strict divorce and either. The con-
version of the Jews, according to Launcelot Gobbo,
merely increased the number of pork-eaters, and,
speaking practically and prosaically, the effect of
exchanging easy divorce for no divorce at all, would
be mainly, I imagine, to increase the number of
natural children ; whereas it is highly probable
that the recent re-enactment of divorce in France
will ere long be found to have produced a salutary
disturbance in the vital statistics of the country.
If this and certain corollaries of the proposition
which will occur to every one more readily than
they can be expressed be true, it is easy to understand how marriage—erected by the church into a
sacrament, and yet frequently found to be actually
intolerable—has hitherto, in France, found less
virtual and sincere acquiescence in its sacred character than elsewhere. Formal respect for it abounds.
Nothing is more shocking to a Frenchman than the
records of our divorce cases. And yet it is as a
convention simply that indissoluble marriage im-

poses itself on his respect, because its sanction is
external, ecclesiastical, and legal, and not spiritual
and natural. He has accordingly the less care for
the fidelity which elsewhere is inextricably associated with it in theory. It would hardly be an
exaggeration to say that for this fidelity he cares,
absolutely speaking, nothing at all. He excuses
himself, or rather he explains his position, by a
reference to nature. The great thing is to be
in harmony with nature, he thinks. In all these
matters he takes very little account of what Goethe
calls culture-conquests except as social institutions,
decorous conventions. Fickleness in women he
admits as a defect, venial or not as the heart happens to be interested, but as much less natural
than the same trait in man as polyandry is less
usual than polygamy. As to man, the universal
French feeling is very well expressed by Mr. Howells in an *obiter dictum* of his "Indian Summer."
In Mr. Howells' public it is always *place aux dames.*
He has so completely won the affection of his women
readers by betraying women's secrets that he is
now and then emboldened to brave their indignation by divulging a secret of the opposite sex, as
he does in this paragraph wherein he represents his
hero, who is in love with two women at the same
time, as "struggling stupidly with a confusion of
desires which every man but no woman will understand." "After eighteen hundred years," he says,
"the man is still imperfectly monogamous." That

strikes us all, male and female alike, as the quintessence of humor. It is not precisely of the same character as that of Tom Jones, a laugh from whom, says
Lamb, "clears the air," but it performs a similar service. Mr. Howells is the *enfant terrible* of realistic fiction, and we can no longer go on pretending that even
American men are strangers to polygamous instincts.
But as an American humorist once remarked of his
church-going propensities, they "can restrain themselves." And doubtless until we have our Flaubert
or our Fielding, as well as our Howells, we shall believe that they do, just as even after that distant
event we shall continue to believe that they should.
But the Frenchman replies that all this is based on
a Puritan systematization of St. Paul's separation of
the law of the members and the law of the mind,
and that it is fantastic. Only in an atmosphere as
colorless and passionless as that in which the characters of "Indian Summer," for example, move, he
maintains, is it possible to carry the question of
rectitude into the region over which the heart presides alone. To violate the heart's dictates, which
are the direct behests of nature, is, in his eyes, either
pedantry or folly ; at all events, an esoteric concern
of monks and nuns. It is not a question at all of a
higher law and the law of the members, but of the
natural instincts of man, which on the one hand he is
to preserve from that depravity universally stigma-
tized as unnatural, and on the other to organize in
such a way as to benefit that highly artificial insti-

tution known as society in the direction of natural
development and not natural restraint.

Hence, plainly, the French idea of marriage as an
institution mainly social. It becomes a convention
like another. If it be combined with a love whose
character guarantees its permanence—a flame which
does not, unlike Campbell's,

> " . . . need renewal
> Of fresh beauty for its fuel "

—so much the better. But love is one thing and
marriage another. This being distinctly understood
it will at once be perceived that the stronger a
people's instincts for social order the more disposition there is to make marriage indissoluble. If
marriage is understood by an entire society not to
be a contrivance to " bind love to last forever," the
principal objection to binding marriage to last forever disappears. Every instinct of form, of propriety, of regularity, every instinct which shrinks from
social disturbance counsels the permanence of marriage, which thus becomes purely an affair of reason.
Family relations, property interests, children's future, the organic solidarity of communities are in
this way distinctly served. It is personal morality
which suffers, because society is immediately adjusted to the notion that marriage is a convention
merely, and that offences against marriage appeal to
the tribunals of manners rather than of morals.
And not only does morality suffer, but marriage un-

questionably tends to become materialized. The two things interact with mutual intensity—marriage is made material by being indissoluble, and it is the material conception of marriage as a social convention which renders its indissolubility attractive. Thus we have both the effect of no divorce and the explanation of it.

I think, therefore, the recent re-enactment of divorce by the French democracy, hedged about as it is with precaution against abuse, cannot fail to have a salutary effect on the personal morality of the community, and that it will also tend to spiritualize the community's conception of marriage. There will be more marriages, and they will be less an affair of reason and more an affair of the heart. This will be the effect, because in taking an irreparable step, however an Anglo-Saxon may prefer the guidance of his instincts and affections, the Frenchman prefers to be directed by his intelligence. And though no one probably thinks of divorce potentialities on his wedding-day, the permanence or dissolubility of the contract undoubtedly makes a great difference in the bachelor's chronic and constitutional attitude toward marriage. One has only to regard the two extremes presented by some of our communities and a Catholic one in this respect. In Southern Europe man is notoriously reluctant to "surrender his liberty;" in some of our communities he can hardly wait to become of age before he crystallizes some passing fancy into matrimony.

On the whole, marriage, divorce, and cognate questions aside, to find the French lacking in moral sense is, I think, to betray confusion. The French themselves, accustomed as they are to such a verdict at our hands, always ascribe it either to prejudice of a particularly unintelligent kind or else to hypocrisy. "The English," says a recent reviewer of George Eliot's life in the "Revue des Deux Mondes," "are no better than other people, but they have a singular desire to appear so." The French, generally, would accept this as a temperate expression of their feeling that any arrogation of superior morality on the part of the Anglo-Saxon is unjustified. We understand morality in many different ways. Some of our most conspicuously moral people believe indeed that it is a rational substitute for religion. A less frigid school finds it impossible to conceive of true morality except as a religious result. Except that the former of these profess the utilitarian ideal and permit themselves little emotion, save of a severely ethical kind, whereas the Frenchman has his susceptibility in constant exercise though under perfect control—except, in other words, that sceptical Puritanism is *sui generis*, and can ill be said to have relations to anything Latin—the French view of morality, the Latin view, may be said to stand midway between these two. French morality is morality in the etymological sense. But because the standard is exterior rather than of conscience, because, as I have already said, the idea of honor to a very considerable degree takes the place of the idea of duty among Frenchmen, because what is there-fore venial with them is sometimes grave with us and *vice versâ*, it by no means follows that the French notion of what is right and what is wrong is any the less strict, precise, and universally binding than our own. And so far as the accord between theory and practice is concerned I suppose it is needless to point out the perfection which has been attained in France in the sphere of morals as well as every-where else. In the sense in which it has been aptly observed that " Coleridge had no morals," French morality is a conspicuous national characteristic.

No, French morality is simply misconceived when it is summarily depreciated as it is our vice to de-preciate it. It is as systematic as our own, and by those most interested believed to be as successful ; it is in France that life is longest and happiness greatest, and well-being most widely diffused. The great distinction between us, the chief characteristic which in this sphere sets off the Frenchman from the Anglo-Saxon, and from the Spaniard also, and the Italian, over whom he triumphs morally, perhaps, is his irreligiousness. I refer of course to the mass of the nation, not to the few who are absorbed by devotion, which is religion intensified. To-day, at all events, the great body of the French people is Voltairian. A better epithet could not be found for irreligious morality. "To Voltaire," says Mr. John Morley, very felicitously, " reason and humanity were but a single word, and love of truth and passion for justice but one emotion." Yet as Emerson observes: "He said of the good Jesus even, 'I pray you never let me hear that man's name again'"— formidable utterance, however interpreted or explained, for disclosing a lack of the religious sense.

Nevertheless he has read to little purpose the greatest humanist of the century of Kant, of Hume, and of Rousseau, who does not perceive the positive force of Voltaire as a moralist. The undercurrent, or rather the substance of all that infinite wit which nearly every English critic of Voltaire warns us to be on our guard against, is moral earnestness, and that he should have been mistaken for a literary artist would have exasperated him as much as a similar popular error grieved the prophet Ezekiel. His word to his fellow-men is this: "Do not make the mistake of thinking life is all of a piece or men either. The world is larger than your philosophy. God is inscrutable but infinitely kind and good. Sin is either stupidity or else a metaphysical invention. Truth is better than the fairest-seeming falsehood, and the fanaticism which lurks in propagandism of all sorts is fatal to it. Absolute happiness is an abstraction. The exaltation which pretends to its possession is either empty or hypocritical. Be content not to be happy, or at least be happy in missing bliss. Be cheerful, be clairvoyant, be kind and good; avoid pedantry even in renouncement, be simple, and above all things remember *il faut cultiver notre jardin.*" The lack of such philosophy is plainly spirituality ; its virtue is clearly good sense. It is not the predominance of the mind over the heart that it teaches, but of both over the soul. Of the two commandments whereon "hang all the law and the prophets," it forgets the first in its devotion to the second. The two are indeed "like unto" each other, and have inextricable mutual relations. But as the second is, except abstractly, not so inevitable a corollary of the first as to render its statement needless, so it is plain that one's duty toward one's neighbor may in practice be very sufficiently performed under the sanctions of a social morality which is nevertheless unillumined by that personal spiritual experience and uncrowned by that "inward glory" particular to the performance of one's duty toward God—particular, that is to say, to religion. It is the personal insufficiency of his philosophy that is responsible for those weaknesses which make M. Scherer call Voltaire "a pitiful character." Voltaire, at all events, could not dispense with religion.

In fine, the French have not the religious temperament, as they have not the analogous poetical or sentimental temperament. The moment one removes from religion the theological element one perceives how differently differently constituted souls may be affected by it ; how, instead of varying, like morality, with energy of character, it varies with temperament ; how some natures are perpetually feeling after and finding its supreme consolations,

and how others are infinitely less satisfied by these.
In general, I think the French temperament fails to
vibrate responsively to them.   There is something
Socratic and self-sustaining about it which demands
the adjustment of life to health and activity, and resents the prominence of solace and healing in an
ideal that contemplates the drawing nigh of evil
days.   As Carlyle said of Socrates, indeed, the
French temperament is "terribly at ease in Zion."
Its ideal is the Epicurean ideal.   Aristotle is its
moralist, not St. Paul—Aristotle asserting, as ex-
posited by Condorcet, that "every virtue is one of
our natural inclinations which reason forbids us
both to resist too much and to obey too implicitly."
All Condorcet's ethics, which are French ethics,
even his sympathetic account of Epicureanism,
which he finds least distant from the truth, are
vitiated for us by our profound conviction that the
maxim, "he that loveth his life shall lose it," is as
empirically sound as it is mysterious.   But that is
religion, and Condorcet and his countrymen concentrate their attention in this sphere on morality.
Instead of conquering the passions they utilize
them.   Instead of resignation they seek distraction ;
and they have so ordered life that such distraction
as with our self-centred individualism we do not
dream of, is within their easy reach.

The gayety we too often associate with levity of
character is, as the French illustrate it, a necessity
of mental health and a kind of goodness.   By no

means is it a mere yielding to sensation, which is
the beginning of dissipation ; but there is about it
something of tension. To be gay a man must live
well, must order his life aright. In many cases
there is a real dissipation in not seeking the means
of gayety, in letting the whole physical system lose
tone for lack of the tension which gayety imparts.
The leading motive of Père La Chaise has a distinct
note of gayety in it. "Man is a sporting as well as
a praying animal," says Dr. Holmes. And, growing
old, M. Renan regrets that in his youth he did not
play enough ; which, to be sure, the "St. James's
Gazette" takes to mean regret for "the serious occupations of the café, the fencing-school, the naviga-
tion of the silvery Seine on Sunday beneath beauty's
favoring smile, and the other occupations of brisk
Parisian adolescence." But every one hasn't the
cockney idea of leisure, of gayety, of every state
which is not the only original Carlylean antidote
for human misery. You see what Satan would find
for the editor of the "St. James's Gazette" to do in
case of idleness, but this does not imply that M.
Renan means debauch, or that French gayety implies it. If the French are deficient in spirituality
and conceive spiritual things materially, it is none
the less true that they look at material things in an
extremely spiritual way. The result is a pervasive
vivacity, a sustained blitheness, whose high key is
preserved with the same delightful ease that one
observes in a painting by Fortuny ; the local color

may have less richness, less variety, but the picture
is more effective ; the individual may " wither," but
the world is indisputably more and more—more and
more important, more and more worthy. And this
ensemble cannot be obtained by frivolous means.
"Il faut souffrir pour voir la comédie," says Doudan.
The French are ready to make any sacrifices in
order to enjoy the utmost attainable. Occasionally
these sacrifices have been of the substance in grasping at the shadow. Occasionally French good sense
has been at fault. During the Second Empire,
whose army imposed one side of Paris on France
entire, the French ideal of the development of the
entire man, under liberal but decorous *mœurs*, was
here and there lost in the "ocean of excess." The
present generation shows marks of this enervation,
but the recovery of moral tonicity after the Napoleonic debauch is most noteworthy and most conspicuous. The rejection of the Reformation is a
still more signal instance of wrong choosing in a
great crisis. We repeat after Michelet, that France
rejected the Reformation because " she would have
no moral reform ;" and we do not enough remember the political necessities of Francis I. and
Catharine de' Medici, and the French origin of
the pollen that fructified the soil out of which
sprang Huss and Wyckliffe. But by France, in this
instance, we really mean, though we are perpetually forgetting it, not the sound heart and core of
the nation, but a luxurious and elegant aristocracy

in the direct current of Renaissance laxity and expansion—such as existed in Germany no more in Luther's time than in any other. Doubtless with an ideal of personal morality France, even then, would have accepted the Reformation, but she is so *solidaire* that she had to await organic and communal agencies. Republican France, that is, France genuine and articulate, has, however irreligious, never been conspicuously immoral.

When we see a people whose qualities are thus national and whose defects are individual, when we consider that the whole is, everywhere but in mathematics, something other than the sum of all its parts, it seems singular that the distinction I have dwelt on between social and personal morality should be so constantly lost sight of. Losing sight of it is, philosophically, the source of that absurd misconception of French morality with which I began, and to lose sight of it both schools of our philosophy are prone. Let me refer once more to Condorcet— an admirably representative Frenchman. " Progress," in Condorcet's mind, says Mr. John Morley, " is exclusively produced by improvement in intelligence"—progress of course being taken to mean progress in morality as well as in enlightenment. Both our metaphysicians and our utilitarians deny this theory. To the former nothing seems more clearly self-evident, or more clearly verified empirically, than the maxim " Education cannot make men moral." Morality depends upon the will ; you can

reach the springs of the will only through the heart.
Sanctification is therefore scientific, as well as religious, doctrine. Progress consists in spreading
sanctification. Systematic minds, ultramontane
avowedly or in disguise, identify Church and State
in the organic unity of mankind whose saving grace
is piety and whose development thus depends on the
centralized and authoritative teaching of religion.
This philosophy, whether illustrated at Rome or
Geneva, at Smithfield or at Salem, has generally
shown itself to be associated with practical disadvantages which, whatever its merits or however perfect its reasoning, have put the Zeitgeist out of conceit with it. For the moment, at all events, this
tyrant is more favorably disposed to the ethics of
the utilitarians, as illustrated in Mr. Morley's criticism of Condorcet for omitting " the natural history
of western morals," which he regards as " a result
of evolution that needed historical explanation" as
much as the evolution of the intelligence—or, as
caricatured by Mr. Adler in finding the ethics of
the shepherds and fishermen of Galilee, two thousand years ago, rudimentary beside the elaborate results reached by Societies of Ethical Culture to-day.
Condorcet would reply to both these positions by
accusing both of confusing social with personal morality. He would perhaps assure Mr. Morley that
as personal morality depends solely upon obedience
to the dictates of a conscience however little enlight-
ened, any mention of its separate evolution as an

element of progress is misleading. In reply to the metaphysicians he would certainly maintain that, although it is perfectly true that "education cannot make men moral," it is equally true that nothing but education can make *mankind* moral. He would argue with President Gilman : "There is no better way known to man for securing intellectual and moral integrity than to encourage those habits, those methods and those pursuits which tend to establish truth." He would probably point out the dangers to social, of a too exclusive devotion to personal, morality ; and indicate the unhappy ethical result of a passionless, unintellectual, unpersonally-investigated, conventional morality, of which the springs are accepted commonplaces. He would assert that, whereas an ignorant man might be as moral as a savant, there is no record of any unenlightened moral community ; that though the existence of an Alexander VI. is compatible with learning it is inconsistent with common schools ; that moral development goes on in the community as a spontaneous concomitant of general intellectual growth, the discovery of one age being the morality of the next ; that the "progress of morality" does not mean the spread of the disposition to do one's duty as one sees it, but the growth of the conception of what duty really is. "Does this or that community conceive this or that to be right or wrong? Is its moral ideal salutary or not ?" are questions whose answers furnish the test of social morality and depend on

6

illumination rather than on conscience. Which best serves the cause of social morality, the Salvation Army or Girard College, Mr. Moody or Harvard University? A community which compasses the prevention of cruelty to animals may conceivably contain a smaller proportion of eminently righteous men than one which burns witches or sanctions the suttee, but its social morality is distinctly higher. As to communities, it is the French notion that the attempt to anticipate the census of the New Jerusalem is idle ; and the discovery, through mental confusion, of Sodoms and Gomorrahs in other epochs and distant lands, a difficult and dangerous proceeding.

III

INTELLIGENCE

INTELLIGENCE

THE sensation which France produces on the impressionable foreigner is first of all that of mental exhilaration. Paris, especially, is electric. Touch it at any point and you receive an awakening shock. Live in it and you lose all lethargy. Nothing stagnates. Everyone visibly and acutely feels himself alive. The universal vivacity is contagious. You find yourself speaking, thinking, moving faster, but without fatigue and without futility. The moral air is tonic, respiration is effortless, and energy is unconscious of exertion. Nowhere is there so much activity; nowhere so little chaos. Nowhere does action follow thought so swiftly, and nowhere is there so much thinking done. Some puissant force, universal in its operation, has manifestly so exalted the spirit of an entire nation, here centred and focussed, as to produce on every hand that phenomenon which Schiller admirably characterizes in declaring that "the last perfection of our qualities is when their activity, without ceasing to be sure and earnest, becomes sport." The very monuments of the past are as steeped in its influences as the boulevard Babel of the present. The grandiose

towers and severe façade of Notre Dame speak the
same thought, in the dialect of their epoch, that the
Panthéon uttered to the eighteenth and the Arc de
l'Étoile declares to our own century. The panorama which spreads out before one from Montmartre or St. Cloud is permeated with this thought
—as distinct to the mental as the scene itself is to
the physical vision. Paris seems to stand for it—as
did the Athens of Pericles and the Florence of the
Renaissance. Like them, she seems to symbolize
the apotheosis of intellect. The present everywhere
asserts itself with superb confidence; the entire
environment is modern, untraditional, self-reliant;
the past steps down from the tyrant's chair and assumes with dignity the pose of history, while students, not votaries, keep it free from the dust of the
hospitable museums that harbor it. Is not each
generation, every moment, provided with the light of
its own mind—that light which Carlyle himself un-
warily calls "the direct inspiration of the Al-
mighty?" Is not consciousness the greatest of
divine gifts to man? Is not intelligence the measure of his distance from the brutes, the bond which
unites him to the gods, the instrument of his salvation?

This confidence in the syllogism, this belief in the
human intelligence, this worship of reason, has been
characteristic of France ever since the nation became conscious of itself as a nation. And the fact
that its special distinction is highly developed in-

telligence is perhaps equally a cause and an effect
of this. The form taken by the Revolution, that
great purge and renewer of the modern world, was
thus wholly natural. It embodied the nation's belief
in the saving power of reason and its impatience
with anomalies and absurdities. The desecration
of the churches, the revolt against religion, the endeavor to infuse life into antique formularies as
jejune as they were classic, the mad terror at the
threatened reimposition by Europe of the old anarchy, Napoleon's career of conquest carrying the
Revolution to all neighboring peoples, whether they
wanted it or not—every feature, in fact, of the great
upheaval is significant of the nation's confidence in
the competence of mind in every crisis. That the
mutual relations of long-existent phenomena could
constitute a subtle harmony quite apart from the
absurd and anomalous character of the phenomena
themselves, and wholly beyond the power of mind
to see, though within the circle of instinctive feeling, France did not feel, and has never felt. The
belief that the "increasing purpose" running
through the ages operates through any other agency
than that of the human intelligence seems fantastic
to French reason. Working out the harmony of
the universe through the "ways of the wicked" or
the unconsciousness of the good it views with complete scepticism. Even now the reactionary Frenchman who would restore the *ancien régime* feels as he
does because he likes the monarchic ideal, and not

because he resents the rude manner of its taking off. And it is this confidence in the efficacy of the intelligence which makes the French so swift to execute their ideas, so anxious to press and impose them. The trait is as noticeable in personal as in public matters, in the social as in the political arena. It is this which makes them so enamoured of the positive and practical truths; and it is their passionate attachment to these, and their desire to make them prevail, which splits parties into groups, reverses ministries, produces revolutions. That a thing should be admitted and not adopted is incomprehensible to the French mind; that it should not be admitted after having been proved, after all that may be said against it has been answered, and simply because of an instinctive distrust in the human reason, is inconceivable to it.

In finding intelligence thus universal in France, and integral in the French nature, I mean, of course, to confound it with neither culture nor erudition. I mean such intelligence as Mr. Hamerton notes in the French peasant when he says that the interval between the French peasant and a Kentish laborer is enormous, densely ignorant as both may be. Or that quality, to take a distinguished example, which enabled Pascal, who had no reading, to anticipate in the seventeenth century such a light of the eighteenth as Kant, and such a light of the nineteenth as Charles Darwin. It is the quality in virtue of which rich and poor, educated and illiterate, priest

and sceptic, can meet on common ground and understand each other. There is, intellectually speaking, far more disinterestedness than elsewhere.
People divide upon ideas, and not upon prejudices,
or even upon interests. Mind enters into everything.
Even the fool reasons—which is perhaps why he is
the most intolerable fool on the footstool. The
" crank " is unknown. Respect for the embodiment
of intelligence in books, science, or art, and for the
distinguished in these lines of effort, pervades all
ranks. M. Prudhomme himself cherishes a deep regard for them. One of his commonplaces is: " La
seule aristocratie, c'est l'aristocratie du talent." The
heroes of French society, taken in the large sense,
are the men who have excelled in some intellectual
field. English qualities, English accomplishments,
are never extolled to them without reminding them
of the contrast in this, to their sense, vital regard
between the materialism of England and their own
civilized ideal. Yet such is the elasticity and sup-
pleness of the French intelligence that whereas Mr.
Froude exclaims bitterly, "In England the literary
class has no standing or influence," M. Philippe Da-
ryl states the phenomenon with much more rational explicitness in saying, " Our neighbors regard
their men of letters simply as specialists fulfilling
their functions in the general work, and having a
just claim, in the division of profits, to their rightful
share of pay and esteem."

It is impossible, in short, to read French books,

to meet French people, to study French history, without perceiving that the unvarying centre of the national target is the truth, the fact, the reality. This is the shining disk at which the Frenchman aims, in criticism as in construction, in art as in science. Milton's grandiose and beautiful images strike M. Scherer especially because they are true as well—because they are, as he says, "toujours justes dans leur beauté." The drawing, the values, justness of tone, redeem any picture, however frivolous its meaning ; errors in these respects condemn any, however noble its sentiment. Far inferior to Donatello and the Greeks, is M. Rodin's judgment of Michael Angelo. Far superior to all painters, is Fromentin's verdict on the Dutch masters. The concluding lines of the " Ode on a Grecian Urn " sum up the French belief with exactness, as they do ours only by extension ; and it is at once the distinction and the defect of French literature that it may be justly called a splendid and varied formulation of this belief. Familiar as well as classic literature bears the same witness. Compare, from the point of view of the intelligence, the "Causeries" of Sainte-Beuve with those of Thackeray. The "Roundabout" chat may have more charm, more philosophy, but the charm and the philosophy are both sentimental. But for their magical style they would be doomed to oblivion long before Sainte-Beuve's judgments reached the fulness of their fame. A great deal has been said—and said in France itself—in praise of the English essay, its delightful indiscretions, its personal intimacy. But when a Frenchman has anything analogous to do, he does it on a plane of the intelligence distinctly higher than that of the vast majority of English essays since their origin in the sentimental "Spectator." M. Renan, M. Pailleron, M. Anatole France, the most diverse French essayists, even in a department of effort which is regarded rather as a digression and diversion, agree in dealing quite exclusively with the thinking power. In this field, as in others, there is undoubtedly a great deal of inferior work done, but it is inferior in a different way from our inferior productions of the kind ; it is pedantic, or superficial, or prosy, or stilted—it is not flat, emotional, and unintelligent. And of the really superior work it is difficult to overestimate the amount or the superiority. For one English or American, German or Italian novelist, *feuilletoniste, chroniqueur,* critic of dignified capacity, there are a dozen, a score, French ones. In Spain and Italy French wares visibly outnumber the native ones in the book-stores. Commerce carries French books to as remote regions as it does Sheffield cutlery or Manchester cottonades. In America we have simply no notion of how in this way the French ideal disseminates itself from Tangier to St. Petersburg. In every country it is an affectation to talk French ; the dullest prig thus feels himself at once artistically occupied. The whole intellectual movement of Latin Europe is

French. Scientifically, of course, France follows
the lead of the Germans, of the English. The eminence of M. Pasteur is somewhat solitary, perhaps.
But science and erudition are special provinces of
accomplishment, and it is in the development, and
diffusion of native intelligence in its general and
humane aspects that the French strength lies. If
M. Pasteur is not one of a group of which he is
primus inter pares, as might have been said of Mr.
Darwin, and as may perhaps be said now of Helmholtz, his vogue is far greater than that of any of his
foreign contemporaries. Millions of Englishmen
never heard of Professor Huxley. Millions of Germans are ignorant of Helmholtz's existence. There
are, in comparison, few Frenchmen, probably, who
do not know that M. Pasteur is one of "les gloires
de la France."

And the national turn for intellectual seriousness
is as conspicuous in the periodical press as in literature. The press, in fact, is literature to a degree
unknown in England and among ourselves. The
"journalist" and the *littérateur* are not distinct, as
one has only to read the journals that flourish and
the journals that struggle to perceive that they are
here. Indeed, our most eminent "journalists," who
seem now to be getting the upperhand of the
"merely literary" writers and establishing themselves as a class, resent being confounded with the
latter, and hold the same opinion of them as Mr.
Cameron, of Pennsylvania. They address them-

selves very little to the intelligence, and exercise
their own wits, which are unsurpassed, in providing
attractive bait for that popular variety of gudgeon
known as "the average man" and "the general
reader," and known to be endowed with only a rudimentary digestive apparatus for the things of the
mind.   They have a corresponding disregard for
French journalism, to which "enterprise" is unknown, and which appeals far more exclusively to
the intelligence. "A new idea every day," Émile de
Girardin maintained was the secret of successful
journalism; following it, he became the most successful journalist of his time. And ideas are, in
Paris, so far more numerous and fecund than are
our kind of sensations, even manufactured sensations, that Paris has on an average some eighty
odd daily papers. If the "Figaro" desires to be especially startling, it gets M. Mirbeau, or M. Grand-
lieu, or M. Saint-Genest, to exalt some disquieting
ineptitude into plausibility; it does not procure bo-
gus interviews, or print a broadside of private letters, or invent a puerile hoax. The police reports
are fewer and infinitely less elaborate. Names and
dates are no more important to the interest of an
actual than to that of an imaginary drama. The
law imposes respect for privacy, but the law has
the full support of the public, which would find
our "Personal" columns, our "Here and There,"
our "Men of To-Day," our "Society" news, and, in
fine, our entire pre-occupation with vapid person-

ality, simply unreadable. The gossip of the French press is pompous and pretentious, but it is not pitched in either the lackey or the parvenu key. Interviewing is still an occasional eccentricity. Who ever has anything interesting to say is able and prefers to say it himself in his own way. And all that is not "enterprise" is very much better done than with us. Criticism follows the movement in art, in literature, and in science far more closely and more discreetly. Of even tolerable criticism we have, speaking strictly, very little; and the best, the very best, is apt to consist of the specific judgment of the specialist concerning the immediate case in hand— a high-class and conscientiously executed "Guide to Bookbuyers," in a word; excellent in its way, but also eloquent of the lack of the humanized public which demands real criticism—criticism of scope, full of generalizations, bringing to bear trained faculties and stored wisdom to the task of that constructive work which shows the relations as well as the character of its subject. Even in political and social discussion our journals show a gingerliness in dealing with generalization, which indicates clearly that it is an article suspected of their customers. The attitude toward it of the latter is evidently very much that of O'Connell's fish-wife to the word "parallelopipedon." Yet of that amplification, historical allusion, elementary erudition, and cheap rhetorical embroidery which some of our successful editorial writers assimilate from their text-book, Ma-

caulay—of that kind of writing, in short, which addresses unintelligent admiration of the things of the
mind, the veriest Gradgrinds of our public seem
never to tire. Of course, the system of signing articles which obtains in France would prick these
bubbles, were they blown there, but it is evident
that the public has no taste for them. The French
public is pleased with its own follies and fatuities ;
it has its own superficiality and its own variety of
provincialism. It suffers especially from that hyper-
trophy of the intelligence, chronic *esprit,* as one of
the prominent but hardly serious journals shows in
melancholy distinction ; every morning it gives one a
picture of the mental wreck, the state of irresponsibility, reached by a concentrated and exclusive development of a talent for *esprit,* of which the first-
fruits were immensely clever, but which culminated
with the Second Empire, whose hollowness it had
done so much to expose. But imagine the subscrib-
ers of " L'Intransigeant," or of " L'Autorité," reading
our journals of the same grade of seriousness. And it
is impossible to take up a French paper of the better
class without being struck by the way in which it is
written, by the security which the writer evidently
feels in the capacity of his readers to understand
him completely, and by his equally evident consciousness that emotional appeals, dialectical sophisms, ingenious beggings of the question, insincere extenuations, impudent exaggerations, and the
rest of this order of artillery which plays so promi-

nent a part in our newspaper-warfare, will avail him
nothing if his reader be not in sympathy with him,
or his presentation of his case be neither sound nor
attractive. There is, in consequence, a sort of
"take it or leave it" air about the French newspaper article that speaks volumes for the intelligence of
its readers. Its moral attitude is that of M. Halévy's
"Insurgé," to whom, even in the supreme crisis of
mortal peril, the idea of influencing his judges by
emotional appeal, or by sophistical distortion of a
plain case, does not even occur.

Very superficial observation, very slight introspection, suffice to assure us, on the other hand,
that we need not go to the press for illustration of
the opposite attitude. In every circle the most
singular paradoxes are current. They are amply
sustained by that ingenuity of dialectic which is a
perversion of one's own and an affront to others' intelligence. "Things are what they are," says Bishop
Butler, "and the consequences of them will be what
they will be. Why, then, should we desire to be
deceived?" Simply because there are other considerations more valuable in our eyes than avoiding
being deceived. If we did not suffer ourselves to be
duped, if we did not at need elaborately dupe ourselves, such is our idea of duty that conscience
would not permit us to do certain things, an irresistible impulsion towards which, according to a
reverend theory, we owe to the momentum of the
fall of our progenitor, Adam. Either these things

do not tempt the Frenchman, or his intelligence perceives their noxiousness, or he yields to them with his eyes open and does not seek to elude punishment in sophistication. Ethically speaking, he thus escapes cant ; but he escapes also, in the entire moral sphere, the dangers arising from mental confusion. He feels that talking, writing, argument, cleverness, can change nothing in the constitution of things, that emotional seriousness will not transform intellectual levity, and consequently he develops no taste for that Anglo-Saxon passion known to him as *thèse*—that is to say, argument for argument's sake. He is not attracted by the supposititious. His mind has no "Pickwickian" phases. His triumph in a contest in intellectual dexterity would be empoisoned by fear lest his skill be taken for sincerity, and his mind, accordingly, supposed ingenious rather than acute, imaginative rather than sure and sound. He avoids thus the confusion of temper and passion in all discussion. Temper and passion mean deviation from the end in view ; they prevent the object from being seen " in itself as it really is ; " emotion is quite dissociated with getting at that, and, therefore, though the social and artistic impulses lead the Frenchman to express a great deal of emotion at times, to become apparently excited in a way which would in our case indicate the submersion of the intelligence by a flood of passion, his emotional expression is generally decorative, so to speak, rather than structural. Withal the French

7

intelligence seems to have almost no frivolous side.
The different varieties of mental arithmetic, guessing-
games, puzzles, puns, spiritualism, theosophy, fa-
naticisms, have no attractions for it. It instinctively
shrinks from all such desultory and futile manifestations of the scientific spirit. When a famous
"mind-reader," who has excited the earnest interest
of both branches of our great race, was in Paris, a
few years ago, one of the papers expressed the general feeling in the suggestion that a pin be hid on a
transport about to sail for Tonquin in order that
the mind-reader's success in finding it might be
the means of taking him definitively away from a
wearied public.

Life is almost never in France taken *en amateur*,
as it is so largely with us at the present epoch. It
is taken, rather, *en connaisseur*. People do not do
things merely from the love of them, without regard
to their capacity for doing them. Every lover of
literature does not make verses. Every lover of the
drama does not write a play. It is not in France a
distinction for a person of particularly literary tastes
not to have attempted a novel. The love of knowledge is not perhaps as insatiable as with us, but it
is infinitely more judicious. Interest in a wide range
of subjects is not accepted by its possessor as the
equivalent of encyclopædic erudition, any more than
it is so accepted with us by the acquaintances of its
possessor. "Aspire to know all things," says M.
Renan to the French youth; "the limits will appear

soon enough." No American Chiron could wisely
give such advice to our Achilleses. And to many
of our universal aspirants the word "limits" can
have really no meaning, since to the appetite of the
pure amateur it has no application. The true con-
noisseur, on the other hand, the Frenchman, proceeds by exclusion. To enjoy, he needs to know ;
and to know, everyone needs to select. We get
along very well without selecting, because even in
the intellectual sphere it is our susceptibility, rather
than our intelligence, that seeks satisfaction. But
about a thousand practical and positive topics the
Frenchman, who speaks from experience and examination, finds our views speculative and imma-
ture. We, who have enough Teutonism in us to enjoy the vague, and of ourselves demand only that it
be also the vast, find him in turn a trifle hard, a
trifle narrow, a trifle professional. He is, in fact,
terribly explicit. His exactness, were it not relieved
by so many humane qualities, would be excessively
unsympathetic. It is not, however, the exactness of
the pedant. It is the precision of perfect candor
and clairvoyance exercised on objects wholly within
its range of vision and undisturbed by anxiety as to
what lies outside. Of that the intelligence gives no
report, and to the Frenchman the "immediate be-
holding" of Kant and Coleridge is the same pure
abstraction that it was to Carlyle. In this way, and
owing to the professional view taken of it, life becomes an exceedingly specialized affair. It lacks

the element of uncertainty. That of each individual
is in great measure prearranged. Given the circumstances, which in France it is not difficult to
predict, and it may even easily be foretold. It will
not be deflected by whim or fancy. Only in rare
instances will it be transfigured by passion. The
individual is too rational to be swerved by sentiment, and it is sentiment that is the great source of
the unforeseen and the unexpected.

Mr. Matthew Arnold was not long ago praising us
for our straight-thinking, or at all events telling his
countrymen that our thinking is straighter than
theirs. The compliment is a gracious one, but to
be told that we think "straighter" than Englishmen
ought not to make us conceited. A comparison of
our own with French thinking, in this respect of
straightness, could not fail to have a less flattering
result. We are not, to be sure, like the English,
handicapped by the dilemma of either thinking
crookedly or else admitting that much of the constitution of our society, its ideals and its ambitions, its
objects of admiration and of ridicule, is anomalous
and antiquated. But to fancy our thinking as free
from prejudice and confusion as that of a society
where cant is unknown, even though its substitute
be fatuity, would be clear optimism. Upon a vast
body of intellectual matters our thinking is not
straight because it is, in these matters, dependent
upon certain firmly held notions which would be
seriously compromised if we were not careful to

keep one eye on them, whatever subject we may be dealing with at the moment. If I admit this in regard to A, what will be the effect of the admission upon the opinion I hold in regard to X? is a common mental reflection with us when brought face to face with certain topics. This is never the mental attitude of the Frenchman, who looks at the matter in hand with absolute directness. He has an instinctive dislike of the confusion which results from thinking of more than one thing at a time, an instinctive disposition to look at it simply and postpone all consideration of its consequences—about which we are in general deeply concerned. He readily makes sacrifices to insure clearness. The American habit of hedging in advance against a possible change of opinion in the event of later information (a clumsy device for avoiding the brutality of downrightness, much in vogue with our "subtler" writers) is unknown to him. One remarks all this in the first discussion among Frenchmen that he listens to or shares. Possibly owing in part to temperament, to a certain *insouciance*, to a conviction that the destinies of empires are not really being decided, the admissions made, the easy acknowledgment of mistake, are surprising. But, mainly, these phenomena are to be ascribed to the straighter thinking of the French mind, to its unembarrassed poise, its genius for clearness, its confidence in itself.

At the bottom of our own peculiarities in the

matter of thinking lies certainly an inherited distrust in the intelligence working thus simply and freely. Of Butler's saying, before cited, namely, that "things are what they are, and the consequences of them will be what they will be," Mr. Arnold admirably affirms that "to take in and to digest such a sentence as that is an education in moral and intellectual veracity." Every Frenchman is thus educated, however, and Mr. Arnold's further remark, that "intensely Butlerian as the sentence is, Butler came to it because he is English," seems fantastic. He came to see the importance of saying it because of his English environment. To a Frenchman it is an accepted commonplace. And, indeed, we, if we withdraw our attention for a moment from the ingrained Anglo-Saxon indisposition to credit it in practice, and look at the maxim clearly and straightforwardly, as at a mere intellectual proposition—as a Frenchman looks at all maxims or other arrangements of words in sentences—we can feel that it loses something of its apparently sensational profundity. But in practice, owing to our English hereditament, we do not simply bring our consciousness to bear upon any point and, after listening to its report, deem our whole duty discharged—even if the point be a maxim which we can, on close inspection, perceive to be axiomatic. In practice our English instinct warns us against being sure that things are what to the unaided intelligence they seem to be; we have no confidence that there is any predetermined law governing their consequences; and if there be, we are not at all sure there is not some excellent reason why we *should* wish to be deceived.   The entire history of the development of the British constitution, which we, in common with Englishmen, admire not more for its results than for the method by which these have been attained, is a conspicuous illustration of this.   No more forcible example of the difference between the French attitude toward the intelligence and our own could be adduced.   The French way of arriving at their constitution we, in fact, do not recognize as a development—as, indeed, for the past two centuries and a half it has not been ; the *Tiers État* knew nearly as well what it wanted in 1615 as it does to-day, and since then the "development" of French society has consisted largely in converting its intelligence into statutory enactments.   But whenever we think of what little we know of this growth of French institutions it is with either contempt or compassion for the French inability to make haste slowly, for their unwise hurry to draw the conclusion after both premises are settled, for their conviction that the order of nature insures things being what they are, for their blindness to Burke's ingenious tabling of discussion in insisting that regard should only be had to "man's nature as modified by his habits," for, in a word, their overweening and short-sighted confidence in the efficacy of the intelligence.   We philosophize in this way about matters of large importance, just as our English cousins do about all matters—from the blessings of inequality to the speciousness of the decimal system.

Nothing, of course, is more foreign to the French mind than this attitude, which it is probably as incapable of appreciating in others as of assuming itself. It never even affects "the humility becoming such doubtful things as human conclusions," to use an English writer's phrase. It regards such "humility" very much as metaphysicians regard the similar distrust of the authority of consciousness which sometimes distresses the beginner in psychology—as distrust, namely, of "the measure," in Coleridge's words, "of everything else which we deem certain." In virtue thus of their taking intelligence seriously, the French make, it must be acknowledged, very much more frequent use of it than we do; and as nothing develops and polishes a quality so much as cultivation, it is not surprising that they strike unprejudiced observers as in this respect our superiors. Englishmen do not in the least mind this, as a rule. An American is perhaps less philosophic. The things of the mind are more esteemed by us. We have more respect for professors and "literary fellows." And although these and their congeners are more numerous in England, and in quality also "average higher" there no doubt, they certainly make less impression upon the philistine mass which surrounds them, and are more completely a class by

themselves than with us. Our vulgarity is of quite
a different type from English vulgarity; having no
" brutalized " class below it, it is less contemptuous,
and having no " materialized " class above it, it is
not obsequious and pusillanimous. It is perhaps,
for these reasons, louder, more full of swagger, more
offensive; but it is manly and intelligent. Our
rapidly increasing leisure class is itself felt to be
more conspicuously lacking in other qualities than
intelligence when it is compared or, rather, con-
trasted (for of course nothing can be so compared)
with the British upper-class. On the whole, occupied in the main as our intelligence may be with
purely material subjects, and ignorant as it may
be of the importance of any others—deficient,
that is to say, as it may be in culture—it is nevertheless one of the great American forces, and is re-
spected as such and gloried in. The ordinary Englishman finds the ordinary American thin, sharp,
stridulous, eager, and nervous, but he also unquestionably finds him clever as well; the defects he
notes are not defects of intelligence.

But after all is said that need be said of us in
this respect, and however greatly our esteem for
intelligence may excel that of the English, the fact
remains that we are in no sort of danger of allowing
this esteem to become excessive. We have nothing
like the confidence in the intelligence which the
French have. It is one of our tools in the work of
society building. With the French it is a talisman.

We do not, in a word, begin to take it as seriously as the French do. The Frenchman would probably address us on this subject somewhat in this wise : "Your intelligence is certainly agile and alert, especially when compared with your English cousins', but you certainly exhibit it frivolously. No extravagance is too great for your thinking. You are constantly trying experiments in thinking, constructing for yourselves notions of this and that—not at all with reference to any experience, but wilfully. Moreover, you have an opinion upon every imaginable topic, and you do not consider it at all necessary to give any substantial reason for it. You have, it is true, a nervous dread of inconsistency, and exercise a great deal of ingenuity to avoid the appearance of it. But the exercise of ingenuity in this way is itself frivolous ; it demonstrates a lack of confidence in the intelligence as such, one of whose chief qualities is flexibility. Flexible, thus, you rarely are, though you are certainly, spite of all your ingenuity, not a little variable. And it is not new light, but a different emotion, which makes you so. Your opinions are very apt to be *partis pris* —not, *à l'anglaise*, out of habit and tradition, but out of pure freak and whim. You are not, in our sense, *sincère*. You are, of course, perfectly honest, but in importing whim and fantasy into the domain of pure intelligence you are not serious ; you are guilty of intellectual levity. You tell us (or, out of caution, the habit of business reserve, civility or what not, you do not tell us) your notions about ourselves, for example. You have, at all events, no hesitation in forming opinions of the most positive kind as to our character, our manners, our art and politics. To mention politics alone, you have strong doubts as to the continuance of the present republic; fancy us in danger of anarchy from unrestricted socialist agitation, yet condemn our cruelty toward Louise Michel; alternately predict a king and a Radical dictator for us; pronounce us grasping in Madagascar, faithless in Tunis, pusillanimous in Egypt; attach weight to M. Rochefort's utterances; anticipate cabinet crises; become 'humorous' over the unexpected duration of the present ministry— all without any such acquaintance with us, our institutions, history, and present condition, as would be necessary really to justify you, if you took such matters seriously, in holding any notions at all in regard to us. You think a great deal. Your intelligence is very active. But you will forgive my frankness in saying that it is, to our sense, a shade lacking in self-respect. Doubtless you have some other touchstone for discovering truth, of which we are ignorant, or perhaps some substitute for truth itself. Your inventiveness is immense. You are the people of the future."

The French quick-wittedness, again, differs from our own as much as their straight-thinking does. Clearness is not more characteristic of French thought than celerity. The constant, unintermittent

activity of the French consciousness assists powerfully to secure this. It keeps the intelligence free
at once from preoccupation and from distraction.
With us the man who sees quickly is apt not to see
clearly. He is rather the man of imagination than
of clairvoyance. He divines, guesses, feels what you
mean. He runs ahead of your thought, anticipates
it wrongly often, if the data of his augury as to
your probable meaning are insufficient. Sometimes
he makes ludicrous errors; sometimes he becomes
very expert at concealing his misconceptions and
appearing acutely sympathetic, with really very
slight title thereto; his agility of appreciation rivals the artificially developed memory of the habitual liar. But all this is presence of mind rather
than quick-wittedness. There is a perversion of
the pure intelligence about it that is almost tragic.
Our truly clairvoyant man sees slowly in comparison with the Frenchman, though I think we may
say in comparison with the Frenchman alone. His
solidity of character gives him an instinctive dislike, an instinctive mistrust, of fragmentariness. He
must first make the circuit of any object before permitting himself really to perceive any of its facets;
he must reflect upon its relations before he can
realize its existence. The Frenchman meantime
has contemplated, comprehended, and forgotten.
Not only is his own intelligence singly developed,
but he lives in an atmosphere in which care for the
intelligence is almost exclusive. He is thus en-

abled to treat propositions by themselves. He does not ask what the propounder is driving at in general, before consenting to comprehend the specific statement at the moment. He would not, for example, before opening his mind to the subject of national characteristics, require to know which ones were personally preferable to the chronicler and commentator. In listening to a speech, in hearing a remark, or in reading a book or an article, he never inquires what are the maker or author's sentiments or opinions on cognate cardinal points. He is a stranger to impulses which impel us to seek Mr. Darwin's views concerning a future life as a preliminary to even apprehending the principle of natural selection, or the positive *credo* of Carlyle before enjoying Carlyle's destructive criticism of Coleridge. As to any important object of mental apprehension, therefore, his road is much shorter and his arrival much quicker. To him, at any rate, it would not be necessary to add that this involves no question of the relative worthiness of the two ways of seeing and thinking.

But it is only the French that we find especially quick-witted, and generally we reach France *via* England ; and, remembering Thackeray's definition of humor as " wit and love," we are apt to express one difference between ourselves, as Anglo-Saxons, and the French in respect of intelligence as the difference between humor and wit. Such a distinction is flattering to us, and it is therefore become classic. It has, however, to be stretched to the utmost of its elastic extent in candid hands to be made to apply in many instances, unless by the "love," which to make humor Thackeray adds to wit, something more intense than geniality and evident kindliness is intended. And more and more this is seen to be the case. Few Anglo-Saxon critics nowadays, of anything like Carlyle's insight, for example, would be tempted to turn an essay on Voltaire, the great destroyer of the old, bad order of things, into a sermon on *persiflage*. To many French writers it would be impossible to deny the possession of a subtle charm qualifying their unmistakable wit, in a way which renders it very cordial and good-humored, if not humorous. Merely "witty," in our sense of the term, they certainly are not. They have an indubitable flavor which is, if not genial, assuredly kindly. Where can even an Anglo-Saxon laugh as he can at a French theatre? Mirth-provoking qualities will, on the French stage, excuse any absurdity. "Say what you like; I admit it," M. Francisque Sarcey, the famous "Temps" critic, repeats a hundred times, "Mais, c'est si amusant; c'est si amusant!" An American would so speak of negro-minstrelsy. "Witty" is a wretched translation of *spirituel*. To be *spirituel* is to be witty in a spiritual way. It involves the active interposition of mind, and what is known as the light touch. Our humor does not depend upon lightness of touch, it need hardly be said. A genial imagination suffices in many instances. Often this need only be possessed by the auditor or the reader to make humor successful. Heartiness on one side, and good-will, on the other, go far toward creating it out of nothing sometimes. Nothing will atone for the lack of this in our eyes ; nothing will atone for the lack of wit in French eyes. This at least it is fair to say. A Frenchman would find Colonel Sellers as *ennuyeux* as Paris found Dundreary. An Anglo-Saxon finds something cynical alloying the mirth of such a master-piece as "Georges Dandin ;" we cannot comfortably enjoy the ridicule of misfortune if it be due to stupidity rather than to moral error. The French attitude is the exact converse, and the fact is exceedingly instructive.

But the French lack of sympathy for our humor does not chiefly spring from the lack of this element of "love" in French *esprit*, for which, indeed, it substitutes a fairly satisfactory geniality; nor does it proceed altogether from impatience with the *voulu* character of this humor, with its occasional heaviness of touch, its ceaseless vigilance for opportunities of exercise, its predominance of high spirits over mental alertness, of body over bouquet. It is in the main due to French dislike of, and perplexity in the presence of, whatever is thoroughly fantastic, unscrupulously exaggerated, wilfully obscure. To illustrate this distinction, a better definition of humor than Thackeray's is quoted by his daughter from Miss Anne Evans, who describes it (wittily,

not humorously) as "Thinking in fun, while we feel
in earnest." Such procedure is in the teeth of
French habit and tradition—does violence to every
French notion of right feeling and thinking. With
them thinking corresponds as exactly to feeling as
talking does to thinking. This is not at all
inconsistent with the subtilest suggestion, intimation, and even a certain amount of superficial indi-
rectness. Suggestion, nevertheless, however subtile, is always strictly and logically inferrible from
the statement which suggests and which may itself
be so delicate as to be easily missed. And however
superficially indirect an intimation may be, it is
never obscure. But we look for the serious feeling beneath the fun in French wit, and it is only by
long practice that we come to perceive that there
is none. "All fables have their morals," says Thoreau somewhere, "but the innocent enjoy the story."
In any department of comedy the French are bound
to seem to us "innocent" in this way. An Anglo-
Saxon reading or witnessing Molière, and inevitably
associating serious feeling with all merriment of
anything like such intellectual eminence as Molière's, is sure to find his amusement alloyed with a
certain dissatisfaction. On the other hand, in the
presence of English or American humor the Frenchman is infallibly at fault. He is accustomed to the
classification and minute division of a literature
highly organized and elaborately developed, where
wit and philosophy have each its province—as dis-

tinctly as history and romance, which with us are
so frequently (and in Macaulay's view, it may be
remembered, so advantageously) commingled.   In
the presence of that portion of our American humor which is unaccompanied by any "feeling in
earnest," and which is so popular in England, we
may perhaps excuse his perplexity, remembering his
partiality for lightness of touch.

What I have been saying is merely another and a
striking attestation of the French sense for proportion, order, clearness.   French wit, like everything
else in French character, is exercised under scientifically developed conditions.   It is never exaggerated in such a way as to lose its strict character as
wit.   "Smiling through tears," after the fashion of
the English comic muse, is little characteristic of
her French cousin.   The French genius for measure
dislikes uncertainty and confusion as thoroughly
as Anglo-Saxon exuberance dislikes being labelled
and pigeon-holed.   Thus, with all their play of
mind, the French seems to us literal, almost *terre-à-
terre* at times—their play of mind is manifested
within such clearly defined limits and exercised on
such carefully classified subjects.   They, in turn,
find us vague, mystic, fantastical.   Our fondness
for viewing things in chance and passing lights
they share in no degree whatever.   What they know,
they possess.   For bias, however brilliant, or imperfect vision, however luminous, they have a native
repugnance.   Therefore we find them frequently defi-

8

cient in imagination, and thus even lacking in their great specialty of appreciation, apprehension, acute observation. M. Taine's criticism of Carlyle, for example, appears to us the very essence of misappreciation. M. Taine is quite blind to that overmastering side of Carlyle's genius, his humor. He takes him too seriously, and not seriously enough ; he takes him literally. At once we say to ourselves, nothing that this critic can say of Carlyle can have real interest and value. And we err on our side ; M. Taine can help us to see how necessary Carlyle's genius is to preserve from triviality, from merely passing interest, all that exaggeration and fantasticality which are just as characteristic of him as his genius and humor.

On the other hand, it is in virtue, rather than in spite, of their distaste for mysticism, that the French display such a rare quality for dealing with subjects whose native realm is the border-land between the positive and the metaphysical. Here their touch is invariably delicate and intuitively just. They prefer the positive ; they deal with the metaphysical positively, or not at all—witness Pascal, witness Descartes, witness the deists of the Encyclopædia, witness Michelet's definition of metaphysics as " l'art de s'égarer avec méthode." But they show immense tact, which can only come from highly developed intelligence unmixed with emotion, in treating that entire range of topics the truth concerning which seems so accessible and is yet, as experience and candor warn us, so elusive—the nebulæ lying, as it were, within the penumbra of perception, neither quite outside its range in the clear light, nor wholly within the shadow where search is as stimulating to the imagination as it is otherwise barren. The field of thought, where the light touch is the magician's wand that opens the mind, though it affords little actual sustenance, and that fortifies the judgment in keeping it within bounds ; where plump statements and definite opinions are out of place ; where the logical conclusion is divined to be incomplete and misleading ; where scores of practical questions concerning love, marriage, manners, morals, criticism are to be discussed without dogmatism, and the clearest view of them is seen to have qualifications—the field, in fine, of airy and avowed paradox, where any emotion is an impertinence and any hard and fast generalization an intrusion, belongs almost wholly to the French. This field they never mistake for the positive. They are no more unconsciously vague here than in the positive field. They treat fancifulness fancifully. They preserve all their perspicacity in dealing with it. Some refinement of the intelligence secures them against the *imposition* of illusion, and enables them to enjoy and illustrate its *art*.

The passion for clearness appears nowhere more manifest than in the French language itself, the clearness of which is a commonplace. It is for this reason, rather than because it is the earliest settled

European idiom, and because of French preponderance in European affairs, that it is the language of diplomacy. It is impossible to be at once correct and obscure in French. Expressed in French, a proposition cannot be ambiguous. Any given collocation of words has a significance that is certain. Permutation of words means a change of ideas. Spanish may have more rhetorical variety ; English a choice between poetic and prose phraseology ; German may state or, rather, " shadow forth " more profundity ; Italian be " richer," as the Italians, who find themselves constrained in French, are always saying ; the synthetic languages may express more concisely certain *nuances* of thought and feeling. None of them is so precise as the French. And this is far from being felt as a defect by the French themselves. One of Victor Hugo's chief titles to fame is his accomplishment in moulding the French language to his thought, in developing its elasticity by making it say new things. This is indeed, perhaps, the only one of his accomplishments that may be called unique. It is universally ascribed by Frenchmen to the miracle of Hugo's genius. Except Gautier, the other romanticists, even, whatever violence they did to traditions of propriety, worked with the old, time-honored tools. Alfred de Musset and Keats are often compared. They have indeed many traits in common. English stylists, admitting at once with Mr. Lowell that Keats is " overlanguaged," nevertheless do not hesitate to find in his luxuriant freedom, and even his license of tropical intensity, one of his most distinguished merits. In Musset's case a French critic, who "hesitates less and less," he says, to term Musset the greatest of French poets, is specially impressed by the correctness, the propriety, of Musset's diction, the grace and power which he exhibits within the lines of conventional grammar. Boileau could reproach him with nothing. His past definites—where Racine himself is weak—are all right. In other words, his precision is faultless ; and whereas this would be nothing in a mere grammarian, in a poet of Musset's spiritual quality it is deemed a merit simply transcendent—so easy is it to give the reins to one's afflatus, and so be hurried beyond the limits of that perfection of style which, whatever else may be present, is absolutely essential to the truest distinction. One sees at once how different the point of view is from our own. One appreciates how the French language itself, with such an ideal as this, conduces to the measure of the French temperament, the clearness of the French mind.

"La Raison," says Voltaire, "n'est pas prolixe." And whether or no the literature in which this admirably clear language is embodied be as important to mankind as other modern literatures, the most superficial study of it reveals the source of that terseness, for which it is known, even of the ignorant, to be remarkable, in its devotion to the qualities of the intelligence rather than to those of the imagination. Inspired by and appealing to the intelligence more exclusively than any other literature, it rarely sins by elaborateness, which is due to the dross of thought, or by an abruptness and inelegance whose conciseness is by no means inconsistent with obscurity. It is thus full without being fragmentary. Inelasticity of form is not a concomitant of its condensation of substance. It is neither vague in idea nor ejaculatory in expression. Born a Frenchman, Emerson, who would surely lose no essential conciseness in a larger sweep and freer flow of phrase, would have been as great a writer as he is a thinker. As for that fulness which is rather over-explicit than fragmentary, and which is indeed rather thinness than fulness, which in every relation but that of teacher and pupil is so relentlessly fatiguing, and of which we enjoy a surfeit in pulpit, platform, press, periodical, and private conversation, it simply does not exist in France. Such analogues of it as do exist are rewarded with the esteem in which all bores are held in a country whose nightmare is *ennui*. Nothing says more for French intelligence. Nothing says more for our own preference of instruction to intelligence than the opposite attitude on our part, which prompts the acceptance of much that is stale and flat in the hope that somehow it may be found not wholly unprofitable.

And French definiteness, like any other illustration of rounded and complete perfection, has great

charm for persons of a quite different temperament
and training.   Take as an instance, among the multitude it would be easy to cite, the conspicuous one
of so thorough an Englishman as Mr. John Morley
in his character of publicist and critic.   The direct
influence of French Encyclopædism upon European
thought has perhaps ceased to be powerful; but as
one of the chief lights of that English school whose
performance is probably mainly responsible for the
late Karl Hillebrand's opinion that the English at
present enjoy the intellectual supremacy in Europe,
Mr. John Morley is an interesting illustration of the
indirect influence which the methods and mental
habits of French rationalism still exert.   Spite of a
thoroughly English temperament and training, Mr.
John Morley's study of the French rationalistic
epoch, upon which he is the authority in English,
induces him to find it "a really singular trait" in
Burke that "to him there actually was an element
of mystery in the cohesion of men in societies, in
political obedience, in the sanctity of contract."
This is certainly a striking instance of the potency
of the French influence in favor of clearness.   But
we have all felt its power and the exhilaration which
comes from submitting to it—all of us who have come
in contact with it.   There is something stimulating
to the faculties in withdrawing them from exercise
in the twilight of mysticism and setting them in
motion in the clear day, and, to cite Mr. Morley again,
upon "matter which is not known at all unless it is

known distinctly." About many things and in many ways a man fond of France and French traits easily gets into the same mode of thinking. Yet there is hardly anything less characteristic of the Anglo-Saxon genius than this purely rationalistic habit of mind. We are, as a rule, a thousand times nearer to Burke than to his critic in native sympathy, and the idea that there is actually an element of mystery in the cohesion of men in societies seems far from singular to us. We not only have a tendency toward the mysticism so foreign to the French mind and temper, but we maintain as a distinctly held tenet the wisdom of taking account of the unaccountable, and find French completeness incomplete in this, to our notion, vitally important regard. But it would be difficult to convince a Frenchman of this wisdom. The rationality of considering only those phenomena of which the origin and laws are discoverable, of eliminating the element of confusion introduced into every discussion by taking, with Wordsworth, "blank misgivings" for "the fountain-light of all our day," accords with his notion of wisdom far more closely. Cardinal Newman's remark, which we find so happy, to the effect that after you have once defined your terms, and cleared your ground, all argument is either needless or useless, seems to him curiously amiss. Then, he thinks, is the very time for argument, when the terms have been defined and the ground cleared, so that candor and clairvoyance may without obstruction be brought to bear upon those natural or social phenomena which will always seem different to different minds until, in this way, the science of them is attained. "But you are not in search of the science of things, you others," he adds; "in virtue of your turn for poetry and your love of mysticism you are, as your Wordsworth says, ' creatures moving about in worlds not realized,' where argument is either useless or needless; and when you do descend to the practical and the actual your mysticism accompanies you even into this realm; and even in occupying yourselves with so actual and practical a matter as social and political reform you refuse, with your Burke, to consider man's nature except as ' modified by his habits,' which, in your fancy, have some mysterious sanction. You wonder that we know so little of your greatest modern poet and your greatest publicist. In literal truth they can be of no service to us. They are too irrational themselves, and they are too contemptuous of merely rational forces." There is indeed little in either Burke or Wordsworth to appeal to the French mind, and the fact itself is as significant as a chapter of analysis.

Let us not take Burke or Wordsworth as witness of the insufficiency of the human intelligence, however. Let us take the clairvoyant Frenchman himself, and let us select two such wholly different witnesses as the late Ximenès Doudan and M. Taine— the sympathetic and the scientific critic, the *esprit délicat* and the incisive and erudite scholar. They are quite in accord. "We cannot get along without vague ideas, and an able man who has only clear ideas is a fool who will never discover anything," says M. Doudan. "When the Frenchman conceives an object," says M. Taine, "he conceives it quickly and distinctly, but he does not perceive it as it really is, complex and entire. He sees portions of it only, and his perception of it is discursive and superficial." Thus, even in the sphere of the intelligence, we find that discovery and perception are not always, even in French eyes, the fruits of French clairvoyance. Nevertheless, nothing is more idly self-indulgent for us whose defects lie in quite other directions than to dwell on the defect of the French quality of clearness ; the French criticisms of clearness themselves, while they illustrate the quality in being made at all, and thus triumphing over prejudice, may be said to illustrate also its defect in being a little too simple and definite. Truth never shows herself to mortals except by glimpses ; concentration and intensity of attention at these moments tend to create forgetfulness of their number and variety—that is, perhaps, all we can truthfully say. It may be impossible to be clear without being limited, but it is entirely possible to be limited without being clear. Limitation belongs rather to the conscious exclusion of essentially vague topics ; clearness, to the unconscious operation of the spirit of order and system. "Clearness," says M. Doudan himself, "not only helps us to make ourselves understood ; it serves also as a demonstration to ourselves that we are not being led astray by confused conceptions." When we consider much of our over-subtle writing, two things are plain—first that there is an unintelligent awkwardness of expression, and, second, that there is an unintelligent confusion of ideas. Reduced to coherence, the meaning is often discovered to be very simple. And the meaning is, after all, what is significant. Yet the emotion associated with its discovery has so heated and fused a fancied new truth that it is distorted to the writer's own view, and he sees it far larger than it is—he sees it unintelligently. French writing is so different from ours in this regard—it is such easy reading, in a word— that, recalling Sheridan's "mot," we are forced to perceive that it may have been hard writing, after all, instead of merely due to limited vision. About, in his "Alsace," prettily reminds Sarcey of a time when he had not "le travail facile, l'esprit rapide, et la main sûre comme aujourd'hui." M. Sarcey's style is limpidity itself; and when we consider what ideas, what *nuances*, what infinite delicacy, are disguised in this limpidity, and in that of others comparable to it, we can see that French clearness by no means necessarily means limitation, but implies a prodigious amount of work done, of rubbish cleared away, a long journey of groping victoriously concluded, and the slough in which our over-subtlety is still struggling left far behind. Clearness! Do we not all know what a badge of intelligence it is; how wearily we strive to attain it; how depressingly we fail; how, when we succeed, we feel a consciousness of triumph and of power? Admit its limitations. The French apotheosis of intellect has its weak side. But it argues an ideal that is immensely attractive because it is perfectly distinct.

IV

SENSE AND SENTIMENT

SENSE AND SENTIMENT

So that "after all," as M. Taine says, "in France the chief power is intellect." More specifically, however, one is tempted to add, it is good-sense. Good-sense is universal. There is no national trait more salient in every individual. One comprehends Franklin's French popularity ; his incarnation of good-sense inevitably suggested to the Parisians the propriety of divine honors. Measure is a French passion. Excess, even of virtue, is distinctly disagreeable to the French nature. Philinte's line in "Le Misanthrope,"

" Et veut que l'on soit sage avec sobriété,"

defines the national feeling in this regard with precision. Exaggeration, exaltation, the fanatic spirit, are extremely rare. Temperance is the almost universal rule in speech, demeanor, taste, and habits. Nothing is less French than eccentricity. The normal attitude is equipoise. Any shock to this Frenchmen instinctively dislike. The unknown has few attractions for them. The positive and systematic ordering of the known absorbs their attention. Their gayety itself is consciously hygienic. Pleasure is their constant occupation mainly because they can extract it out of everything, and make it such an avowed motive. But that intensification of pleasure which, either by attaining joy and bliss, on the one hand, or degenerating into riot, on the other, involves a complete surrender of one's self to impulse, they rarely experience. They organize their amusement, and take it deliberately. They cultivate carefully a capacity for enjoyment. They strike us as, one and all, calculators. They leave nothing to chance, and trust the unforeseen so little that the unexpected disconcerts them. They are alert rather than spontaneous. To our recklessness they appear to coddle themselves, but we speedily discern that in nothing is their good-sense more salutary ; they conceive hygiene as we do therapeutics. Similarly with their economy, which is conspicuous and all-pervading. If you are bent on pleasure, a frugal mind is a necessity. Frugality is noticeable everywhere. It is the source of the self-respect of the poor ; it keeps Paris purged of slums ; it decorates respectability, and sobers wealth ; it enables the entire community to get the utmost out of life. Economy extends even into the manner of eating. *Les Américains gâchent tout* is a frequent French reflection upon our neglect of the gravy and lack of thoroughness in the matter of mutton-chops. With them good-sense triumphs over grace itself. In dress, economy is as common as sobriety of taste. French-women would no more pay for, than they would wear, our dresses. Frenchmen make the opera-hat do duty in the afternoon promenade, and would resent the rigor of our " spring and fall styles."

This wide-spread diffusion of good-sense has, how-ever, one inevitable concomitant—namely, a corre-sponding deficiency of sentiment. So preponderant is rationality in the French nature that Frenchmen strike us, sometimes, as a curious compound of the Quaker and the Hebrew. We are used to less alert-ness, to more relaxation. Bathos, enervation are foreign to their atmosphere, and are speedily trans-formed amid its bracing breezes. But it is impos-sible to be so completely unsentimental as the French are without missing some of the quality of which sentimentality is really but the excess. The perfume of this they certainly miss. There are characters in Anglo-Saxondom—not to seek the *Ge-müthlichkeit* of Germany—that are completely pene-trated with this fine aroma. Neither are they rare ; every man's acquaintance includes such. Their lives are full of a sweet, indefinable charm. Whatever the exterior, and often it is rugged and forbidding, the real nature within glows with a delightful and temperate fervor that irradiates everywhere the circle in which they exist and move. Whatever, in-deed, the intellectual fibre or equipment, the " mel-low fruitfulness" of disposition and demeanor is potently seductive. Still further, one may find the quality in question illuminating and rendering

9

subtly attractive most deviously tortuous moral im-
perfections. And in France this quality hardly
exists. In very few varieties of French type is it to
be found, even in dilution. Even then it is apt to be
imported. Rousseau was Swiss, and his heart and
imagination had been touched by the deep colors
and mysterious spaces of the Jura with a magic
which it is vain to seek under the gray skies of
Northern, or amid the " sunburnt mirth," the "dance
and Provençal song," of Southern Gaul. Passionately patriotic as was the chief of Rousseau's successors, it is undoubtedly to her Northern blood that
she owes her sentiment. About her French side,
the side which came to the surface chiefly in her life,
as the other did in her books, there was, if we may
believe M. Paul de Musset and other *chroniqueurs*,
very little sentiment indeed. In any event it is an
exception, and not a type, that George Sand illustrates as a Frenchwoman. Her great contemporary,
Balzac, remarkable and original as he was, is a
thousand times more French. But it is idle to cite
instances. After all one may say of the De Guérins,
of Senancour, of Joubert, Doudan, Renan, the fact
remains that the French one meets, the people we
mean when we think of Frenchmen, the great mass
of the nation and its characteristic racial types, strike
our Anglo-Saxon sense too sharply and clearly, with
too ringing and vibrant a note, to appear to us otherwise than distinctly, integrally, and ineradicably
unsentimental. It is this principally, I think, which

makes the Anglo-Saxon feel so little at home in France—that is to say, the Anglo-Saxon who does thus feel, and who, I suspect, is in the majority. Paris is certainly very agreeable. Americans especially, having none of the jealousy of French institutions which makes a Tory of the most liberal Englishman while he is in Paris, find all sorts of *agréments* there as well as *en province*. But it is notorious that of both those who merely make flying visits, and those who form the American colony and move about in its rather narrow circle, there are very few who come into close contact with Frenchmen or make acquaintances of any degree of intimacy among them. And both to the few who do and to the many who do not come to know them well, I suppose that French people are not, in general, acutely sympathetic.

The reason is not the difference in manners or in morals. Italian *mœurs* are as unlike American as are French habits and character. There are a dozen points of reciprocity between Frenchmen and ourselves which do not exist between us and the rest of the Latin race. Indeed, from our excessively industrial point of view, it seems as if it were only since 1870 that the Italians had belonged to the modern world at all—that world of which, from the same point of view, we are the present light and the future hope. Yet I do not doubt that nine out of every ten travelling Americans find the Italians more sympathetic, and that those who cross the

Pyrenees get a more cordial feeling for the Spaniards. The reason is that the moral atmosphere south of the Pyrenees and the Alps is saturated with sentiment. As, journeying northward, one passes into the vine-clad prairie of Languedoc, or into the rose-decked arbor of Provence, one exchanges the deep Iberian tone and intense color, and the soft sweetness and suave grace which but gather substance without changing character in their *crescendo* from Naples to Turin, for a flood of bright light and clear freshness that fall somewhat chill on American relaxation. One exchanges the air of sentimental expansion for that of mental exhilaration, and only when some definite work is to be done do we, in general, enjoy external bracing of this sort. And in France, where industry, sobriety, measure, good-sense, hold remorselessly unremittent sway, where the chronic state of mind seems to him keyed up to the emergency standard, where no one is idle in Lamb's sense, where day-dreams are unknown and pleasure is an action rather than a state, where " merely to bask and ripen " is rarely "the student's wiser business "—where, in a word, everything in the moral sphere appears terribly dynamic, the American inevitably feels himself somewhat at sea.

We have, of course, our unsentimental man, but he differs essentially from the Frenchman He is practical, pragmatical—his enemies are inclined to add, pharisaical. To any one of a radically different intellectual outfit he is intensely unsympathetic. He constantly expresses or betrays scorn for sentiment, which he associates with weakness of character ; and for weakness of character he has nothing but contempt. Yet it is plain that he has, at bottom, more sentiment than the most sentimental Frenchman. His contempt for sentimentality, in fact, is thoroughly sentimental, and due to an instinctive dread of cheapening a force and a consolation which he secretly cherishes and jealously guards. And the contrast is as marked among the vicious as among the virtuous or along the commonplace level of respectable merit. The well-known association of Thackeray's Rebecca with Balzac's Valérie Marneffe, by which M. Taine illustrates radical differences in the art of the respective authors, serves better still, to my sense, to mark the radical difference in respect of sentiment between the French and English variants of the same type. Madame Marneffe is far less complex, far colder, more deliberately designing, more cynical, less remorseful. She is cleverer and infinitely more charming, to be sure, but the charm is wholly external. Rebecca's perversion is deeper, because her nature is more emotional. She is a hypocrite in a sense and to a degree that would undoubtedly surprise Madame Marneffe, about whom there is no cant at all. Her circumstances develop none. Her victims succumbed to other weapons. The absence of cant is itself unfavorable to sentiment, from which, at all events, cant is inseparable—an invariable excrescence, if not in one form or another and to some degree a more integral accompaniment. As a matter of fact, the social naturalist infers it where sentiment is found in luxuriant growth, and from its absence argues the certain presence of cynicism. No two things are more reciprocally hostile than cynicism and cant, unless it be cynicism and sentiment. We come logically, thus, to find the absence of sentiment, involved in the French freedom from cant, express itself in what strikes the Anglo-Saxon as positive cynicism. Examples are abundant in contemporary literature. The Parisian widow of his "Four Meetings,"—one of Mr. Henry James's masterpieces, and designated by him, with malicious felicity, "quelque chose de la vieille Europe"—surpasses Madame Marneffe ; but easily the mistress of both, and here a marvel of pertinence, is the inimitable, the irresistible Madame Cardinal.

"Who has not the inestimable advantage," says Thackeray, "of possessing a Mrs. Nickleby in his own family?" Morals apart, what French family, one may inquire in a similarly loose and approximate spirit, cannot boast at least a distant connection with Madame Cardinal. This creation of M. Ludovic Halévy merits the high praise of association with Mrs. Nickleby. Morals apart, she is quite as frequent a French type as Mrs. Nickleby is an Anglo-Saxon one ; and it is to be remarked that she is as unmixed an embodiment of sense as Mrs. Nickleby is of sensibility. There is a side of French nature, and of French nature alone, which Madame Cardinal illustrates in an eminent degree and with a *désinvolture* that is delightfully indiscreet. In his Academy address of welcome to M. Halévy, M. Pailleron spoke with sternness of the Cardinal *ménage*, and praised its chronicler as a moralist. But for a foreigner the moral is evident enough without insistence upon it, and the point of her portrait—aside from its exquisite technic—is not that Madame Cardinal is deeply perverted, but that she is national. She is national to this extent, that in the vast majority of her compatriots who are, in correctness of conduct and respectability of position, wholly removed from her sphere, who are as worthy as she is scandalous, there is, nevertheless, something acutely sympathetic with that trait of her character in virtue of which her rationality infallibly triumphs over the subtlest attacks of sentiment. Strictly from the point of view of sentiment, we may say, I think, that the average Frenchman makes the same impression on us that she probably makes on the average Frenchman.

Be the situation never so sentimental, it never overpowers her omnipresent good-sense. *La santé avant tout* is not only her watchword, but that of millions of her countrymen. It is as potent to conjure with as the *Marseillaise*—and in the same way; one would say it aroused the same kind of feeling. The famous scene at table on Good-Friday, when Madame Cardinal takes a hand in the conversation, and brings the most delicate and elusive topics

into the cold, relentless light of reason, is exquisite
comedy, but it is satire as well. This brief two
pages of *genre* will live as long as any masterpiece
of the kind in literature, but its interest is not
merely artistic. It is a contemporary national
document of the first-class, beside which M. Zola's
are often trite and superficial. There are present
M. and Madame Cardinal, their two daughters,
both *danseuses* at the Opéra, and the Italian marquis, who has a wife and children in Italy, but who
prefers living with the elder Mademoiselle Cardinal
in Paris—an arrangement secured by the maternal
solicitude of Madame Cardinal herself. Frequent
quarrels disturb the serenity of this interior, however, despite the exclusively practical and unsentimental origin of the relationship. The marquis
is reactionary. M. Cardinal is radical. The occasion of Good-Friday provokes a clerical discussion. M. Cardinal abuses priests. The marquis
forbids him to speak ill of his religion, announcing
that he is a Catholic and has two bishops in his
family. "Tenez," breaks in Madame Cardinal,
"vous nous faites pitié avec votre religion ! Ayez
donc de la morale avant d'avoir de la religion.
. . . Comment, voilà un homme marié, qui a une
femme, trois enfants, qui laisse tout ça végéter en
Italie pour venir vivre à Paris avec une danseuse.
Et puis il parle de ses sentiments religieux. Non,
vrai ! ça me coupe l'appétit ; "—"See here, you make
us perfectly sick with your religion ! Get some

morality before having so much religion. . . .
What ! a married man with a wife and three children who lets all that vegetate in Italy, while he
himself comes to Paris to live with an opera-dancer.
And he talks about his religious sentiments ! It
spoils my appetite." Sentimentally speaking, this
has the sublime irrelevance of Mrs. Nickleby's com-
mon-sense. Otherwise considered, it is the very
acme of sense, reached under what, to anyone but
Madame Cardinal, would be extremely discouraging
conditions. How great must be the tension and
how constant the alertness in which it is necessary
to keep the purely intellectual faculties in order not
to be distracted from impulsively denouncing in
another the contemptible conduct for which you
have rendered yourself expressly responsible by far
greater baseness. In what a pitiful light does the
sentimental marquis appear beside this victorious
imperviousness to the sophisms of mere *délicatesse !*
His exculpatory talk about his wife's wrongs toward
him takes away our appetite as well as that of Madame Cardinal. As Périchole says, " Oui, bonnes
gens, sautez dessus ; " he is, in effect, " par trop
bête."

It is, indeed, very noticeable that the social circumstances responsible for the evolution of such
creatures as the Cardinals should have succeeded in
debasing merely the emotional side of their nature.
The will is not enervated, the conscience is doubtless readjusted rather than repudiated altogether,

and the mental faculties are, to a perfectly sane sense, perhaps, abnormally developed. No one would think of calling Madame Cardinal *bête.* She has the whole jargon of sentimentality at her tongue's end, and makes artistic use of it. The effect is somewhat hard and brassy ; but justness of tone in such matters is for people of Madame Cardinal's station an affair of the susceptibility. A Madame Cardinal of any other nationality would be simply abominable, since to her moral obliquity she would inevitably add the mental degradation fatal to the last vestiges of self-respect. As it is, the caricature of one side of the French nature which M. Halévy's admirable portrait furnishes serves the purpose of a lens of high magnifying power in exhibiting the weakness of the French ideal of *délicatesse.* Its weakness appears equally clear when Madame Cardinal is grossly and absurdly flouting it, as in the above *boutade,* and when, as is generally the case, she is grossly and absurdly affecting it. *Délicatesse* is a social and intellectual virtue—not a personal and moral one. It is the refinement of good-sense under the direction of the art instinct. It is, in a word, conscientiousness minus sentiment. What is the quality of conscientiousness—almost as frequent with us as its correlative opposite, cant—but the result of adding sentiment, that is, serious emotion, to a disposition to right conduct ? And the French lack of conscientiousness in its deeper and subtler sense, and their substitution for it of *délicatesse,* indicates very strikingly a profound lack of sentiment also—an adjustment of the susceptibility to social expansion instead of to personal concentration. Rousseau's notion of gaining a fortune by pressing a button which should kill a mandarin has no attractions for us. The irresponsible levity of M. Sarcey's chagrin at having killed a servant of brain-fever, by trying vainly to teach him to read, gives us a slight shock. We have, very likely, too much conscientiousness. Everyone will recall absurd instances of its unhappy exaggeration. But our possession of both the quality and its defect is one of our differences from the French. *Délicatesse*, of which unquestionably we have too little, is in comparison decidedly an external and rational quality. Violation of its precepts results in mortification, but not remorse. A coarse person may become thoroughly *délicat* by careful observation of his acts, by considerateness, by attention, by intellectual conviction of its worldly wisdom. The chances are against his success, of course, because of the well-known difficulty of making silk purses out of anything but silk—but it is not impossible ; whereas to "become" conscientious is a nonsense except through a change of heart and the aid of sentiment and emotion.

Certainly the frequency of French allusions to so delicate a thing as delicacy jars on a sensitiveness that is acute rather than rational—rude rather than civilized the French would perhaps say. You feel like the little boy who, being taken to visit a family

of very articulate piety, protested in confidence to
his mother that so much open talk about God
sounded to his sense too much like "bragging."
Such words and phrases as *honneur, gloire, excessive-
ment scrupuleux, très honorable, extrêmement délicat*
seem to us over-frequent in French usage, because
we always use them with emotion, and with personal
emotion (sincere or perfunctory), and so fail to see
that the French use them scientifically. An American miner—not such a one as the grotesque Clark-
son of M. Dumas fils's imagination, but such an un-
cut diamond as Bret Harte's Kaintuck—would undoubtedly find M. Augier's Marquis de Presles lacking in true sensitiveness in boasting of his pedigree
and prating of his honor. On the other hand, the
delicacy of Una's lion itself probably seems a little
fantastic to the Frenchman, who would be sure also
to share the feeling of the Marseillais for that of
Inghomar. His highly developed social instinct,
his remarkable intelligence, his good-sense, his lack
of sentiment, enable him to disport freely and even
gracefully on what appears to our eyes the thinnest
of thin ice ; he talks with great frankness of intimate
things, makes confidently all manner of delicate allusions, seems to menace an assault upon the very
citadel of your privacy, asks with inimitable *aplomb*
questions of an indiscretion which makes your own
awkwardness fairly gasp—all because his interest in
these things is purely impersonal and uncolored with
a tinge of sentiment. Take, for example, the in-

stance of money. The French consider America
El Dorado ; and having regard to the comparative
ease with which money is made here, they are quite
right. But they entirely mistake our interest in
money, which they imagine to be intensely philistine, whereas it is not so much that we care for
money as that we care as a nation for little else.
Money is, on the other hand, only one of the far
more numerous and multifarious interests of the
French ; but they talk about it as we never do, and
as, in fact, sounds cynical to American ears. Money-
making is so much a matter of course with the vast
majority of our people that without being paradoxical we may call our preoccupation with it in a measure disinterested. We pursue the end of money-
getting more or less artistically, in a word, and the
extravagance and recklessness with which we spend
it proceeds from this and not from vulgarity, as
Europeans, whose experience tells them nothing on
this point, believe. It is, in fine, with us an end
rather than a means, and consequently enables us
to escape that sordidness which does not fail to
shock us abroad. Our attitude is thus irrational beside that of the French, and causes their frank eager-
ness of acquisition and undisguised economy of
spending to seem extremely *terre-à-terre* to us.
"Coal-oil-Johnny" is really a less vulgar figure than
the more sensible Père Grandet, and he is perhaps
a less frequent type with us than Balzac's miser is in
France. As business is a less definite pursuit with

the French, it becomes in dilution even more general ; it is followed as art is with us—not only by the profession, but by an innumerable army of amateurs. And it is largely with these that the American visitor comes into contact. His mental note-book is naturally, thus, crowded with disagreeable and exasperating data of what seems to his haste indelicacy carried beyond the honorable limit. But it is to be observed that these instances rarely illustrate an offence committed against the unwritten law of the French community itself, and that therefore dishonorable is an inapplicable epithet. To expect a community to change its customs in these regards for the benefit of your *naïveté* would be to exhibit still greater *naïveté ;* but it is impossible not to argue from them an indisposition to permit good-sense any sentimental relaxation whatever, even in circumstances of the utmost seductiveness to a sensitive nature.

The French community is destitute of many sentimental influences which are very potent with us. The home, for instance, in England and among ourselves is a nursery of sentiment to a degree which it certainly is not in France—right as the French are in resenting our absurd misconception of their home-life. Mother and children are not, in France, brought into such sympathetic and sentimental relations. The reciprocal affection is, of course, just as sure and puissant, but its sinews are rational. She does not efface herself so much, and aspire to live only in them. They are educationally and otherwise occupied instead of developing emotional precocity. There are no long readings winter evenings, and none of that intimate companionship so often productive of what, physiologically speaking, has been so aptly termed " emotional prodigality." Our society is in considerable measure leavened by young men who, chiefly through this prodigality, have at one time or another contemplated entering the ministry, and have abandoned the notion only after the momentous struggle which leaves lasting traces on the sensibility. French youth do not know what solitude is ; their only " communings " are communication. They naturally have less aptitude for the spiritual side of life than for its sensual and rational sides. The heart and the passions are of course as highly, if not as exclusively, developed in France as elsewhere, but in the elevation I have already mentioned—in considering French morality —of the mind over the soul the tendency to materialism is never far from the surface.

In fine, when the French enter the realm of sentiment they do not seem quite at home. They are in danger of becoming either fantastic or conventional. " Les deux tours de Notre Dame sont le H de Hugo ! " exclaims, one day, Auguste Vacquerie to Jules Claretie, and Claretie chronicles the remark as an impressive one. Similar extravagances pass muster in the sphere of art, though only where sentiment is concerned. On the other hand, though nowhere is beauty admired more fanatically—adored more abjectly, one may almost say—the idea of it is often conventional enough. Expression, sentiment, do not count for so much as regularity. *Le charme prime la beauté* is a French adage, but what constitutes charm is the real question. As the vocabularies disclose, a single French word answers to "beautiful, fine, handsome." Sometimes charm is mere *chic*, *cachet*, style, order and movement in carriage. That at any rate is, as a matter of fact, the great Parisian substitute for beauty, and has doubtless become so by natural selection. Accordingly, for the most part they confine their activities to the sphere of the intelligence, where they are never fantastic and rarely perfunctory ; and they find no difficulty whatever in doing this, because the atmosphere of the intelligence is their natural element.

Notice, for example, the diction of French acting. It is the sense and not the sentiment of the verse or prose that is savored by the actor and the audience. The voice never caresses the emotion evoked by the significance of the lines beyond the point needful for complete expression. The personal feeling by which such an actor as Salvini infuses warmth and glow into his most polished impersonations, the boards of the Comédie Française never witness. It is an impersonal, that is to say, a purely intellectual enjoyment that one obtains from the delicious voice and admirable acting of Madame Sarah Bernhardt, when she is at her best, when she is most contained, when she appeals most strongly to the Parisian. There is absolutely no sentiment whatever in that quintessence of the exquisite which has made Madame Judic the most popular actress of Paris. An American or Englishman, and I should suppose, *a fortiori,* a German, is infallibly much impressed in his early stages of French theatre-going at the absence of intensity in the love passages ; the absence of all that kissing, clasping, enfolding, rushing together, gazing into the depths of each other's eyes—in fine, all that effort to enact the unutterable which is so characteristic of our stage as to have become thoroughly perfunctory. That this sort of thing does not exist on the French stage is partly due, to be sure, to a nicer sense of propriety, which dictates the limits of what is fit subject for artistic representation ; but mainly it is to be ascribed to the predominance of good-sense over sentiment in the French appetite. One of the most refined pleasures that this world furnishes to the educated intellectual palate is the acting of Mademoiselle Susanne Reichemberg. It is not only delicious in its *ingénue* quality, but it has an ampleness—what the French call *envergure*—wholly remarkable in this kind of art. Yet the foreigner undoubtedly, during a long apprenticeship, finds Mademoiselle Reichemberg's art a little faint, a little thin, a little elusive, because of the ethereality with which it hovers over the region of sentiment, without ever alighting so that he may repose his apprehensive faculties an instant and devote himself to purely sensuous enjoy-

10

ment. There is no pause, no intermission in which to meditate, as we say—the word often being a euphemism for "dream." In the presence of a worthy object, the Frenchman's pleasure is produced by the act of apprehension itself ; ours by the stimulus apprehension gives to the sensibility. We like the light touch, but we like it to linger. Take such a piece as M. Augier's charming trifle, called "Le Post-Scriptum." It is impossible for the American to repress a wish that there were more of it ; the *dénouement* occurs just as sentiment enters the scene. The Frenchman can imagine the rest; so can we, but we want it imagined for us all the same —we are more sentimental. The French public would never have demanded the epilogue of "The Newcomes."

Pathos and grandeur and their adequate presentation are by no means unknown to the French stage, though assuredly they are not its strong points. But it is always unmistakably apparent that these are never pursued outside the realm of pure intelligence, and driven to a refuge in that of pure emotion. Even in such a torrent of passion as that which Got portrays in "Les Rantzau," for example —certainly, as he presents it, one of the most powerful scenes to be found in the contemporary drama— the spectator is throughout acutely conscious of the illusion in virtue of which art is art and not a vulgarization of nature. In other words, however the feelings may be stirred, the mind is maintained in continuous activity, and never abdicates in favor of the momentum of pure emotion. Exactly the opposite is the experience of the spectator who witnesses Miss Morris's remarkable impersonation of Cora, in "Article 47," say—in seeing which the nerves vibrate long after the moral susceptibility is too benumbed to react. Similar contrasts are noticeable in every department of activity.

The absence of anything answering to our negro-minstrelsy presents a very striking one. Few things could be less alike than the sensations obtainable from the *café-concert* entertainment and those produced by the melancholy songs and the burnt-cork buffoonery under whose benign influence the Anglo-Saxon sensibility is so wont to expand. "They have gazed," said Thackeray of his spectacles, "at dozens of tragedy-queens, dying on the stage and expiring in appropriate blank verse, and I never wanted to wipe them. They have looked up, with deep respect be it said, at many scores of clergymen in pulpits, and without being dimmed ; and behold ! a vagabond, with a corked face and a banjo, sings a little song, strikes a wild note which sets the whole heart thrilling with happy pity." It would be difficult, I think, to explain to a Frenchman the significance of "thrilling with happy pity ; " or the value in general of idle tears drawn from the depths of never so divine a despair ; or the connection of this kind of emotion with that with which Thackeray associates it in saying, in the same paragraph which records the dimming of his spectacles by a sentimental ditty, "I have seen great, whiskered Frenchmen warbling the 'Bonne Vieille,' the 'Soldats, au pas, au pas,' with tears rolling down their mustaches." "Is there then," one can fancy him asking in perplexity, "no difference between the respective ways in which Béranger and a banjoist affect the English sensibility?"

We miss unction in the expression with which the French read even the lyric and emotional verse and prose of their own authors. A Frenchman seems to see in such idyls as Daudet's "Lettres de Mon Moulin" a wholly different kind of charm from that which penetrates us. What we call unction would undoubtedly seem to him unctuousness—especially should he listen to some of our professional elocutionists, who bear on so hard as to make the tenderer sentiments fairly squeak. Even in personal matters, sentiment with the French does not outlast the intellectual occasion of it. In the sincerest grief they are easily consoled. Their sanity comes speedily to their rescue from the peril of morbidness, which, from their point of view, it is so clearly a duty to avoid that they devote themselves to it consciously and expressly. Inconstancy is therefore not a trait to be ashamed of. Certain forms of constancy, on the other hand, seem puerile and rudimentary. Be constant just so long as instinct, reason, and passion dictate. *L'amour* becomes *l'amitié* with appalling swiftness. There are, perhaps, as many "John An-

dersons "—Daudet's "Les Vieux" is as touching as
the Scotch poem—but they are not given to senti-
mentalizing.   In the average Parisian the horror of
old age has something almost hysterical about it.
For them, more than for anyone else, the days of
their youth are the days of their glory.

The feeling for landscape is said to be a modern
sentiment.   In a Wordsworthian degree of intensity
it may be ; though from Sophocles to Shakespeare
there is not wanting abundant evidence of the power
of nature over human emotions.   But here, at any
rate, is a field in which the imagination has full sway,
in which the feeling for what *is* can be indulged un-
hampered by what is *made*, where the mind is led
captive by the sense and the sense itself seduced by
the fancy, where sentiment, uncurbed by either the
intellect or the will, reacts under the effect of nature's
beauty in such a way as to transfigure the cause itself of so much emotion and transform the actual
aspect of nature into celestial mirage.   Mention that
phenomenon to the Frenchman, and you will be
sure to find his civility hardly capable of concealing
his scepticism.   You will discover in him something
of the feeling you yourself experience in the presence of certain manifestations of German sentiment.
It has been said, indeed, of Théodore Rousseau that
whereas other men loved nature, he was in love with
her ; but Rousseau was a specialist, and, like George
Sand, remains wholly exceptional.   Daudet's Bom-
pard, who finds Switzerland " un paysage de conven-

tion," is the type. In the presence of nature even
the Provençal is *recueilli*. The true Frenchman,
who is socially and intellectually expansion itself, is
no more touched by green fields and new pastures
than such English exceptions as Sydney Smith or
Doctor Johnson. Only by an excess of sentiment
over the thinking power can one surrender himself
fully to the pantheistic charm of landscape, or share
that passion for "scenery" which rules strongly in
the breast of even our philistine.

As with nature, so in art—a domain wherein the
modern Frenchman believes himself supreme, and
wherein, indeed, he is on many sides unrivalled. In
architecture, painting, sculpture, and poetry, one
may almost say that whereas the antique and the
Renaissance art appealed to the mind through the
sense, the French genius reaches the sense through
the mind. The mind at all events is first satisfied.
It is the science rather than the sentiment of perhaps the most emotional plastic art in the world—
mediæval architecture, namely—that strikes most
powerfully its most eminent expositor, M. Viollet-le-
Duc, as appears not merely in his admirable "Dis-
courses," but especially in his restorations, which
are as cold as the stone that composes them. French
æsthetic criticism in all departments is pervaded by
this spirit. And as criticism far more than imaginative writing demands standards and canons in order
to attain coherence and effectiveness, it is perhaps
for this reason that French criticism is altogether

unequalled.   Competence may be measured, but
sentiment is less palpable ; accordingly, in every
artistic province competence mainly is what is
looked for, seen, and discussed.   Accordingly, too,
it mainly is what is found.   Not only is the technic
more interesting as a rule than the idea, the treatment worthier than the motive.   This is a consequence of highly developed education, which, though
it may not stifle inspiration, yet infallibly disturbs
the relation which, under more rudimentary conditions of training, conception and execution reciprocally sustain.   But what is more noteworthy and
more natively characteristic of French art is that the
technic itself is sapient rather than sensuous.   Your
respect for it reaches admiration ; but exceptions like
Vollon, whose touch seduces you by its charm, are
rare.   Manet and the whole impressionist school,
Degas apart, whose art begins and ends in technic,
are in the last analysis admirable rather than moving ; the mass of the school, indeed, still handles its
brush polemically.   Observe the difference between
Diaz (who is essentially not Spanish but French) and
Monticelli (who is essentially not French but Italian)
in the matter of sentiment.   There can be no doubt
which is the saner painter, which has the larger
method, but there are chords of infinite refinement in
the other's poetic register that Diaz never reaches ;
his fine ladies and gallants are very courtly, they
have the grand air, but they have not the exquisite
suavity of Monticelli's, and do not breathe the same

ether. The great annual exhibition at the Palais de l'Industrie contains no sentiment like that of the Venetian Nono, the English Burne-Jones, the American Martin; there is no tone like Segantini's, no color like La Farge's. Even in the crucial instances of Corot and Millet—not to mention Troyon and Daubigny—even in the case of the Fontainebleau coterie, which contrasts so strongly with the mass of French art, and which is thoroughly poetic, there is still visible the high, clear prevalence of French style, French distinction, French reserve, order, measure. Corot is, I think, yet more eminent for style than for sentiment. Millet's sentiment is a trifle morbid; his melancholy is not intense and spontaneous, but pervasive and discouraged. It is not quite, I think, the spontaneous, natural note which produces the poetry of "Turner's seas and Reynolds's children," comparatively impotent as the technic is in either English case. It has a philosophical touch in it; it is mentally preoccupied. The French peasant is, in fine, too exclusively Millet's subject. Even in the Fontainebleau coterie the thinking power dominates.

Of course the same characteristic is quite as noticeable in poetry as in plastic art. French tragedy is not what the younger Crébillon called it—"the most perfect farce ever invented by the human mind"—but it has incontestably the qualities of prose; it has even the defects of prose. As a rule it is clear, placid, measured; the emotional element quite lost in its contained and cadenced expression ; or else it is *emphase.* We, at least, cannot quite understand what is meant by what the French say about the rude grandeur of Corneille, except by contrasting him with the ingenious and refined but, to our notion, not deeply poetic Racine ; and, of course, such a contrast has nothing in the way of positive judgment in it. Still it is the fashion to misappreciate French classic poetry in English, and to misappreciate it very grossly and absurdly ; the affectation of over-estimating it is very recent and, as yet, very little disseminated. We have far more to learn from the French admiration of it than we commonly imagine. It is singular that we should be as temerarious as we are in judging an art with whose medium of expression we are so little familiar. Plastic art is a universal language. The French idiom is perhaps the modern tongue whose idiosyncrasies are most highly developed, in the first place, and, in the second, the most inaccessible to the foreigner. But one thing is plain, an English-speaking person is apt to underestimate its poetic capacity because of the peculiar composition of his own language. How much of the poetic quality of English verse and prose is due to the fact that we have a double vocabulary it would be difficult to determine. It is certainly very considerable. The play of mind and emotion afforded by this easy method of avoiding prosaic associations by using the Saxon or the Latin word or phrase, or both, or varying their proportions, as the shade of sense may prompt, is very great. We rely so unconsciously on this advantage that we feel its absence as the French, who do not know it, of course cannot, and as it is, equally of course, wholly unjust to feel in the case of French poetry. When Creon exclaims to Œdipus, who has the madness to appear in Thebes, "Quelle imprudence extrême!" the English-speaking spectator, who misses the value of the tone, adjudges the poetic quality of the ejaculation about equivalent to that of a reproach addressed to a man who should have had the imprudence to brave the night-air without an overcoat. He does not see that such a word as *imprudence* is, so far as its poetic quality is concerned, a totally different word from "imprudence." Even a critic of so nice a sense and a French scholar of such distinction as Mr. Arnold complains that the only word the French have for "fustian" is *emphase*—our word for emphasis. But *emphase* in the proper circumstances means to a Frenchman precisely what fustian means to us; it does not mean emphasis at all. It would be as pertinent to find the French lack of musical instinct attested by their making chanticleer *chanter* instead of "crow." We cannot proceed too cautiously where the shades of the French language are concerned. There is no *feu follet* which equals it.

Nevertheless, let us note that this applies mainly to technic; and that after we have admitted our incompetence to pronounce upon the poetic quality

of the medium, and come as directly as thus we
may to the substance of French poetry, we almost
infallibly find this to have the quality of rhetoric
rather than of absolute poetry, as we understand
the term. Its stuff is assuredly not star-dust.
Keats's conjunction of the two words "Cold pasto-
ral!" shows the power of the alchemist who fuses
thought and emotion at the white heat requisite for
producing the quintessence of poetry. Beside them
Victor Hugo's naively admired characterization of
death as "La grande endormeuse" is the rhetorical
variant of a classic commonplace. On the other
hand, where elevation rather than intensity of poetic
emotion is in question, the rhetorical quality of
French poetry is still more apparent; it is perfect
rhetoric, but its rational and finite alloy is still more
noticeable. Is there anything in Victor Hugo's
trinity of Rabelais, Molière, and Voltaire, or in
"soft Racine and grave Corneille," that strikes precisely the same note as Lear turning from his dead
Cordelia with "Pray you, undo this button—thank
you, sir!"? Yet you may find in English prose the
same sudden poetic harmonizing with the calm and
simplicity of nature herself when personal emotion
has spent its exaltation; for example, where Henry
Esmond, after his tirade to the Prince, turns to his
cousin with "Frank will do the same, won't you,
cousin?"

Lack of sentiment, too, seems to me directly responsible for that intrusion of philosophy into the

domain of art, which is a French eccentricity—just
as, perhaps, to an excess of sentiment is to be attributed the tendency of the Anglo-Saxon artist to
infiltrate his work with moralizing. Balzac and
Thackeray contrast in illustration of this as in so
many other respects. In either instance art loses—
in the one because sentiment overshadows the artistic sense, in the other because there is no qualifying sentiment to prevent paradox through the medium of tact and feeling. Dreary pages of Balzac
would have been spared his readers had his intelligence been sentimentally modified. But it is in
such instances as that which the younger Dumas
presents that this characteristic effect is best seen.
The younger Dumas is taken very seriously in
France. He is the first of French social philosophers. He uses the stage as a professor does his
desk. His plays are philosophical deliverances;
and, in spite of their immense cleverness of artistic
artifice, they are invariably artistic paradoxes. Invariably the sentiment revolts at the first act, and
the rest of the piece is an acted argument to prove
the illogicality of this repugnance, its philosophical
unsoundness. A similar note is observable in much
of Hugo's work. The catastrophe of "Hernani" is
very powerfully buttressed, but sentimentally it is
paradoxical and sterile. The same is true of the
way in which the King wins the love of his victim
in "Le roi s'amuse;" it is very likely sound em-
pirical philosophy, but artistically it is an intrusion.

"Les Misérables" is full of analogous error, owing
to the same cause.   And in fact, nothing is so hostile to the *emphase* which is admittedly the great
bane of Hugo's writing, as the subtle sense of fitness
born of feeling alone ; where he is instinctive and
truly sentimental, Hugo is superb.   Finally, take
the still more conspicuous instance of a writer who
passes in general for very nearly a pure sentiment-
alist, and who is certainly an artist of the first class
—M. Renan.   He is quite right in classing that
curious part of his work, of which " L'Abbesse de
Jouarre " may figure as the most striking representative, as pure diversion ; it is related to the
mass of his admirable accomplishment on no side.
French criticism itself finds "L'Abbesse de Jouarre " displeasing ; and it is displeasing because in
it M. Renan virtually reverses his usual process, and
instead of philosophy penetrated with sentiment,
gives us art invaded by philosophy.   The philosophy of "L'Abbesse de Jouarre" is, perhaps, not
fantastic as philosophy, but as art the piece is fatally
lacking in sentiment ; although it deals with love
itself, it deals with it argumentatively ; it defends
a thesis ; it is what the French call *thèse*.   Perhaps
did the world believe its last hour come there would
be a universal outburst of sexual love.   Perhaps for
people in general love is a passion capable of enough
sublimity for supreme crises.   But though we may
grant this, we do not feel it.   Yet with the most
sentimental of French philosophers the intellect so

dominates the susceptibility that in a professed
work of art the subject is taken on its curious side,
even at the expense of revolting the sentiment.
And if we examine in this regard a great deal of
current French literature—the immensely clever
and impressive work of M. Guy de Maupassant and
M. Richepin, for example—it is impossible not to
note the frequency with which this motive recurs :
namely, illustration of the warfare between truth
and sentiment, of the incompatibility between zest
for the real and affection for the attractive, and, as
a constant undertone, the superior dignity of the
former in either instance. The spirit and temper
of this literature are eccentric only in degree ; they
are only accentuations of the national turn for the
domination of sentiment by sense.

What has become of the Celtic strain in the
French nature? How superficial of Karl Hillebrand
to assert, "Grattez le Français et vous trouverez
l'Irlandais!" And how little impression the Frank
seems to have made on the true French character !
When Sieyès exclaimed of the aristocracy, "Let us
send them back to their German marshes !" he had
not only the nation, but the French nature itself, at
his back. The fusion of the Gaul and Roman seems
to have been as complete in character as in institutions. Whatever is runic, bardic, weird, barbaric,
is as repugnant to the Frenchman of to-day as to
the Roman of the age of Augustus. It was even
repugnant to the Frenchman of the epoch of "The

Romaunt of the Rose." The romance and chivalry
of Francis I.'s time were in great measure, doubtless, a Merovingian legacy ; and their survival in
duels and deliberate gallantry nowadays, amid so
much that is *terre-à-terre* and eminently unromantic,
constitutes an odd conjunction. Of the Renaissance
ideals, nearly the only one spared by the Revolution
is the substitution of honor for duty in the sphere
of morals. Otherwise even the *jeunesse dorée* of the
day is more *bourgeoise* than cavalier. It does not
include many Bayards. As equality, tolerance,
civilization, material comfort move forward, sentiment evaporates. Rabelais gives place to Zola.
Where *esprit* prevails, sentiment necessarily suffers.
Wit is hostile to the penumbra of poetic feeling
inseparable from humor. Fond as the French are
of intellectual *nuances*, they have in the sphere of
sentiment singularly few. And for such sentiment
as may be divined or anticipated—for axiomatic or
commonplace sentiment, in fine—their contemptuousness is marked. Voltaire's peevish reproach to
the rival responsible for his mistress's death is a
characteristic illustration ; the circumstances so
plainly justified indignation that the only resort of
the intellectual instinct was in petulance. A society's need of sentiment, we may perhaps say, having
regard at any rate to its expression, varies inversely
with its solidarity, with its homogeneity of feeling ;
and it is the highly developed social instinct of the
French that dispenses them from all dependence

upon that *épanchement*, that sentimental effusion, which we find so necessary to the enjoyment of social intercourse—of which with us, indeed, it is the very essence.

This certainly is the notion of the French themselves. The *abandon* of feeling and impulse, which is characteristically Celtic, they regard as uncivilized. Their apparent excitement on occasion, political and other, contains a large artistic element, even when it is not the natural accompaniment of deliberate action. Their entire sentimental attitude they themselves believe to be the antique attitude. According to De Maistre, Racine is simply a Greek talking French. M. Taine points out the similarity between the prominent Athenian traits and those of his countrymen. The parallelism indisputably holds good in many points; but there is an important difference. The French have the antique sanity; they have neither the serenity nor the spirituality of the antique world. The immense complexity of the modern world ; the tremendous task of clearing away the débris of the Middle Age, which has left permanent scars, and is still incomplete ; the substitution of diffusion for concentration of culture and intelligence—are all hostile to national serenity, to national spirituality. The force which overwhelmed the antique civilization was a prodigious effusion of feeling. The people that issued soonest and farthest from the night that succeeded naturally freed itself most completely from the mediæval trait of mind dominated by emotion.   So, amid all the gayety and brilliant *verve* of French life at its flood, we feel inevitably with Arnold, exclaiming in Montmartre, that "amiable home of the dead"—

> So, how often from hot
> Paris drawing-rooms, and lamps
> Blazing, and brilliant crowds,
> Starred and jewell'd, of men
> Famous, of women the queens
> Of dazzling converse—from fumes
> Of praise, hot, heady fumes, to the poor brain
> That mount, that madden—how oft
> Heine's spirit, outworn,
> Long'd itself out of the din,
> Back to the tranquil, the cool,
> Far German home of his youth!

And Heine, who belonged plainly to Paris by his intellectual side, had undoubtedly that un-Parisian sentiment which, when he was sick unto death and everything external seemed trivial to him, drew him irresistibly toward his old German grandmother, in spite of the exasperation with which, in his prime, her ingrained philistinism had filled him.   How much more, then, do we, about whose intelligence there is very little that is Parisian, who have no such capacity as Heine for breathing with exhilaration the rarefied French atmosphere, feel therein the lack of that sentiment which is to us the universal solvent and the supreme consolation.

11

But do not imagine that the French themselves feel this insufficiency. Do not even fancy that they quite respect our contentment with vague emotion, however exquisite, as a substitute for the bracing air of those heights where the mind exerts itself freely and the consciousness disports itself at its ease. To them Parnassus—or the Parisian variety of it—is far more attractive than the fireside. They are no more " maddened " by the "heady fumes of praise" than the eagle is blinded by the sun, or the owl dismayed by the darkness, or any other creature disabled by its natural element. One of Edmond About's eulogists exclaimed at his funeral, with a fine burst of eloquence, referring to his Alsatian birth : " Peut-il être le produit d'une terre allemande ! " I think if we take Heine as an evidence that the French ideal is unsatisfactory to the Germanic foreigner best disposed thereto by nature and training, About may be taken as the type of the highly organized and really noble nature to which this ideal seems complete, and which reminds us that if the French are the least poetic, they are the sanest of modern peoples. The nation itself deserves Hugo's praise of Paris : " Paris a été trempé dans le bon sens, ce Styx qui ne laisse point passer les ombres "—" *Paris has been dipped in good-sense —that Styx which lets no phantoms pass.*"

V

MANNERS

MANNERS

FRENCH manners are artistic, they are systematized and uniform ; they are not excessive as we erroneously imagine ; they are frank ; they are gay and gentle, but they are above all else impersonal. In this sense the French are not merely the most polite nation in the world. They are the only people who of the communication of man with man distinctly and formally make a recognized medium, an objective "third somewhat," in metaphysical phrase, in which the speech and action of each communicant encounter those of the other without in any degree involving either individuality behind them—which is, on the contrary, left pointedly alone in its separate and independent sphere. With regard to this last indeed, there is never, except in violation of the social code, any curiosity manifested, unless the degree of intimacy is such that manners themselves are of no importance, or the individuality is of so particular a type as to escape divination—both of which contingencies are rare. And it is perhaps this indifference that is mainly accountable for the general Anglo-Saxon position concerning French politeness, for our esteeming

it incurably artificial. We no more like to submit
to the perfect unconcern as to the subtler points
of our individuality which we cannot fail to remark
in the way in which the politest Frenchman treats
us, than we like the persistence with which he appears to esteem his own personality a matter of no
moment to anyone but himself. We are as solicitous to impress him with our qualities as he seems
to be to impress us with his accomplishments ; and
we resent what we insist on considering his careful-
ness to conceal his real opinions, disposition, character in the same measure in which we are piqued
by his concentration upon our own superficial
graces—or our lack of any. Ingrained frivolity, absolute superficiality, is invariably our verdict—secret or outspoken according to the degree of our
weakness for seeing the charm of purely objective
and impersonal intercourse illustrated by others in
a perfection only consistent, as we profoundly,
though perfunctorily, believe, with a lack of deep
and large sincerity of character. It is so difficult
for us to realize that in manners, as the French understand them, there is no more question of character than there is in any other fine-art. They illustrate the individual's ideal, not himself ; his aspirations, not his qualities ; and his ideal and aspirations in an absolutely impersonal sphere where
what serves as stimulus, and all that is at stake are
the sense of external propriety and the artistic fitness of things.

How exquisitely adapted the French are to excel in precisely this sphere is indicated, I think, by the thread of this essay. The social instinct which subordinates the individual and suppresses eccentricity, the social and tolerant nature of a morality which dictates conformity to general rather than personal standards, a highly developed intelligence and the absence of that sentimentality in conjunction with which it is impossible to find the refinement of manners which is based on reason, however it may inspire that *politesse de cœur* in which Prince Bismarck finds the French lacking, afford precisely the conditions for producing in perfection an impersonal, artificial, graceful, and efficient medium of social intercourse. And, in fact, of manners, as the French understand and illustrate them, it may be said that we lack even the conception. Of other manifestations of the artistic spirit we at least permit ourselves the luxury of an ideal. It does not "cost much anyhow," we say ; and indeed it does not, much of it ; our painting and sculpture and poetry and music have cost as little probably as the fine-art of any nation of the world that has devoted any attention whatever to fine-art. Our amateurs and artists are nevertheless active and numerous, and it can no longer be said of us that fine-art does not occupy a considerable share of our attention. In what is sometimes esoterically called "household art" we are even already distinguished. A few New York palaces vie with those of Genoa—whose "household art" had a similar origin ; on the other hand the chromo and the Christmas-card have penetrated social strata which in France enjoy only white and blue wash. But as for the manifestation of this same artistic expansiveness in social life and manners, the idea simply never occurs to us. It would be a pardonably fanciful exaggeration to say that by manners we are very generally apt to understand "table manners ;" it is at least true that we use the terms manners and etiquette interconvertibly, and in a narrowly specific sense. In "table manners," as a rule, we excel. We are not perhaps so distinguished as the English, from whom we inherit the conception, but it is generally conceded in France I suppose that the English and Americans "eat better" than the rest of the world. "Table manners," however, as Anglo-Saxons illustrate them, are rather a department of science than of fine-art. A solecism in them has a fatal importance, and a mistake is mathematically an error ; they offer no field for that human quality which is necessary to constitute art. The French certainly do not "eat well ;" that is to say, as a rule. French people would at table permit themselves, and overlook in others, phenomena which Anglo-Saxons of the same social grade would not permit themselves and still less overlook in others. But in other ways they certainly carry manners to an extent we but vaguely appreciate and perhaps a little disapprove. It is indeed noteworthy that all other manifestations of the artistic spirit they are

apt to make subsidiary and subservient to manners ;
whereas we consider these ends in themselves very
often, as the Talmud does study, and the English
neopagans consider dress. In France they are popularly regarded as humanizing agents, a higher
class of social influences perfecting the mind and
temper and preparing them for success in the one
great art of life from the French standpoint—social
intercourse. The opera, the *Salons*, the *expositions
rétrospectives*, the *concours hippiques* and *agronom-
iques*, classical concerts, the theatre itself afford to
countless people—secondarily, to be sure, a great
deal of indirect enjoyment, more intelligent enjoyment, very certainly, than is anywhere else to be
witnessed, as the occasion of it is almost invariably
superior to such things elsewhere—but, primarily
and directly, social rendezvous on a large scale and
of a gay character. Artists complain loudly of this.
The Théâtre Français is, two days in the week,
transformed into a social court, as it were, before
which the actors play as, *mutatis mutandis,* their
predecessors used to before Louis XIV. ; the play
is distinctly not " the thing ; " the thing is the rendezvous. The two arts in which the French excel
all peoples, ancient or modern, with possibly the exception of the Athenians for a brief period, comedy
and conversation, namely, are particularly adapted
to French excellence because of their intimate and
inextricable connection with manners. Painting
and music and poetry are all very well, but they

necessarily take the second rank after manners in French esteem, and French proficiency as well, because as professions they are limited, whereas in manners all Frenchmen are artists.

What degree of perfection comedy has reached in France it would be a wholly superfluous undertaking to point out. It is conceived in a larger, more universal way than elsewhere. The muse of comedy presides over every Thespian temple. Tragedy still has her stilts on, not because the French have never heard of Euripides and Shakespeare, but because everything not distinctly grandiose falls naturally into the domain of comedy. The mere titles la Comédie Française, la Comédie Humaine, l'Opéra Comique—where Auber and Hérold dominate Offenbach and Lecocq—indicate the extension given to the term which thus includes every mimic representation of reality from *Le Misanthrope* to the veriest vaudeville. And the stream of French comedy inundates and fertilizes all Europe. From Stockholm to Seville and from London to Moscow it is a commonplace that every stage-manager and every dramatic author looks constantly toward Paris, where each has learned his trade and whence most have borrowed their substance. And in the art of conversation, which plays in private life the part of colloquy on the stage, the nation is equally unrivalled. All the French activities are called into exercise, and all French qualities are illustrated in the conversational crackle and sparkle of daily in-

tercourse, in which constant practice and ceaseless
pleasure lead to a marvellous artistic proficiency.
At the table, in the drawing-room, in the cafés, in
the open-air public rendezvous which abound everywhere and vary in importance but hardly in character from the Champs Élysées or the *potinière* of
the Avenue du Bois de Boulogne to the little *place*
or *boulevard extérieur* of a village *en province*, at
every leisure moment of the day—and overflowing
into the hours of industry, which themselves, indeed,
are never, even in their most secret recesses, shel-
tered from its spray—the stream of conversation rip-
ples ceaselessly on and on.   All Frenchmen breathe
the atmosphere thus affected and, however great
their differences, are thus subject in common to a
potent unifying influence ; so that each individual,
even supposing him to have no natural bent therefor, no Gallic alertness and lingual felicity, becomes an educated artist in the great French art.
To be convinced of this, one does not need to remind himself of the Hôtel Rambouillet, of the *salons*
which since Richelieu's time have flourished on every
hand, of the society of the *grand siècle ;* one has
only to enter a café or even a cabaret, or chat with
an omnibus-driver, or one's next neighbor in black
coat or *blouse* on a seat in a public square.

About this conversation there are two striking peculiarities : It is in the first place literally *conversation*, and in the second it is, like any other fine-art,
practised for its own sake.   It need hardly be said

that in each of these respects French conversation differs from our own. What in general passes for good conversation with us is really monologue— sometimes, in fact, so circumscribed as to constitute a sort of informal lecture ; what the French, indeed (who are strangers to our lyceum, for which they substitute a considerable higher education), call a *conférence*. This is the sense in which it is discussed by Dr. Holmes, than whom no one has touched the subject with a lighter charm. Dr. Holmes's view of conversation is extremely autocratic, and would be intolerable to a democratic people like the French. In his opinion the cardinal offence is interruption ; the literal and unimaginative interrupter is the individual he denounces, but it is plain that it is the fact of the interruption not the interruption of fact (as he might say) that really exasperates him. French conversation is in great part made up of interruptions. Its essence consists in "give and take." The most brilliant conversationalist is he, or she (for in France women practise this art as well as men) who succeeds best in *donner la réplique*. Hence epigram and repartee abound. With us the analogous triumph is to state some truth, sentiment, fact most felicitously and to draw from it some apposite conclusion. Hence the little preachments, anecdotes, sermonettes which season our dinners. As for *post*-prandial eloquence, in which our prandial conversation so often culminates upon the slightest excuse, to which it is merely the

modest prelude, and toward which it tends with increasing momentum from the soup on, it is nearly
unknown in France. Imagine Mr. Evarts at a
French dinner. On such an occasion his "speech"
(for which the French language has no word) would,
we may be sure, be qualified with an epithet for
which the English tongue has no equivalent ; it
would be pronounced *assommant*. And after the
formal speaking at a Delmonico dinner, say, is over,
and the toasts (another word which illustrates the
poverty of the French vocabulary) have all been
drunk, and what we understand by general conversation again sets in, conducted by General Horace
Porter, that prince of anecdotists, the Frenchman
would certainly find himself at fault. In an analogous position at home he would be sure to interrupt.
The French *raconteur* is, it is true, a well-known
type, but he is oftener than not, perhaps, a bore, owing in great measure to the perfection to which he
has carried his style, which tempts him to apply it
to the decorative presentment of wholly trivial substance. And in France when a man is a bore the
fact is discovered with electric promptitude. And
in any event, bore or not, the *raconteur* never enjoys
the esteem of our "good-story-teller," who frequently possesses not merely a local but a national
reputation, as it is called. The introduction of the
personal note is distinctly disagreeable. The force
of our "good-story-teller" though always personal
is often histrionic, and the French have, it is true, a

talent and a passion for acting. But even in act.
ing they care most for the *ensemble*. On the stage
an actor who should force his part into the fore-
ground would displease, however admirable in itself his performance might be. And in actual life
the social comes to the aid of the artistic instinct
in protecting an entire company from resolving
itself into a lyceum audience and an amateur lec-
turer.

French conversation thus is social and artistic
first of all—never personal and utilitarian. Communication being its end, it is moreover always admirably clear. Precision is as eminent a characteristic
of spoken as of written French. Each *nuance*, and
nuances abound, is unmistakable. More even than
by its grace and its vivacity, it contrasts with our
own more serious conversation in absolute exactness.
The exactness is in expression merely ; it never becomes literal and exacting. When a trivial mistake
is made, a sophism uttered, a person or thing un-
fairly ridiculed or ridiculously praised, the Frenchman does not experience the temptation, so irresistible with us, to set wrong right at any expense to
the conversation. The conversation itself is the object of his solicitude. Besides, he realizes that out of
the pulpit *persiflage* is as potent as preaching. His
expertness in treating serious subjects with the
light touch that avoids flippancy has its moral side
as, imitating Carlyle's obtuseness about Voltaire,
we are slow to perceive. With us it is the essential

levity of the subject discussed rather than a deft and
lively treatment of it that causes the superficial
sparkle. We associate the two things so closely as
to infer one from the presence of the other, an error
which French clearness avoids. Hence French
conversation is far freer than ours. It not only
compromises no personality, and essays no ulterior
result, but its scope and style are in consequence
very extensive and very varied. It has terms sum-
ming up phases of social life, to characterize which
we should need long phrases, and employs them as
counters, as bankers do checks and drafts instead of
exchanging coin. It tends naturally out of its abundance to include topics with which we easily dispense, in mixed company at all events. It is very
outspoken without being brutal. It makes, indeed,
such a specialty of suggestion for the sake of the
art itself as sometimes to lose all sense of the substance suggested ; otherwise at least some allusions
are unaccountable. And this freedom, which occasionally no doubt fringes license—but probably less
often than with us offends the proprieties conven-
tionally determined—helps to confer the great
charm of naturalness upon French intercourse.
One's impulses find themselves less restrained in
being more explicitly directed. The manner is as
artificial as you choose, the matter is apt to be genuine and to lack the quality which constitutes pose.
On a high level and in a rarefied atmosphere there
is far more naturalness because there is a greater

sense of freedom than in the lower regions, amid denser air, in which the sense of freedom is really the lack of energy, and to issue out of which demands discipline and attention.

"But are they sincere?" is the universal Anglo-Saxon demand in reply to all that one can say in characterization of French manners and of their articulate manifestation in the exquisite art of French conversation. On this point we are, apparently, all agreed. Charming, intelligent, graceful, everything else you will that is admirable; at that vague quality known to us as sincerity we draw the line. A recent clever book makes a character say that "French sincerity is a subject he never cares to enter upon. He likes too many French people." That is the utmost concession I at least have ever seen made. Yet an intelligent observer familiar with the French must, I think, whether he like them or not, feel disposed to plead weariness whenever the time-honored question of French sincerity is mooted anew. One sympathizes with Hawthorne's exasperation at the public curiosity concerning the ears of his Donatello. In this instance also a delightful and delicate thing is being brutally treated. The stupidity is carried so far as to awaken that sense of helpless resentment which one feels in the presence of wilful wrongheadedness on a large scale among intelligent people. The truth is the French are as sincere as any other people, only they manifest the virtue in their own way. French manners include a great deal of compliment, and compliment is taken literally only by the savage. To argue individual insincerity from the perfection which compliment has reached among the French is like arguing that every American who pays his bills in silver dollars is personally corrupt. Compliment is merely the current coin of the French social realm. Nor in nine cases out of ten is it actually debased. Very slight familiarity with French compliment is sufficient to enable one to see that the French sense of intellectual self-respect almost invariably prevents them from trusting solely to the intelligence of the complimented for a complete understanding of the fact that the accuracy of compliment is not that of algebra. Somewhere in most French compliments you are sure to find the intellectual corrective of their sensuous charm. Your unfamiliarity with this circumstance and your failure to notice it may lead you to blush at the moment of receiving a genuine French compliment yourself, but subsequent reflection is apt to make you blush at having blushed ; there was really, you will infallibly perceive, less cause for confusion than you imagined. Take, for example, a typical compliment by a characteristically courteous and sincere Frenchman. During a visit to England in 1868 the late Prévost-Paradol was received " avec ces empressements flatteurs," says a French writer, " que la société anglaise sait si bien prodiguer pour peu que l'envie lui en prenne "—" with those flattering at-

12

tentions which English society knows so well how to lavish when it happens to take a notion to do so." Ladies contended for the honor of being taken down to dinner by the brilliant French journalist. The London press commenting on this *engouement*, and on its striking contrast with the lack of consideration manifested for English journalists of equal parts, called attention anew to the important rôle which the esteem of his compatriots permits the French journalist personally to play in his own country;—to which the Frenchman naturally replied by a compliment. "Un Français," said he, "a rarement une passion réelle pour le véritable pouvoir ou pour la fortune. Son ambition vise surtout à la réputation, à l'éloge, à l'espoir de donner une haute idée de lui à ses concitoyens, ou même à un cercle étroit de familiers ; il se console aisément de bien des déboires s'il peut croire que ceux qui l'entourent le considèrent comme supérieur à sa fortune. . . . Il donne le premier rang aux plaisirs de l'esprit ; "—"A Frenchman rarely has a sincere passion for real power or for fortune. His ambition is above all else to achieve a reputation, to win eulogiums, to succeed in giving a high idea of himself to his fellow-citizens, or even to a narrow circle of intimate friends. He is easily consoled for many mortifications if he can convince himself that those who surround him consider him superior to his fortune. He gives the first place to the pleasures of the mind." Fancy the audience to which that compliment was addressed speculating as to its sincerity!

The truth is that the matter of personal genuineness is not at all in question. So far as sincerity in compliment is concerned it depends upon the specific truth or falsity of the words employed and their impersonal suggestion. Of course the French do intrude the personal equation into this sphere; they do occasionally endeavor to make one believe they mean what they say in a special and intense sense; the phenomenon is not absolutely unknown. But it is far less common than with us; and it invariably denotes in the practitioner a lower grade of person. The large part played by the emotions in our activities of this kind causes us to regard the passage from compliment to flattery as venial whenever the heart is in the right place. The circumstance that compliment is in France a fine-art makes the same error there far more grave, and consequently far less frequent. It becomes a sign of *grossièreté*—which is the French unpardonable sin.

Furthermore the French compliment never means more than it says. The national turn for intelligence serves as a great safeguard for sincerity here, whereas if we examine closely our own way of allowing the heart to dictate to the judgment, we cannot fail to see how inexact our sincerity often becomes. The Frenchman if he wishes to compliment you will select some point about you that will bear it. His language regarding this may at first (and, as I have indicated, only at first) seem exaggerated, but the basis of it will be sound. With us in sincere instances the process is this : a genuine esteem precedes the desire to please ; the desire to please takes the form of an expression of this general feeling of esteem ; this form itself has nothing more to do with the facts it states than had the compliant admissions of Polonius to Hamlet, "very like a whale," "it is backed like a weasel"—which furnish a not bad illustration indeed of our ordinary form of compliment, all question of Polonius's fundamental sincerity, of course, aside.

The foreigner's notion that the French "do everything with an air" is perfectly sound. The author of "Living Paris," who is an unusually liberal observer, adds that "they do it all the same." This is quite true. If there was ever a practical and positive people under the sun it is the French. But it answers only an elementary vulgar error. A more plausible yet equally erroneous notion is that this "air" is affected and theatrical. Theatrical it may sometimes become in that excess which is uncongenial to the French character and therefore rare. But the noticeable thing about it is that it is not theatrical. Such poses, tones, and gesture as are common to our stage and occasionally overflow into so opposite a place as our pulpit would excite amazement at a *théâtre de banlieue*. Dramatic is the true epithet for that systematization of expression noticeable in the French. The "air" with

which they do everything has nothing of ill-regu-
lated emotion in it; nor, on the other hand, is it
often characterized by that sensuous magic inseparable from Italian native grace. It is in nowise sentimental; it is simply expressive. It may be more or
less ornate, now structural, now decorative, as individuals differ. But what is to be noted is that it is
invariably the "air" which the individual deems appropriate, and that fitness is his sole criterion. The
reason for our failure to perceive this is that in every
serious matter we rely on the impression produced
by personal character to convey its importance to
the listener or spectator. The more weighty the
substance the more condensed the statement, the
more poetic the theme the balder, or at least the
briefer, its expression. In fine our idea of expression is repression. We appeal to the imagination,
not to the sense or the reason. We find the French
"air" theatrical instead of logically and aptly dramatic, because our ideal is to have no "air" at all.
We are egoists, not artists; it is not what we say or
do that we wish to count, but ourselves.

Hence manifestly the confusion of which we are
guilty in accusing the French of affectation at the
same time that we speak of them as naturally theatrical. But they are no more affected than they are
theatrical. By our exaltation of character over manners, by our adjusting of manners to personal expression, by our sentimental and inartistic substitution
of a thoroughly contained and intense air for the nat-

ural and spontaneous one which fits the thought, we are in far graver peril from this subtle foe than is the Frenchman, whose manner alone, at any rate, is attacked and whose character escapes. Tell over scrupulously the list of your friends, American or English. How many of them are there who do not affect some character or other, some moral rôle foreign to their native disposition, with which their effort to harmonize their demeanor is quite as obvious as it is successful? In one's own case this may be aspiration, but in that of others it is invariably affectation. And the attempt to impose it results in a kind of pervasive and general hypocrisy beside which the explicit and definite *cafardise* of the French has the merit of being a frank foe. In France a man's valuation of himself is much more nearly that which his friends set upon him. Even in the French manner what we mistake for affectation is merely intention. To bring all one's physical activities into the sphere of culture and reason, to suit the gesture to the word and the word to the thought, to stand and walk and sit decorously, to enter a room, to bow to a lady, to carry on a tête-à-tête, or share a general conversation, to avoid controversy, to attain repose—to do all this respectably requires intention. So far as communities are concerned fine natural manners are a myth, but this probably does not prevent the Sioux and Apaches from considering our manners artificial, or us from finding affectation in those of the French, owing to

the distinctness which unfamiliarity gives to intention in either instance, and to the failure in each
case to appreciate the importance of intention in
everything of importance.

In fine the vulgar mistrust of French sincerity is
based on nothing more nor less than the fact that
French manners are studied, artificial, conventional,
which does not of course mean that they are of
necessity inelastic or excessive or superficial, but
that the French put the same intention into manners
that all civilized peoples do into language, and have
systematized them with the same care for correctness
on the one hand and pliability on the other. We
have no exactly equivalent word for what the French
call *tenue*, and if we have exactly the thing, it is infinitely less developed and less nearly universal than
in France, where it is as characteristic of manners as
are the impersonal and artistic spirit. *Tenue* means
restraint, order, measure, style, consciousness, intention in demeanor and bearing. Owing to his natural turn for these qualities the Frenchman is rarely
tempted to permit himself indiscretions. He is not
solicited by whimsical impulses. He has no desire
for relaxation, and does not chafe under restraint.
It is not difficult for him to feel at ease in an erect
posture ; he supports the greater muscular tension
involved with less evident fatigue ; his hands do not
automatically seek his trousers' pockets nor his knees
cross one another. Consciousness and self-consciousness are not identical terms to him. Nor does the

artificiality of the drawing-room atmosphere oppress
him and entice him into mistaking buffoonery for
the talismanic touch of thawing nature, into spas-
modic laughter, into long stories, into that amusement of the *ensemble*, which involves neglect of the
members, of the company. Of course perfect breeding is perfect breeding the world over. But the perfectly bred man is born, not bred, if the paradox
may be permitted. The mass of mankind have no
more genius for manners than for tight-rope dancing, but it is easy to see that the mass of Frenchmen
have a talent for them in adding a talent for *tenue* to
the social and the artistic instincts.

It would be difficult to find in any *bourgeois* interior the entire absence of form characteristic of many
of our own average homes.   Not that in moments—
or hours—of mutual *ennui* and common *délassement*,
the average *bourgeois* interior does not, from the
point of view of pure form, leave something to be desired.   But, in seasons of entire sanity, the respective shapes expansiveness takes in a French home
and in one of our own differ prodigiously.   Take a
large French family reunion. Few social pictures
are prettier. There is very likely an entire absence
of that hearty familiarity which characterizes our
Thanksgiving or Christmas gatherings.   The children do not romp, the grown people do not appear
as if at last the moment had come when all outward
restraint and formality could be thrown aside with a
clear conscience.   The visitors do not "make them-

selves perfectly at home," the hosts do not invite them to do so, or treat them as if such were the case. There is everywhere perfectly apparent the French veneer of artificial courtesy. Children are treated with politeness and not hugged ; babies are banished—are generally, in fact, in a state of chronic exile ; if at times everyone is talking at once it is evidently because of the social desire to contribute to the conversation, rather than because of the unsocial disposition to neglect one's neighbor's appreciations— an abysmal difference in itself ; there are no uncomfortable silences passed in simply "sitting 'round" and cudgelling one's brains as to what to do next ; the great art and enjoyment of social life being conversation—exchange of ideas, or notions, original or trite, but always cast in more or less careful form— games are far seldomer than among us resorted to as a substitute, and being invariably for money probably owe their popularity to the ingrained French disposition toward avarice ; an avarice which always seems curious to us but about which in its milder manifestations there is never any concealment. Games themselves are never conducted in silence. The solemn stillness that with us accompanies the rubber of whist which is more and more tending to become, even as played by the young and frivolous, a tremendously serious thing, and which indicates clearly that the game is an end in itself and not a pastime, is unknown outside the clubs in France. An occasional old gentleman, who when the stakes

are high insists on a subordination of talk and vigorously represses his partner's tendency to discursive-
ness, is voted a nuisance. Naturally thus, there is
nowhere to be seen, perhaps, such wretched whist-
playing as in French *salons*.

Universally in French interiors an American perceives at once the absence of effort at "entertaining
people," in our phrase. The entertainment is a phenomenon spontaneously generated when people come
together. The various social amusements are certainly cultivated ; dancing and singing and the piano
are, of course, merely subordinated, not suppressed
—one cannot converse forever. But dancing is nowhere the passion that it is with us ; if it were, the
French, who dance detestably, would perhaps dance
better. People dance, but then, also, occasionally,
they desist from dancing ; in the cotillion the pretti-
ness of the figure occupies much more attention than
its duration. As for music the French are decidedly
ahead of us. They already very generally recognize
the caricature which ordinary amateur effort is; they
are well known to have far less respect than our race
for what bores them ; and now that so much professional effort is had at *soirées* they have become exacting and only extraordinary amateur skill is tolerated. As for our readings, Browning societies, and
in general the class of literary entertainment provided by the thousands of provincial and rural
"sociables" from one end of our country to the
other—many of these half-acknowledged *pisallers*

would seem grotesque to the most long-suffering
Latin ; in France, especially, elocution and erudition,
general and special information and all cognate
acquirements are taken seriously. The end and
aim of society is in fact simply human intercourse,
decorated with infinite variety but never needing to
be buttressed—recognized as a natural satisfaction
of a profound instinct and needing no extraneous
stimulus, only a careful and elaborate development
and ordering.

This ordering necessarily results in uniformity of
manners, and uniformity is as foreign to our manners
as is the impersonal, artistic, or conventional spirit.
But it is to be observed that uniformity of manners
is a great humanizer. It is perhaps the simplest
means of bringing persons of different idiosyncrasies into sympathetic relations. Our own diversity
is grotesque and is responsible for much estrange-
ment between our different sections. A Chicago
journal, for example, treating of courtship, apos-
trophizes plaintively " the turned-down light, the
single chair," but it would be idle to pretend that
the *milieu* thus briefly characterized is congenial to
all of us. As yet with us every man is his own
Chesterfield. We have individuals with the charm
which in Emerson struck Carlyle as elaborate, not
to say excessive. We have the average rural New
Englander whom Emerson found picturesque, but
whose charm is distinctly not excessive. We have
the entire gamut run by the Southron describing a

dinner party composed to his sense of "an elegant
gentleman from Virginia, a gentleman from Ken-
tucky, a man from Ohio, a fellow from New York,
and a galoot from Boston." Our society thus has
the advantage of not being monotonous to the artist ;
but the dead level of steel rails has this superiority
over the interesting diversity of corduroy roads that
it makes travel easier and arrival more hopeful.
The avoidance of friction secured is incalculably delightful. The social machinery so scrupulously
attended to runs far more smoothly than ours, which
we imagine will quite take care of itself if we fulfil
the condition that made such a carver of men's cas-
ques of the sword and such a sure-thruster of the
lance of the pure-hearted Sir Galahad. No Frenchman to whom you talk punctuates your sentences
with an eager and admonitory " yes, yes, yes." Nor
does appreciation of his own wit or of yours involve
distracting excursions. Nor does he show you
plainly how hard it is for him to wait till you have
finished, or let his attention wander, or try to save
time by the surreptitious reading of a letter or a
glance at a newspaper heading, or indicate in any
way as so many of us do, the manner varying with
individual character, that conversation is not the
most important affair in the world. He knows that
for the moment it is.

On the other hand susceptibilities escape wound-
ing with a completeness that seems as wonderful as
the means by which it is secured is seen to be simple.

In France it is in the first place bad manners to be too
susceptible ; in the second place it is a mark of that
conceit always ascribed to a lack of intelligence; in
the third place one's susceptibility is justly wounded
only when an offence has been committed against the
code of manners. These sound like commonplaces.
But they are practically not accepted by us. Practically we believe in " taking no offence where none is
intended ; " and we really think that when the social
code of the Golden Age comes to be discovered, this
will be found to have been its spirit too. On the
contrary giving unintentionally just ground for
offence is precisely what the French find it impossible
to support. Provided with a conventional and uniform code, they concentrate their attention upon the
grossièreté—to them the most repugnant quality in
the world—of the offence, and whether or no it be
accompanied by design, by *malhonnêteté*, is a subordinate consideration. Accompanied by *malhonnêteté* it may or may not be, but aggravated by it or
by anything, it cannot. In this way the French
avoid the habit so prevalent with us of always seeking the motive of everyone's speech or behavior and
the suspicion, the morbid sensitiveness, which is the
inevitable result of this habit. So long as the *con-
venances* remain undisturbed people's motives are
assumed to be amiable. It is our notion on the contrary that observance of conventions can mean very
little, and our own experience, in fact, teaches us
that they are often extremely deceptive indices of

both the feelings and the character. So long, accordingly, as we are sure that a person is well-disposed and worthy, he may, within certain ill-defined limits, say and do what he chooses; so long as we are convinced that right feeling presides at their sacrifice our solicitude for conventions ceases. We do not in this way reach much eminence in what is strictly defined as civility, but that is a common-place which does not greatly disturb us; we readily reconcile ourselves to the impeachment; we easily console ourselves with the notion that we possess what is far more important and perhaps after all inconsistent with that "outward grace" which Mr. Lowell assures us we know to be but "dust." But this attitude compels us to be continually "making allowances" for people who are, though kind, still uncouth or inconsiderate; and uncouthness and inconsiderateness, are, however tolerable, nowhere agreeable qualities in a positive sense. And one cannot continually "make allowances" or have them made for him without great detriment to his dignity. Consequently we do feel a vague discomfort, which the French with their concentration on the dust of outward grace are spared, in a hundred more or less trifling details of social intercourse. And occasionally, when an individual of either of the two great branches of our race contemplates such an individual of the other as chance may be trusted now and then to bring into contact with him—in encounters of this sort with which every travelled

American or Englishman is familiar, scales seem to
fall from his eyes. French manners appear transfigured to him. Mere "outward grace" rises prodigiously in his esteem. Few cultivated Englishmen
probably have escaped a shock when subjected for
the first time to the unrestrained familiarity and the
empty-headed effusiveness characteristic of many of
our compatriots. Few Americans probably have
not flushed with a sense of outrage at the tactless
incivility of the worthy but forbidding Briton. The
American "drummer" narrating his experiences and
making his "effect" at a Continental *table d'hôte*, and
the English lady opposite him visibly wondering how
he can eat butter with hot meats and carefully mani-
festing an exaggerated disgust in consequence, tend,
for example, to excite in each other a feeling of toleration for manners as the French conceive them—
manners which in seasons of calmer weather they
find excessive.

Nothing, however, could be more erroneous than
the popular Anglo-Saxon notion that French manners are excessive. Like all our notions about the
French this is with us an inheritance. English
manners are in general reserved, brusque, embarrassed perhaps in reality, if you choose to examine
into the real nature of puerilities, but superficially—
that is to say in the sole sphere of their action—
splenetic, bald, absurdly uncivilized as manifested
toward strangers, and characterized in intimacy by
what Emerson calls "unbuttoned ease." By force

of contrast French manners are bound to appear excessive to Englishmen. Positively speaking, of all possible qualities that of excess is the most foreign to French demeanor as it is to the French mind. The Italian manner is excessive, if you choose—and are ill-natured enough to mention it. And curiously enough our own and that of the English— when any value is attached to it, when account is really taken of it, when we wish to be "especially polite," as the singular phrase is—may certainly be thus described. But French manners are saved from excess by the very fact that they are so thoroughly conventional. Nowhere is convention more esteemed, although nowhere are its terms more elastic. Nowhere, as one has occasion to remark there at every turn, is a given convention so frankly accepted as the formulated opinion of mankind concerning the subject of it. To dispute it, to advance individual notions in modification of it, is clearly regarded as more *naïf* than even courageous. That "common consent of mankind" which certain moralists make the arbiter in ethics is in France applied to almost every conceivable act of man with an elaborateness and system that rival those of the Code Napoléon itself. Nowhere, perhaps, outside the precincts of the Court of Castile, is etiquette, that codified system of manners, carried so far ; nowhere is an offence against it more quickly noticed. Violations of it are readily excused if justifiable ; there is no pedantry : there is even a special interest exhibited in *originalité*—a word which it is significant that we have to render by eccentricity. But violations are invariably remarked and the proper deduction made therefrom.

Nevertheless, etiquette itself being not a court affair but something thoroughly understood and practised by everybody, French manners are thereby saved from excess, as they are from every other form of eccentricity. They strike one, rather, as being almost business-like ; at any rate their design is clearly to remove friction as well as to decorate intercourse. The "grimacing dancing-master," the "bowing and scraping" simply do not exist ; not because the French are incapable of such insincere artificiality, but because they do not like it. It does not seem to them a good thing in itself. The degree to which they have carried the evolution of manners has left it far behind. It is an offence against measure and it is undemocratic—either circumstance being enough to condemn it in French esteem. In Peking, doubtless, the French manner would seem meagre. In Virginia, "before the war," the Frenchman would certainly have found much in that courtly and elaborate bearing of which we still read in Southern literature and of which we observe the majestic remains whenever a Southern orator delivers a set speech, which would have seemed to him Oriental. Indeed, one may remark in passing, Claverhouse himself would have been greatly surprised at the abundance of manner in the " de-

13

scendants of the cavaliers." The grandiose is almost never to be encountered in France—except in art or literature where it is sought of set purpose and expressly, as who should say "let us now intone instead of simply speaking." On the other hand the sincerely familiar manner, that manner which is the absolute absence of manner, is quite as uncommon. Drop into the little stuffy hall in the Boulevard des Capucines of a Thursday evening, and listen to one of M. Francisque Sarcey's charming *conférences* on the stage, on poetry, on literature. M. Sarcey's manner is admirably free from pose of any kind ; it passes in Paris for the manner suited to a *bonhomie* almost, if not quite, *bourgeoise*. It is familiar in a sense unknown to our lyceum ; M. Sarcey, who is in the first place seated, stops over a citation to laugh or admire with his auditors : occasionally one of these hazards a suggestion to which the *conférencier* bows agreement or shrugs dissent ; one is almost *en famille*. But the family is clearly a French family. There is no relaxation, no unbending, no flaccid *abandon*. Of familiarity as we understand the term and as we illustrate it on the rostrum, as well as in the "back-store," there is none at all. Quite as watchful a guard is kept over the moral muscles as if the occasion were a wholly different one. M. Sarcey and his auditors are as much on "dress-parade," as we sometimes say of this attitude, as the soldiers at a Longchamps review. They have simply, morally speaking,

learned so well to use their faculties by the habit
which is a second nature, that that first nature which
as Pascal observed is perhaps only a first habit,
seems to them rudimentary rather than specifically
natural, as it appears to us. Suppose—if such a
thing can be supposed—M. Sarcey forming one of
the late Mr. Beecher's audience at Plymouth Church
on a Sunday morning. The time, the place, the
theme are sacred, but he would be certain to find a
lack of correspondence between this fact and the
manners of the occasion—he would be sure to esteem unfair any criticism of French manners as excessive which should be based on the standard
there confronting and surrounding him. He would
be sure, on the other hand, to find excess in the occasion's absence of *tenue*. He would reflect : "Our
manner is business-like rather than Italian ; it is direct rather than rococo. We are familiar, we are
free, we are frank, we are gay ; but we are not gay
like *that*."

Finally, French manners are gentle. A certain
mildness of demeanor, which is, among us, mainly
confined to such individuals as do not fear the consequences of failure in self-assertion, is everywhere
observable. The fiercely mustachioed concierge
shares it with the bland academician. It is the
rarest imaginable chance to hear an oath. There is
something feeble and inefficient, an acknowledgment
of inarticulateness, about the intenser sort of exple-
tives, which are wholly foreign to the French tem-

per, accustomed to perfect facility and adequacy of
expression. Similarly with slang. French *argot* is
almost a language by itself. Slang as we comprehend the term, and as Walt Whitman eulogizes and
employs it—namely, as the riotous medium of the
under-languaged, is unknown. One may in a week
hear more oaths and more slang of the coarse and
stupid sort in Wall Street, at the seaside, in the
hotel corridors and street-cars and along the sidewalks of New York and Philadelphia, say, and in
public generally among us than in the length and
breadth of France in a year. There is not the same
burlesque of "heartiness," the same slapping on the
back, the same insistent invitations to drink, the
same *brutalité ;* in fine there is infinitely more gentleness. Their occasional savagery strikes us as ineffective and amateur, their fury seems fustian.
The "rapier-thrusts" of sarcasm, the kind of writing and talking to which some of our newspapers
apply their most eulogistic epithet, "scathing," the
bitter banter to which not a few of the best bred of
our young girls seem just now especially addicted
would excite amazement in France. *Persiflage,*
there, is never personal when it is not also good-
natured. In any event there is far less of it than
of compliment; and this compliment is less factitious than are our personalities of the uncompli-
mentary kind. The difference shows an important
temperamental distinction as well as anything can.
The French are as inclined to the amiable, the agree-

able, the social, the impersonal as we are to avoid
being the dupe of these qualities ; perhaps they are
less duped than we are, and at any rate the amount
of fruitless friction which they save over us is very
great.   Indeed with us this friction grows by natural selection ; it is popular because, conscious of immense kindliness at bottom and our own withers being for the moment unwrung, we like to see the
galled jade wince.   The Chamber of Deputies is
sometimes a bear garden, and the air is thick with
denunciation, but such a speech as Mr. Blaine's
famous characterization of Mr. Conkling or Mr.
Conkling's of Mr. Curtis was never heard there.   In
private life there is more refined *malice*, more gayety,
and more gossip—if possible—in a Paris *salon* than
in a Fifth Avenue drawing-room, or on a Newport
piazza ; but there is nothing of what we have come
to know as personal "rallying," and the gossip is
about the absent.

We, on the other hand, are all familiar, Mr. Arnold reminds us, with the notion of "hewing Agag
in pieces," and our ungentleness of manners proceeds largely from the astonishing way in which
this Teutonic and Puritan passion has penetrated
our very nature.   How English literature witnesses
this from the time of Milton to the very latest number
of "The Saturday Review " we all know.   The greatest and kindliest natures are not exempt from it on
the other side of the water.   Not only does Macaulay riot in it, but such a good-natured soul as

Mr. James Yellowplush indulges in many a swing of
the axe—when Agag is for the moment personated
by Bulwer, let us say.   Not only is the hewing done
with the grandiose strokes of Carlylean brutality,
but it is amiably and dexterously performed by the
advocate *par excellence* of "sweet reasonableness"
and the chief critic of the custom, Mr. Matthew Arnold himself.   The description of Mr. Swinburne as
"sitting in a sewer and adding to it," attributed to
Carlyle, differs mainly by its outrageousness from the
implacable way in which a long catalogue of saints
and sinners is subjected at the hands of Mr. Arnold
to an illumination as indiscreet as it is discriminat-
ing.   There is much discussion as to whether it is as
a critic or a poet that he will appeal to "the next
ages," but there is a side of his admirable and elevated genius in virtue of which it is not difficult occasionally to fancy him gracing the Pantheon of the
future in the harmonious guise of Apollo flaying
Marsyas.   No Anglo-Saxon would wish Mr. Arnold
different, but it is worth pointing out that the respectably sized and felicitously executed "Dunciad"
which might be collected from his works is incontestably due to the personal attitude, the personal
way of looking at many questions and discussing
many subjects.   His gentleness in consequence is
rather express than ingrained, and now and then
has something feline in its velvety caress.

In this country, I think, we are less disposed to
censoriousness.   At any rate our more refined spir-

its are—from the various reasons which spring from the American differentiation of the race. We have more room, and more equality. Our manners are affected by our greater amenity. But we do not need the abundant testimony of the daily journals to assure us how thoroughly personal is, in general, our point of view, how instinctive is our protest against the impersonal and artistic way of discussing and deciding any serious problem, how distrustful we are of the earnestness of whatever bears no personal indorsement. "It makes a great difference to a sentence," says Emerson somewhere, "whether or no there be a man behind it." That is our universal feeling. It is impossible to conceive the serene and charitable Emerson finding the flaying of Marsyas work so congenial as to be worthy his best and most vivacious effort, but it cannot be doubted that the operation would awaken his interest and, if neatly performed, win his approval. To the most malicious Frenchman on the other hand, the flaying of Marsyas by Apollo would seem a work of supererogation. Neither in literature nor in life does he practise it. "That is a fine legend, a most significant myth," he would remark to us, "but you materialize it atrociously. The only part of it with which we are directly and actively concerned is the contest—that part which Raphael painted with a real personal feeling, as you may see in the Louvre. The consequences to incompetence of its insolence are, as he has conventionalized them in the Vatican, natural and necessary ; they follow without the interposition of the god, who was born for higher things. Agag is sure to be satisfactorily hewn in pieces, and the work is accomplished by the matter-of-course operation of impersonal forces. Individually and socially we are only concerned with recognizing Agag when we see him and with showing ourselves superior to him. He is so little liked among us, his following is so entirely inconsiderable compared with that he can boast among you that his fate, indeed, is sealed from the beginning. To denounce him would be to utter platitudes."

VI

WOMEN

WOMEN

WRITING over a hundred years ago, Sébastien Mercier, whose "Tableau de Paris" was once a very popular work, says of his countrywomen : " Frenchwomen are remarkable for piercing, mischievous eyes, elegant figures, and sprightly countenances, but fine heads are very rare amongst them." The type has not varied greatly since then and it may be safely asserted that at present large eyes and beautiful faces are as rare among Frenchwomen as are poor figures. They are admired, too, in France with an intensity not untinctured with envy. For large eyes especially this admiration is universally unmeasured—no woman's eyes seem too large to be beautiful ; from the lay-figures of fashion plates to the goddesses of the *Salon,* Grévin's beauties, the wax-figures of shop-windows—every ideal type whether vulgar or refined is sure to possess large eyes. American girls have not this peculiarity, it is well known, as frequently as those of several other races, but in Paris they are nearly as noted for it as for any other feature of their pretty faces. An American returning home after a long sojourn in France is himself struck by the number of " ox-eyed

Junos " in which his country may glory and which
he had not before suspected. Pretty faces are not,
perhaps, more abundant in France than large eyes.
They are rarer among women of a certain age than
among young girls—so much rarer indeed than is
the case with us that one naturally infers the de-
teriorating effect of French life and manners upon
the fresher and more delicate beauties of feature
and color. Of this Frenchwomen seem themselves
convinced, and they begin early the endeavor to
circumvent the ungallant influences of passing years.
It is a bold thing to say, they are themselves such
excellent judges in these matters, but it is probable
that in this they commit a grave error, and, by
meeting them half-way, really aid in the ungra-
cious work of these influences. Balzac cynically
divides Parisians into the two classes of the young
and the old who attempt to appear young. As to
women alone he does not seem, to a foreign observer, very far out of the way. There are doubtless large numbers of men who do not attempt to
regain the youthful aspect they could not retain,
but almost no women.

It is not by any means exclusively vanity that furnishes the motive for this unequal struggle with
nature. Partly, to be sure, it is a poignant repugnance to loss of consideration which, in a society
where the great prize of life is the esteem of others,
is of great importance. But in the main it proceeds
from a passionate desire to preserve even the sem-

blance of the period when one feels at one's best,
when one can enjoy most thoroughly, and when one
wastes one's life the least. Some day perhaps gray
hair will become as fashionable in Paris as it is in
New York, but hitherto there are no signs of its favor. The number of women one sees who have
dyed hair is very large, and, till one remarks a corresponding rarity of gray hair, very odd. At first
one's respect for Parisian taste receives a severe
shock. The dye used, however—apparently the
same all over Paris—is far superior to the hideous
russets we are accustomed to note in the beard and
hair of an occasional under-bred old man, and when
fresh is, except for its evident artificiality, a not at
all bad looking dark-chestnut. After a few days it
becomes easily less beautiful, and it is certainly not
renewed often enough. The *ennui* of the process
and economy, the sense for both of which is quite
as keen as that of coquetry in France, are against
its frequent renewal. Before long one becomes
used to the general phenomenon and is in two
minds about agreeing with the Parisians as to its
preferability to gray hair, which certainly does not
suit all complexions and makes the person not naturally distinguished appear insignificant ; and except
in rare cases it ages rather than renders piquant the
youthfulness it sometimes accompanies. As for the
mauvaise honte of resorting to artificial aids to
beauty, one inclines to get over that in breathing
the Parisian atmosphere where such a feeling is

wholly unknown and would probably be incomprehensible.   Women with us certainly resort to wigs
in case of baldness and to rice powder in the event
of any grave defect in complexion.   The line between the palliation of natural blemishes and the
adornment of natural features is difficult to draw.
A society which has a great deal of regard for form
will insist on the latter, while a society perpetually
on its guard against permitting form to out-weigh
substance will hardly excuse the former.

The truth is that coquetry, which is a defect in
our eyes, is a quality of the Frenchwoman.   It is a
virtue which consecrates as it were the possession of
natural attractions.   In France always *le charme
prime la beauté,* and coquetry there is the science of
charm in women.   Charm in this special sense our
women do not greatly study ; and its crude exhibi-
tions oftener than not occur in conjunction with an
absence of those natural attractions so much better
and so universally appreciated by the opposite sex
that there is no atoning for the lack of them nor any
need of enhancing them.   But in France to paint
the lily is not regarded as a paradox.   The result is
not without a certain specious felicity, it must be
confessed ; as indeed many American men who have
been honored in any degree with French feminine
society could probably testify.   On the other hand
it is not to be inferred that from our point of view
the French lily needs to be painted.   Her natural
charms are many and great, and they would be po-

tent even in a *milieu* which would distinctly frown
upon her mobilization and manœuvring of them, so to
speak. Her complexion is, in general—before it has
submitted to the inexorable necessities arising from
competition with the heightened and accentuated
tints that best sustain the gaslight (or rather can-
dle-light) splendor of opera, balls, and soirées—very
nearly perfection. Less florid than the red and
white freshness so greatly admired as witnessing
quite as much as decorating the superb health of
English women, it is nevertheless full of color, readily changeable, and of a purity unaffected either by
its occasional leaning toward olive or by its more
frequent shading into pink. Muddy or sallow it
never is. The Parisienne is perhaps often *étiolée*—
there is much croaking in the journals about the effect of the *vie fiévreuse et excitante* of Paris ; but ane-
mia as a chronic condition is infrequent. She has
a disgust for invalidism rare among American women, who would find her on this score terribly unsympathetic—"cold and hard" in fact. Unlike so
many American women, who esteem her *blasée* in
consequence, *elle n'est pas née d'hier*, in French
phrase, and she perfectly appreciates the intimate
connection between invalidism and hysteria. To be
pitied forms no part of her programme, and to be
pitied on such grounds would be unendurable to
her. The "rest cure" is probably unknown in
France.

But quite as much as such commiseration she

undoubtedly dreads the loss of physical attractiveness which invalidism involves. She devotes indeed a share of attention to the conservation of her beauty in every respect which the American woman would esteem excessive. Her hand, oftener expressive perhaps than *mignonne,* but in general shapely and well-attached, shows the advantages of this attention. Her foot on the other hand shows its disadvantages ; it is as a rule if larger than the corresponding American foot (which is not to be denied) smaller by a greater discrepancy still than that of the Englishwoman, and there seems really no excuse for compressing it, as is so universally done, into the fashionable but transparent deception known as the Louis Quinze boot. Under this treatment, little different in kind from that which is *de rigueur* in China, it assumes an aspect totally devoid of graceful contour, to be characterized only by what Carlyle would describe as " mere hoofiness." Still for a moment—the moment during which alone perhaps the feminine foot should be remarked—the effect is possibly to diminish apparent size ; and here again, as in the instances of paint and powder and dyes, one should hesitate before proffering advice to so excellent a judge as the Frenchwoman. The point remains, in Candide's words, "une grande question." Coquetry itself, however, can offer nothing to enhance what is beyond all question the Frenchwoman's most admirable physical endowment, namely her incomparable figure. *Embonpoint,* it is true, is

a danger to be contemplated as one approaches
middle age. Beyond this period of life France undoubtedly possesses her full share of ample and ma-
tronly femininity. The opposite tendency may safely be scouted ; Madame Bernhardt herself is well-
known to be what is called a *fausse maigre.* But in
any assemblage of Frenchwomen from a ball in the
Faubourg St. Germain to a *bal de l' Opéra* the number
of admirable figures is very striking ; the face may
be positively common, but the figure is nearly sure
to be superb. The wasp-waist so much affected
across the Channel is apparently confined to fashion-
plates designed for exportation. The unwisdom of
tight-lacing is evidently not more perfectly appreciated than its unsightliness, though the relations of
hygiene to beauty are thoroughly understood ; it is
doubtless often resorted to, but mainly as a corrective. With this excellence of figure generally goes
a corresponding excellence of carriage ; in this respect the skill with which the Louis Quinze heel is
circumvented is beyond praise. And with regard
to the tact and taste displayed in the garb which
decorates this figure and carriage, the world is, I suppose, as well agreed now as in the time when the Em-
press Eugénie set its fashions for it in a more inexorable way than the women of the present republic can
pretend to. France is still, if not the only country
in the world where dress is an art, at least the only
one where the dressmaker and the milliner are artists.

14

It is as unquestionably the country in which women think most of dress. The fact is often enough made a reproach to the Frenchwoman, and nothing is commoner than to hear Englishmen, Germans, Spaniards, and Italians, as well as Americans, in Paris referring to it as indicating her character and defining the limit of her activities. Her toilet occupies the Parisienne too exclusively, is nearly the universal foreign opinion—even among those foreigners who are themselves most attracted by the graces and felicities of the toilet in question as well as least serious themselves. The difficulty of transmuting such a trait into that domesticity which the Southern Latin ready to *se ranger* prizes as highly as the Teuton or Anglo-Saxon who makes it a part of his feminine ideal, is a frequent theme of purely disinterested speculation among these social philosophers. It is a difficulty nevertheless which does not puzzle the Frenchman. The conditions of French life are such that domesticity is either not understood in precisely the sense in which it is accepted elsewhere, or is not given the same overmastering importance as an absolute quality. The domesticity aimed at by the Spanish convent and cultivated by the Germanic hearth and chimney-corner is in no sense the object of the Frenchman's ambition for the Frenchwoman. Here as elsewhere his social instinct triumphs over every other, and he regards the family circle as altogether too narrow a sphere for the activities of a being who occupies so much of his mind and heart, and in whose consideration he is as much concerned as she in his. To be the mother of his children and the nurse of his declining years is a destiny which, unrelieved by the gratification of her own instincts of expansion, he would as little wish for her as she would for herself. To be the ornament of a society, to awake perpetual interest, to be perpetually and universally charming, to contribute powerfully to the general aims of her environment, never to lose her character as woman in any of the phases or functions of womanly existence, even in wifehood or maternity—this central motive of the Frenchwoman's existence is cordially approved by the Frenchman. In fact it is because he approves and insists upon it that she is what she is. It is for this reason that she devotes so much attention to dress, which in her thus, spite of those surface indications that mislead the foreigner, is almost never due to the passion for dress in itself to which similar preoccupation infallibly testifies in the women of other societies. A New York belle dresses for her rivals—when she does not, like the aborigines of her species, dress for herself alone. Mr. Henry James acutely represents the Mrs. Westgate of his "International Episode" as "sighing to think the Duchess would never know how well she was dressed." To induce analogous regret in a Frenchwoman a corresponding masculine obtuseness would be absolutely indispensable. And this among her own countrymen she would never encounter. Her dress, then, is a part of her coquetry —one of the most important weapons in a tolerably well-stocked arsenal; but it is nothing more, and it in no degree betokens frivolity. Like her figure and her carriage it is a continual ocular demonstration and a strong ally of her instinct, her genius, for *style*. In these three regards she is unapproachable, and in every other attribute of style she is certainly unsurpassed. In elegance, in intelligence, in self-possession, in poise, it would be difficult to find exceptions in other countries to rival the average Parisienne. And her coquetry, which endues her style with the element of charm (of which it is, as I said, the science), is neither more nor less than the instinct to please highly developed. It is not, as certainly coquetry elsewhere may sometimes be called, the instinct to please deeply perverted. The French coquette does not flirt. Her frivolity, her superficiality, may be great in many directions—in religion, in moral steadfastness, in renunciation, in constancy, even in sensibility—but in coquetry she is never superficial; the dimly veiled, half-acknowledged insincerity of what is known as flirtation would seem to her frivolous to a degree unsuspected by her American contemporary. To her as to her countrymen the relations of men and women are too important and too interesting not to be at bottom entirely serious.

In fine to estimate the Frenchwoman's moral nature with any approach to adequacy it is necessary entirely to avoid viewing her from an Anglo-Saxon standpoint. Apart from her *milieu* she is not to be understood at all. The ideals of woman in general held by this *milieu* are wholly different from our ideals. To see how and wherein, let us inquire of some frank French friend. "We shall never agree about women," he will be sure to admit at the outset ; and he may be imagined to continue very much in this strain : "We Frenchmen have a repugnance, both instinctive and explicit, to your propensity to make *companionability* the essential quality of the ideal woman. Consciously or unconsciously this is precisely what you do. It is in virtue of their being more companionable, and in an essentially masculine sense, that the best of your women, the serious ones, shine superior in your eyes to their frivolous or pedantic rivals. You seem to us, in fact, to approach far more nearly than your English cousins to the ideal in this respect of your common Gothic ancestors. Your ideal is pretty closely the Alruna woman—an august creature spiritually endowed with inflexible purity and lofty, respect-compelling virtues, performing the office of a 'guiding-star' amid the perplexities of life, whose approval or censure is important in a thousand moral exigencies, and one's feeling for whom is always strongly tinctured —even in the days of courtship—with something akin to filial feeling. In your daily life this ideal becomes, of course, familiarized—you do not need to be reminded that 'familiarized' is, indeed, an ex-

tenuating term to describe the effect upon many of
your ideals when they are brought into the atmosphere of your daily life, that the contrast between
American ideals and American practice frequently
strikes us as grotesque. In the atmosphere of your
daily life the Alruna woman becomes a good fellow.
She despises girls who flirt, as you yourselves de-
spise our dandies and our *petits jeunes gens.* She
despises with equal vigor the lackadaisical, the hysterical, the affected in any way. She plays a good
game of tennis ; it is one of her ambitions to cast a
fly adroitly, to handle an oar well. She is by no
means a Di Vernon. She has a thoroughly masculine antipathy to the romantic, and is embarrassed
in its presence. She reads the journals ; she has
opinions, which, unlike her inferior sisters, she
rarely obtrudes. She is tremendously efficient and
never poses. She is saved from masculinity by
great tact, great delicacy in essentials, by her beauty
which is markedly feminine, by her immensely narrower sphere, and by Divine Providence. She is
thus thoroughly companionable, and she is after all
a woman. This makes her immensely attractive to
you. But nothing could be less seductive to us than
this predominance of companionableness over the
feminine element, the element of sex. Of our
women, ideal and real (which you know in France,
the country of equality, of homogeneity, of averages,
is nearly the same thing) we could better say that
they are thoroughly feminine and that they are,

after all, companionable. Indeed, if what I understand by 'companionable' be correct, i. e., *rien que
s'entendre*, they are quite as much so as their American sisters, though in a very different way, it is
true.

"Let me explain. The strictness of your social
code effectually shuts off the American woman from
interest in, and the American girl from knowledge
of, what is really the essential part of nearly half of
life ; I mean from any mental occupation except in
their more superficial aspects with the innumerable
phenomena attending one of the two great instincts
from which modern science has taught us to derive
all the moral perceptions and habits of human life.
This is explainable no doubt by the unwritten but
puissant law which informs every article of your social constitution that relates to women : namely, the
law that insures the precedence of the young girl
over the married woman. With you, indeed, the
young girl has *le haut du pavé* in what seems to us
a very terrible degree. Your literature, for example, is held by her in a bondage which to us seems
abject, and makes us esteem it superficial. 'Since
the author of "Tom Jones" no one has been permitted to depict a man as he really is,' complains
Thackeray. With you it is even worse because the
young girl exercises an even greater tyranny than
in England. Nothing so forcibly illustrates her position at the head of your society, however—not
even her overwhelming predominance in all your

social reunions within and without doors, winter and summer, at luncheons, dinners, lawn-parties, balls, receptions, lectures, and church—as the circumstance that you endeavor successfully to keep her a girl after she has become a woman. You desire and contrive that your wives shall be virgins in word, thought, and aspiration. That this should be the case before marriage everyone comprehends. That is the end of our endeavor equally with yours. In every civilized society men wish to be themselves the introducers and instructors of their wives in a realm of such real and vital interest as that of which marriage, everywhere but in your country, opens the door. But with us the young girl is constantly looking forward to becoming, and envying the condition of, a woman. That is the source of our restrictions, of our conventual regulations, which seem to you so absurd, even so dishonoring. You are saved from having such, however, by the fact that with you the young girl is the rounded and complete ideal, the type of womanhood, and that it is her condition, spiritually speaking, that the wife and even the mother emulate. And you desire ardently that they should. You do not 'see any necessity,' as you say in your utilitarian phraseology, of a woman's 'losing' anything of the fresh and clear charm which perfumes the existence of the young girl. You have a short way of disposing of our notion that a woman is the flower and fulfilment of that of which the young girl is the bud and the promise. You esteem this notion a piece of sophistry designed to conceal our really immoral desire to rob our women of the innocence and *naïveté* which we insist upon in the young girl, in order that our social life may be more highly spiced. Your view is wholly different from that of your race at the epoch of its most considerable achievements in the 'criticism of life' and antecedent to the Anglo-Saxon invention of prudery as a bulwark of virtue. It is a view which seems to spring directly from the Puritan system of each individual managing independently his own spiritual affairs without any of the reciprocal aids and the division of labor provided for in the more elaborate scheme of Catholicism, in consequence of which each individual left in this way wholly to himself is forced into a timid and distrustful attitude toward temptation. Nothing is more noticeable in your women, thus, than a certain suspicious and timorous exclusion from the field of contemplation of anything unsuited to the attention of the young girl. It is as if they feared contamination for virtue if the attitude and habit of mind belonging to innocence were once abandoned. They probably do fear vaguely that you fear it for them, that your feminine ideal excludes it.

"Now it is very evident that however admirable in its results this position may be, and however sound in itself, it involves an important limitation of that very companionableness which you so much insist on in your women. In this sense, the average Frenchwoman is an equal, a companion, to a degree almost never witnessed with you. After an hour of feminine society we do not repair to the club for a relaxation of mind and spirit, for a respiration of expansion, and to find in unrestrained freedom an enjoyment that has the additional sense of being a relief. Our clubs are in fact mere excuses for gambling, not refuges for bored husbands and homeless bachelors. Conversation among men is perhaps grosser in quality, the *équivoque* is perhaps not so delicate, so *spirituelle*, but they do not differ in kind from the conversational tissue in mixed company, as with you they do so widely. With you this difference in kind is notoriously an abyss. In virtue of our invention of treating delicate topics with innuendo, our mixed society gains immensely in interest and attractiveness, and our women are more intimately companionable than yours. You Americans take easily to innuendo from your habit of mind, which is sensitive and subtile. You are unaccountably unlike the English in this respect. As a rule, one of you who should know French and understand French character as well as Thackeray, would not like him be depressed by what he was pleased to call 'all that dreary *double-entendre*.' Still, when you attempt the application of it to delicate topics, I can myself recall instances of your leaving, as we say, something to be desired. In such an instance it is natural that a feeling of ill-

success should produce a conviction that the topic
is too delicate to be handled at all ; seeing another
person handle it with triumphant gingerliness does
not unsettle such a conviction—the '*double-entendre*'
becomes irretrievably "dreary.' But, in point of
fact, it is only a contrivance of ours to extend the
range of conversation in mixed company ; you can
do without it because you limit any conversation
with a wide range to one sex, to your clubs and
business offices—where, apparently, it is not needed.
It seems to many of you, doubtless, a device for confining the talk in mixed company to what are called
delicate topics. But that side of our talk really appears magnified to you because of its absolute
novelty. In strictness there is in mixed company
quite as much conversation upon politics, letters,
art, and affairs in Paris as even in Boston. Our
équivoque simply takes the place of your silences.
The point is that from the circumstance that we do
not exclude it, the conversational tissue in mixed
company is with us immensely varied, and that
when a Frenchman finds himself in the presence of
a woman—in 'ladies' society' as you express it—
whether *à deux* or in a general gathering, he experiences no more restraint—except that which polishes
his periods and refines his expression—than an
American does at his club or office. His 'instinct
for expansion' suffers no repression. Society becomes a very different thing from 'ladies' society.'
It is not a medium for the exploitation of the young

girl and the woman who emulates and follows her *haud passibus œquis ;* nor is it a realm 'presided over' by 'the fair sex'; it is an association of men and women for the interchange of ideas on all topics, and the texture out of which the drama of life is woven. In saying that your ideal of companionableness in woman was defective this was what I had in mind. Even in companionableness we find our women much more to our mind.

"But this is, after all, a detail. Even if your women were intimately companionable they would none the less radically differ from our own; we should still reproach them with a certain masculine quality in the elevated, and a certain prosaic note in the familiar, types. By masculine, I certainly do not here intend the signification you give to your derisive epithet 'strong-minded.' In affirming that there is a generous ampleness in the feminine quality of our women unobservable in yours, I do not mean to charge them with inferiority in what you call 'pure mentality ;' in intelligence and capacities we believe them unequalled the world over. But they are essentially less masculine in avoiding strictly all competition with men, in conserving all their individuality of sex and following their own bent. Nothing is more common than to hear American women lament their lack of opportunity, envy the opportunity of men. Nothing is rarer with us. It never occurs to a Frenchwoman to regret her sex. It is probable that almost every American woman with any pretensions to 'pure mentality,' feels, on the contrary, that her sex is a limitation and wishes, with that varying ardor and intermittent energy which characterize her, that she were a man and had a man's opportunity. In a thousand ways she is the man's rival, which with us she never is. Hence the popularity with you of the agitation for woman-suffrage, practically unknown in France. Your society probably wholly undervalues this movement, and frowns upon it with a forcible feebleness that is often ludicrously unjust. You do not perceive that it furnishes almost the only outlet for the ambition and the energy of such of your women as are persistently and not spasmodically energetic and ambitious, and that its worst foe with you is the great mass of women themselves, which is governed by timorousness, by intellectual indolence, and by the habit born of long-continued subordination in all serious matters. To a disinterested observer of the complacence with which your society contemplates 'Folly set in place exalted,' in this matter, it is impossible not to remark the secret sympathy with the movement entertained by serious women and concealed in deference to the opinion of the mass, whose fiat in all matters related to 'good taste' is necessarily final. They probably fear that the mass of their countrywomen, spite of the indefinite multiplication of female colleges, will never become really and responsibly intelligent without the

suffrage ; and in effect with you this must become
the great practical argument for it. Animated as
the most serious of American women unquestionably
are by a sense of rivalry with men, they instinctively
feel this handicap, and instinctively desire for their
sex the dignity and seriousness conferred by power
and the sense of responsibility power involves. But
I wish I could make plain to you how differently
the Frenchwoman feels, how radically different the
Frenchwoman is. Being in no sense, and never
feeling herself to be, the rival of man and the emu-
lator of his opportunities, to her seriousness and
dignity the suffrage could add nothing whatever.
Her power and responsibility lie in quite another
direction, and that they do is quite clear to her. It
has in fact been so clear to her in the past, that we
have hitherto made the mistake of giving her in
general an extremely superficial education. Madame
Dubarry got along very well without any at all.
This is an error we are just now systematically re-
pairing. And we have our croakers who oppose the
reform, entitle their gloomy vaticinations 'Plus de
femmes,' and predict that our women will become
Americanized. They are needlessly alarmed ; for
this Americanization involves the quality of masculinity which does not exist at all, either in the nature or in the ideal of our women. It is neither
their disposition nor their aspiration to enter that
condition of friendly rivalry with men, to become
members of that 'mutual protective association,'

which plays so large a part in the existence and imagination of your more serious women.

"The difference is nowhere so luminously illustrated as in the respective attitudes of French and American women toward the institution of marriage. With us from the hour when she begins first to think at all of her future—an epoch which arrives probably much earlier than with you—marriage is the end and aim of a woman's existence. And it is so, consciously and deliberately. A large part of her conduct is influenced by this particular prospect. It is the conscious and deliberate aim also of her parents or guardians for her. They constantly remind her of it. Failure to attain it is considered by her and by them as the one great failure, to avoid which every effort should tend, every aspiration be directed. In its excess this becomes either ludicrous or repulsive as one looks at it. 'Si tu veux te marier, ne fais jamais ça '—' Cela t'empêchera de te marier '—who has not been fatigued with such maternal admonitions which resound in interiors by no means always of the *basse classe*. But the result is that marriage occupies a share of the young girl's mind and meditation which to your young girls would undoubtedly seem disproportionate, and indeed involve a sense of shame. There is no more provision in the French social constitution than in the order of nature itself for the old maid. Her fate is eternal eccentricity, and is correspondingly dreaded among us who dread nothing more than ex-

clusion from the sympathies of society and a share
in its organized activities. Marriage once attained,
the young girl, though become by it a woman, is
not of course essentially changed but only more
highly organized in her original direction. You
may be surprised to hear that sometimes it suffices
her—as it suffices English, and used to American
women ; though it must be admitted that our society
does not make of even marriage an excuse for exacting the sum of a woman's activities which it is
the Anglo-Saxon tendency to do, and that thus her
merit is less conspicuous. If marriage do not suffice her, it is not in 'Sorosis' or Dorcas or Browning
societies, or art or books that she seeks distraction,
but in the consolation strictly cognate to that of
marriage which society offers her. Accordingly,
whatever goes to make up the distinctively feminine
side of woman's nature tends with us to become
highly developed. It acquires a refinement, a sub-
tlety, of organization quite unknown to societies
whose ideal women inspire filial feeling. We have
as a rule very few Cornelias. Our mothers themselves are far from being Spartan. The Gothic goddess is practically unknown in France. 'Woman's
sphere,' as you call it, is totally distinct from man's.
The action and reaction of the two which produce
the occupation, the amusement, the life of society
are far more intimate than with you, but they are
the exact reverse of homogeneous.

"It is an inevitable corollary from this that that

sentimental side which you seem to us to be endeavoring to subordinate in your more serious
women, receives in the Frenchwoman that greatest
of all benefits, a harmonious and natural development. Before and after marriage, and however
marriage may turn for her, it is her disposition to
love and her capacity for loving which are stimulated
constantly by her surroundings, and which are really
the measure of the esteem in which she is held.   To
love intensely and passionately is her ideal.   It is so
much her ideal that if marriage does not enable her
to attain it, it is a virtue rather than a demerit in
her eyes to seek it elsewhere.   Not to die before
having attained in its fulness this end of the law of
her being is often the source of the Frenchwoman's
tragic disasters.   But even when indubitable disaster arrives to her it is at least tragic, and a tragedy
of this kind is in itself glorious.   To remain spiritually an *être incomplet* is to her nearly as dreadful a
fate as to become a monstrosity.   Both are equally
hostile to nature, and we have a national passion for
being in harmony with nature.   It is probably impossible to make you comprehend how far this is
carried by us.   Take the life of George Sand as an
instance.   It was incontestably the inspiration of
her works, and to us it is the reverse of reprehensi-
ble, 'for she loved much ;' it is not her elopement
with Musset but her desertion of him that indicates
to our mind her weak side.   In this way the attitude of the Frenchwoman toward love is one of

15

perfect frankness. So far from dissembling its nature—either transcendentally or pietistically, after the fashion of your maidens, or mystically, after the fashion in the *pays de Gretchen*—she appreciates it directly and simply as a passion, and for her the most potent of the passions, the passion whose praise has been the burden of all the poets since the morning stars first sang together, and whose possession shares equally with the possession of superior intelligence the honor of distinguishing man from the lower animals. This is why to our women, as much as to our men, your literature, your 'criticism of life,' seems pale, as we say—pale and superficial. This is why we had such an *engouement* for your Byron and never heard of your Wordsworth. This is why we occupy ourselves so much with cognate subjects as you will have remarked.

"And the sentimental side, being thus naturally and harmoniously developed, becomes thus naturally and spontaneously the instrument of woman's power and the source of her dignity. Through it she seeks her triumphs and attains her ends. To it is due not her influence over men—as with your inveterate habit of either divorcing the sexes into a friendly rivalry or associating them upon the old-fashioned, English, harem-like basis, you would inevitably express it—but her influence upon society. This results in a great gain to women themselves— increases indefinitely their dignity and power. It is axiomatic that anything inevitable and not in it-

self an evil it is far better to utilize than to resist.
Everyone acknowledges the eminence of the sentimental side in woman's nature, the great part which
it plays in her conduct, the great influence it has
upon her motives. And since it has, therefore, inevitably to be reckoned with, its development accomplishes for women results which could not be
hoped for if sentiment were merely treated as an
inevitable handicap to be modified and mitigated.
Your own logic seems to us exceedingly singular.
You argue that men and women should be equal,
that the present regrettable inequality with you is
due to the greater influence of sentiment on women's minds in viewing purely intellectual matters
(you are constantly throwing this up to your woman suffragists), and that therefore the way in which
women are to be improved and elevated (as you curiously express it) is clearly by the repression of
their sentiment. It is the old story : you are constantly teaching your women to envy the opportunities of men, to regret their 'inferiority' hitherto,
and to endeavor to emulate masculine virtues by
mastering their emotions and suppressing their
sentiment ; that is to say, you are constantly doing
this by indirection and unconsciously, at least, and
by betraying the fact that such is your ideal for
them. You never seem to think they can be treated
as a fundamentally different order of capacity and
disposition. I remember listening for two hours to
one of your cleverest women lecturing on Joan of

Arc, and the thesis of her lecture was that there was no mystery at all about the Maid and her accomplishments, except the eternal mystery of transcendent military genius, that she was in fact a female Napoleon and that it was the 'accident of sex' simply that had prevented her from being so esteemed by the purblind masculine prejudice which had theretofore dominated people's minds. Thinking of what Jeanne d'Arc stands for to us Frenchmen, of her place in our imaginations, of the way in which she illustrates for us the puisssance of the essentially feminine element in humanity, I said to myself 'No, the Americans and we will never agree about women.'"

The Frenchman is apt to become eloquent in allusions to Joan of Arc, and French eloquence, like any other, is sometimes misleading. One may be permitted to object to our French friend's implication here, that the resemblance between Joan of Arc however conceived and the average Parisienne is at least not a superficial one. At the same time, making every allowance for the difference between things "as they really are" and as they seem to the persons irreparably committed to support of them, it is undoubtedly true that if not love at least interest in the other sex plays a considerably larger part in the life of the French than in that of the American woman. It is certain that she never, as so frequently happens with us, considers herself independently,

that she has no occupations or projects from which
men are excluded, that she never contemplates a
single life, for example, except as a fate hardly to be
borne with philosophy and likely to prove too
much for her *sagesse*. Society makes no provision
for the *vieille fille*, in the first place; in the second,
society occupies almost the whole of life, absorbs
almost every effort—two enormous differences from
ourselves. The attractiveness of the spinster with
us and the position she occupies in our society are
well-known. Of how many "homes" is she not the
delight, of how many "firesides" is she not the decorously decorative adornment! She may or may
not have had her romance; she may, that is to say,
have courted or have drifted into her position of
dignified singleness; it is in either case equally sure
that she has not considered her estate so "incomplete" in itself, or so disengaged from the structure
of society, as to furnish in itself reason and motive
of exchange for another distinguished quite as much
by another kind of duties as by another order of
opportunities. And not only is the Frenchwoman
prevented from taking such a view as this by the
society which surrounds her and of which it is a
prime necessity of her nature that she should form
an integral part, but she is constitutionally incapable
of contentedly fulfilling such a destiny. All her
instincts of expansion—and she possesses these in
greater intensity than we are apt to fancy is natural
to women—are hostile to it. The genius for renun-

ciation so conspicuous in many of our New England
women is, in her composition, quite lacking. Such
concentration as she possesses is, to speak paradoxically, expended upon the exploitation of her expansiveness. If by chance she becomes *vieille fille* she
has a clear sense of failure. This certainly happens,
comparatively rare as it seems to us. And the
French spinster is apt to be an enjoyable person—
as for that matter who in France is not? But it
cannot have failed to strike any Anglo-Saxon observer that she is a wholly different kind of a person
from her Anglo-Saxon analogue. Almost invariably
she is either *dévote* or *gauloise*. Most people's experience probably is that she is generally *gauloise*,
and one may even be permitted to note that in that
event she is apt to be exaggeratedly *gauloise*. Pru-
dishness is hardly ever exhibited by her except in
conjunction with religious devotion. The *dévotes*
apart, almost every *vieille fille* after a certain age is
reached—the age when marriage is no longer to
be contemplated—feeling the formal eccentricity of
her position in society, makes a distinct break with
her rôle of *jeune fille*, and tacitly suffers her already
cynically disposed *milieu* to infer that she does not
really merit the ridicule she would inevitably receive upon the supposition of her total unfamiliarity, even by reputation, with the fruit of the tree of
the knowledge of good and evil.

Single women, however, are, after all, exceptions
in France, and it is only the great contrast which

France presents in this respect to those portions of America which are socially most highly developed that makes a consideration of the character and position of the *vieille fille* interesting or significant. Its significance really consists in what it suggests and implies as to the fundamental differences which separate French and Anglo-Saxon societies. Married women, of course, constitute the great bulk of the feminine portion of French society. But when it is remembered that the interest in the other sex just referred to is as characteristic of them as of their unmarried sisters, it will be immediately perceived that French society contrasts positively as well as negatively with our own. With us, it is well known, feminine interest in the other sex ceases at marriage. It is frequently active enough before that event, but its cessation with the wedding ceremony is nearly universal. To many men this change comes with a suddenness that is appalling. Each season witnesses shoals of our society beaux left stranded by it. They seem never to be able to prepare for it in advance, inevitable as they must know it to be; to them the disappearance from the social circle (the arena, it might be called) of a young girl who seems to have made her selection and thenceforward to forget that there was ever any competition, comes always with the force of a shock. Furthermore with us feminine interest in men ceases at marriage as absolutely, with as complete remorselessness, when the marriage is of the

former beau as when it is of the former belle.   To
this our young men will probably never be able to
habituate themselves with philosophy.   However it
may be with American women, American men are
very much like other men, like Frenchmen even in
some respects, and the average "society man's"
sense of sudden loss, of a support withdrawn, an
activity paralyzed, immediately consequent upon his
marriage must be of a nature calculated to effect,
in the long run, substantial changes in the existing
social constitution.   To many young men with us
marriage involves not perhaps a loss of caste, but
indubitably a loss of that constant consideration,
direct and indirect, which makes the possession of
caste desirable ; and this circumstance is perhaps
the most serious menace by which the view of society as a device for bringing marriageable young
people together is at present threatened.   Our
young men have nothing approaching the genius
for renunciation of our young women, and though
they may long tolerate the retirement at marriage
of women from society—being largely reconciled
thereto by the thought of thus attaining superior
domesticity in their own wives—to continue to submit throughout the course of our social evolution
to instant personal effacement at marriage, to drop
at once in universal feminine consideration from
the position of Adonis to that of Vulcan, would undoubtedly be too much to expect of them.

In neither of these ways, it need hardly be said,

does marriage affect French society. Marriage is, on the contrary, the cardinal condition of society in France. It might almost be called the young girl's "coming-out party." It is, if anything, to a woman's sense an added attraction in a man; he is *rangé* certainly, but certainly none the less a man, association with whom is, *cæteris paribus*, as much more agreeable than association with a woman as the elective affinity of nature has contrived it. Women's general interest in men, that is to say, is so far from being repressed or even restricted by marriage that it is quickened by it, and thus society in general receives the stimulus of a powerful force which with us is well known to be almost altogether lacking. The entire French conception of marriage differs so fundamentally from our own that it is really difficult for us to appreciate it. Probably most Americans who have been attracted toward the French have, at some period of their study of French manners, said to themselves: "There must be some error in our understanding of French marriages. According to all accounts they are invariably and exclusively *de convenance*. They must therefore be loveless marriages. No healthful social life such as *must* exist in France can be based upon strict conformity to such a system. It must be, therefore, that the accounts exaggerate. In this detail, as in others, we must have been misled by English prejudices." But the fact is literally as it is understood to be. Exceptions to the rule of *mariages de convenance* are so rare as really not to count at all. To comprehend, however, that this does not inevitably lead to social stoppage and disaster, it is necessary to perceive that the same thing which might result very badly for us does not necessarily result badly for people who are so very different from us as the French are. And this is an extremely difficult matter ; it is always difficult to realize that maxims which we have conquered for ourselves have not a universal validity. The conception of *mariage de convenance* by no means excludes the idea of love. Neither does the practice. No young girl in France looks forward to not loving her husband. She simply expects to learn to love him after marriage as our young girls are expected to do before as well. As a matter of fact, in the vast majority of cases this expectation is justified. Parents and society see to it that it shall be justifiable, and the result—always of course a lottery—is made dependent on old heads instead of on young hearts. To our criticism of the working of their system, the French retort in kind with unconvinced obstinacy. They assert that certain lamentable and undeniable phenomena are direct results of our system and observe, truly enough, that from these at least theirs is free. To our rejoinder that this may be so, but that their conception of marriage, however salutary, is terribly unromantic, their answer would undoubtedly be that we are altogether too romantic. And this is really our difference from the French in this matter—that we conceive marriage sentimentally, namely, and they as an affair of reason ; and from reason to *convenance* is always an incredibly short step in France. Individualism is a force so nearly unknown in France, collective and corporate authority is such a constant and intimate one, the entire social structure is so elaborately organized for the general rather than the particular good, that to leave even so particular a matter as marriage wholly to the whim of the persons directly interested would be foreign to the national proclivities. No sentiment is too sacred, no feeling too intimate, to be thus centrally administered, as it were, by society. If they are sacred and intimate enough and for any reason—often for a reason which might to us appear frivolous—intensely enough recalcitrant to the code, their violation of it will be tolerated and even applauded. But the notion that the code should not deal with the subject at all would be esteemed as absurd as we should esteem it to disparage marriage though permitting divorce.

The French marriage being thus distinctly not the affair of sentiment which it is with us, the ideal formed for a woman's deportment within its bonds differs proportionally from that to which we hold our married women. Of the strictness of the latter one hardly needs to be reminded. The husband himself insists upon it with virtuous sufficiency. The wife herself admires this attitude in him. He becomes in a way her spiritual director, and she in some sense his penitent. Following his idea of

making a companion of her, he arranges her reading, counsels the disposition of her leisure, modifies
the list of her acquaintance, in proportion as he attaches value to these things. If her family have
been of a different political or religious faith from
his own, he devotes no small labor to the subtle un-
dermining of her prejudices. She is *his* wife, pre-
siding over *his* household, entertaining *his* friends.
She sees the world through his spectacles—such of
it as he permits. Her amusements are such as he
approves, her study such as he directs. Her destiny
and glory are to be the mother of his children, the
ornament of his fireside, his help-meet. This at
least the Teutonism underlying our American chivalry makes our ideal in many instances, and in
these instances it is realized by our women with a
grace and dignity which ought, perhaps, to do more
than they do to keep our men up to the mark of
realizing its counterpart. There are with us of
course very few average men who do not expect
their wives to take them at their own valuation—
very few average women who do not thus take their
husbands, at least until they become grandmothers.
Indeed the mental acuteness and moral independence of our women are in many cases pitched to a
considerably lower key than even this ; they are expected to and do take their husbands not merely at
the self-valuation of these latter, but at the valuation fixed by marital diplomacy as well as by marital conceit. There is indeed to some extent with us

an unconfessed but perfectly recognized freemasonry of husbands, having for its object the preservation in the fairer sex of illusions as to the
sterner. Treachery to this is extremely uncommon,
and is regarded as almost base by the occasional
traitor himself. It is painful to the American husband to witness the absence of similar illusions in
the Frenchwoman. The discovery of her opinion of
the opposite sex and her complacent acquiescence
therein comes to him with a certain shock ; it is
some time before he recovers from it and again permits himself to be attracted by what to him seems
the uncomfortable paradox of *blasée* femininity. It
is important to distinguish, however, that the absence of illusions in the Frenchwoman as to masculine qualities by no means implies, as a similar absence might be taken to imply with us, a more or less
brutal disillusionizing process as having taken place
and left its scar and stain upon feminine freshness.
The Frenchwoman is simply almost never *naïve,* in
great things any more than in small. The French
ideal excludes *naïveté,* and from a French point of
view she is never more *femme* than when she is least
naïve ; to be *naïf* is the next thing to being insignificant, and to be insignificant is ignominy.

One effect of this attitude is to make the Frenchwoman much more serious in an intellectual sense
than is possible to women whose cherishing of illusions is systematic. They are far more nearly at
the centre of the situation ; their comprehension of

motives is far wider, their acquaintance with socio-
logical data and causes far more intimate. They
are far less dependent upon their emotions in the
exercise of their judgment ; and thus a perfect acquaintance with the facts and their bearings in any
given case, and with the great mass of material to
which secondarily and indirectly any given case is
to be referred, and by which in large measure it is
to be judged, relieves them of this one great reproach which among us is constantly addressed to
women who make any attempt to discuss serious topics. They are in no wise driven to the makeshift of
making up by the intensity of emotion for imperfect
comprehension. In fine, whereas we seek the artificial stimulus for certain virtues in what may be fancifully called a "protective policy" as applied to
women, the French are believers in social free trade,
with individual competition and survival of the socially fittest the only winnowing principle recognized.

And the characteristic effect of each theory is by
no means confined to women alone, or to women and
what passes for society in general. It is very marked upon the men considered apart—as with us they
have to be considered in so many relations. It is of
course impossible to make of an entire sex a class
by itself which, unconsidered in any but the domestic and decorative functions of life, shall have no influence upon the habits of thought and the courses
of conduct of the other sex in even those matters
with which the latter exclusively charges itself. In

a general and vague way we are so far from denying this that we make a merit of sustaining the contrary. It is indeed because we value so much what is called "the purifying influence of woman" that we like to keep her so far removed from the dust and stain of street or forum discussion. But now and then this remoteness not only acts upon themselves in the way just indicated—throws them back upon pure feeling in matters of pure judgment, that is to say; it gives a decided twist, a divergence of marked eccentricity to the movement of exclusively masculine thought and discussion. Men who are very much with women and very little in the world betray this influence upon their philosophy quite as much, often, as they illustrate in their conduct the general "purifying influence." Instances are within the recalling of every reflecting observer. They illustrate a state of mind and temper analogous to that of the dweller in the country, as compared with the metropolitan, or if one chooses, the "cockney" temper and mind ; or that of the Middle Ages philosopher compared with the modern sociologist. D'Alembert, says Mr. John Morley, adopted instead of the old monastic vow of poverty, chastity, obedience, "the manlier substitute of poverty, truth, liberty." The substitute may be more manly ; undoubtedly the modern world, breaking more and more completely with Middle Age ideals, tends more and more so to believe. But it is certainly not more womanly, as we understand the term, and in our society, owing to the influence aforesaid, many men feel that there is something radically defective in any social philosophy to which women—and women as we make them—do not subscribe.

Very slight analogy of this influence is to be encountered in France. And the reason, many persons will say, is because women as such have no influence in France, because France is socially organized entirely with a view to the interest and pleasure of men. One hears that constantly from Americans in Paris. Women are not admitted to the orchestra chairs of some of the theatres. In omnibuses and tramways *place aux dames* is a satirical phrase denoting a civility far from the heart of the ordinary French male. The cabs charge upon both sexes alike. The divorce law, so long withheld in the interest of men, with its proposition odiously unjust to women so nearly adopted, the arguments on either side during the debate, were excellent illustrations of the general feeling. The vice most inimical to women is licensed and regulated for the benefit of men. Women's fate in the highest as well as in the lowest social circle is to be pursued by man—pursued, too, brutally and prosaically. In marriage it is the men who are mercenary. What American in France, I say, has not heard a great deal of this from his travelling countrywomen? The Frenchman's answer to it all is that it is superficial and unintelligent, and he attributes such criticism to what he deems our habit of separating the sexes in thought and in fact, which in its turn he thinks attributable to our not having fully emerged from the pioneer stage of civilization wherein men and women have markedly distinct functions to perform and demand markedly distinct treatment and consideration. In an old society such careful and conscious distinctions are not needed ; like the marching of regulars the adjustment takes care of itself. At all events what we refer to as women's influence upon man is in such a society less formal, less immediately recognizable. Co-operation between the sexes is so complete in France that their reciprocal influences are, so far as they are obviously traceable, mere matters of detail. The position of woman in France at the present time is certainly one of the results of modern civilization working upon, socially speaking, the most highly developed people of a race which "invented the muses and chivalry and the Madonna"—and of that race the people which has produced by far the greatest number of eminent women. And if it seem to us and especially to our travelling countrywomen an unworthy position, and inferior to that which women hold with us, the reason is not to be sought in the absence of a marked and rigid distinction between the sexes, in which we ourselves would have to yield the palm to the Semitic and polygamous peoples, who have carried the idea to a perfection of logical development undreamed of by us.

However, the real answer to this is that French-

16

women themselves are perfectly satisfied with this position. They do not find it humiliating, as it is hardly likely they would fail to do, being tolerably susceptible, if there were not some error about its being really humiliating. Their influence upon men is perhaps not the less real for being less marked. If it is not what we mean by "purifying" it is assuredly refining. It is as hostile to grossness as women's influence with us is to immorality. Indeed it is to this influence that is to be distinctly ascribed the losing by vice of half its evil, to recall Burke's phrase. "His wife, I find, is acquainted with the whole affair. This is the woman's country!" exclaims Gouverneur Morris in his Paris diary in 1789 ; and it is only a Frenchman, I fancy, who would agree with M. Jules Lemaître, who said the other day that if he could be just what he chose he would be first of all a beautiful woman. The conditions of the active operation of feminine influence in France are nearly the opposite of those with us. They consist in the co-operation before alluded to between the sexes, in the possession of the same social philosophy by men and women, the same opportunities, the same knowledge of motives and data, of facts and general principles. Just as with us these conditions consist in a separation and exaltation of woman's sphere far above contact with the rude strife of natural passions and complex interests, the intricate and absorbing conflict of business, politics, amusement, and *ennui* of which the real drama of human life is composed.

VII

THE ART INSTINCT

THE ART INSTINCT

"IN art," exclaims a French critic, M. Jacques de Biez, "we care more for the true than even for the beautiful"—*ce qu'il nous faut, c'est le vrai dans l'art plus encore que le beau.* Nothing could be more just. It is precisely for this reason that sentimental and poetical peoples have hitherto wholly surpassed the French in art, where the beautiful is of even more importance than the true; Italy in plastic art, for example, the Germans in music, the English in poetry. In vain does Victor Hugo, running down the list of great poets, associate Voltaire with Dante and Shakespeare; in vain does every French writer on art, having occasion, in any general way, to mention Raphael, habitually add the name of Poussin: none but Frenchmen are deceived. Corneille, Racine, Jouvenet, Le Sueur, Lebrun, Watteau, Puget, Jean Goujon, Mignard, Houdon are glorious names, but they are not to be imposed as names of the first class, ranking with Velasquez, with Rembrandt, with Milton, Donatello, Leonardo, Goethe, when it is "the art of art" that is in question. What foreigner has not been struck by the struggle which the French canvases in the *Salon carré* of the Louvre make to justify

their places in the serene and lofty company of the
great Flemish, Dutch, Venetian masterpieces? One
looks at Jouvenet's fine "Descent from the Cross,"
and thinks of Rubens's at Antwerp, of Daniele da
Volterra's at Rome, of Sodoma's at Sienna, of Rembrandt's at Munich. A glance from Le Sueur's soft
"Saint Scholastica" to the gorgeous Rubens above
it, from Poussin's portrait of himself to Rembrandt's
"Saskia," from Rigaud's "Bossuet" to Holbein's
"Erasmus," from Gaspar Poussin's rural idyl to
Giorgione's, brings one into a wholly different æsthetic atmosphere ; just as turning from "Hernani,"
or "Le roi s'amuse," to Wordsworth or Keats, or
from "Fra Diavolo" to "Oberon," does in other departments of fine art. It is the change from the atmosphere of the intelligence to that of poetry, from
an atmosphere in which the true is insisted on to
the region where the sense of discovery, the imagination, genius with its unexpectedness and its aspirations, are overmasteringly occupied with beauty.
Metaphysical critics will deny the distinction, perhaps, and remind us of Plato's definition of beauty
as merely "the splendor of truth," but plain-think-
ing minds will readily perceive the practical difference arising between the art of a nation which devotes itself to the splendor, and that of one concerned
chiefly about the constitution, of truth. When the
latter attitude of mind, indeed, becomes excessive,
as it has become in France, the very intelligence
which is the object of such direct and concentrated

cultivation suffers obscuration, and the faculty itself of appreciation loses the keenness of its edge. Thus Stendhal, who passed his life among the master-pieces of Italian art, and who had a passion for the beautiful which made him the bitterest of the critics of pure rhetoric—Stendhal is perpetually finding the sum of all pictorial qualities in Guido. And Fromentin, an *esprit délicat*, if ever there was one, discovers with every mark of surprise, and proclaims with every sign of conscious temerity, that Rem-brandt was an idealist in disguise. Why in dis-guise? asks every reader but the Frenchman, the devotee of order and measure, who finds it astonish-ing that poetry should be extracted from ordinarily prosaic material. Down to Delacroix, French paint-ing is mainly a continuation of the Bolognese school.

It is precisely for the same reason that the French art of the present day, while it interests everyone extremely, moves and touches so little anyone but the French themselves. It is true that French painting and sculpture stand at the head of contem-porary plastic art. It is true that such sculptors as M. Rodin and M. Dalou recall the best days of the Italian Renaissance ; and that from Delacroix to Degas is a line of painters whose works are as sure of the admiration of posterity as of their present fame. And nowhere else is there anything in con-temporary art to be seriously compared with the productions of these men. There is a fine landscape school at The Hague. Mr. Alma Tadema is an ex-

tremely clever painter, and Mr. Poynter and Mr.
Burne-Jones are men indisputably provided with
what the French call a " temperament." There are
Mr. Whistler and Mr. La Farge, who are unclassifia-
ble, and so entirely individual that to argue from
them to their respective *milieus* would be unwarrantable. There are Signor Nono in Venice, and Signor
Segantini in Milan, truly poetic artists as well as
thoroughly equipped painters, who are sure one day
of a fame of wider than Italian extent. But putting
all these together (and adding even, if any reader
chooses, the painting professors of Germany), it is
evident that they make but an insignificant showing
beside the names first mentioned and those with
which these are associated—Carpeaux, Rude, Barye,
Corot, Courbet, Rousseau, Troyon, and Millet.
These men, however, are wholly exceptional, not
only in the possession of conspicuous genius, but in
the quality of their genius. It cannot be said that
this is not French—it is certainly nothing else ; but
it is the kind of genius that is the rare exception
in France, and that makes its way there, not amid
the favoring and forwarding influences of popular
sympathy, but against the current of opinion and
the whole drift of feeling. Make their way, too,
these men have all done. The Institute might frown
on Barye, and the *Salon* juries reject Millet ; but it
is idle to argue from this hostility, as ignorance so
frequently does, that France has often failed to appreciate her most admirable artists, her most poetic

and truly exalted talent. Invariably they "arrive," as the phrase is; and they arrive first in Paris, where they have indeed, from the first, never failed of supporters. M. Rodin's most pronounced and most uncompromising work is now in the Luxembourg; we may one day expect to see a work by Manet in the Louvre. The French mind is elastic, and French public opinion tolerant to a degree which shames the prejudice of other peoples.

All these considerations, however, do not at all obscure the fact that it is not M. Puvis de Chavannes that Paris really admires, but—let us not say M. Bouguereau, for that would be unfair, or M. Cabanel, or even M. Gérôme, though each of these painters is honored in his own country in a way which it is difficult for a foreigner to understand. Let us say M. Meissonier. M. Meissonier presides without a rival in French estimation generally; his qualities are precisely those which appeal to French admiration—sanity, flawless workmanship, thoroughly adequate expression of a wholly clear and dignified pictorial motive. Or, if his defective sense for what is poetic be pointed out, the Parisian will in turn point to M. Henner, with whose art he has in general less sympathy, but whose poetic sense he feels must be striking enough for anyone's taste. And it is undeniable that the *Salon*, or even the greater part of the Luxembourg, seems, to the sensitive foreigner the æsthetic side of whose nature is developed in any considerable degree, particularly lacking in those elements which place the plastic arts in the same category with music and poetry. The trail of the conventional is apparent on every hand. Original inspiration, of whatever character, is infrequent. The faculties are, in the vast majority of instances, mainly occupied and occasionally exhausted in technical expression. With the idea, the sentiment, the theme, the artist does not concern himself in anything like the same degree. As to this, he selects rather than invents, and his material is inexhaustible. France is the only country which has kept alive the Renaissance tradition, and consequently education in France means familiarity with a far greater number of artistic generalizations, of precedents, and authorities, than exist elsewhere. Speaking loosely, it may be said that, of every problem which the French artist attacks, he knows in advance various authoritative and accepted solutions. Irresistibly he is impelled to take advantage of these. He could not, if he would, go over the whole ground for himself as if it were virgin soil. Inevitably his zest for discovery is less vivacious, and the edge of his impulse dulled. He counts the less personally for his acquisitions ; his equipment saps his original force ; he cares less about subject and more about treatment. Incompetence is what he most dreads in the general competition. To avoid appearing ridiculous is as much an anxiety of the artist as of any other Frenchman. He holds himself, therefore, well in hand, and proceeds systematically. He surrenders himself to no afflatus but that of science. In every department of artistic effort, then, where training is salutary and education possible—that is to say, not merely in method but in general attitude—the French artist excels. Freak, fantasticality, emotional exuberance are nearly unknown. *Les incohérents* are mainly practical jokers, and the rest gain no acceptance. In this way, as the epoch changes in taste, seriousness, ideas, objects of interests, Lebrun, Boucher, David, M. Meissonier, are successively developed. And to-day the French appreciation of M. Meissonier—the French feeling that he is the fine flower of what in France is most confidently believed in—has become in fact a cult. It would scarcely be fanciful to find something religious in the intelligent idolatry of the daily crowd at M. Meissonier's exhibition of his works a few years ago. The Galerie Petit was a temple. M. Meissonier himself conceives his mission in eminently hierarchical fashion.

In fine, the lack of personal quality born of the social instinct, and illustrated in French manners, shows itself in French art as well, and has done so from the time of Francis I., when classicism was born in full panoply instead of, like its Italian foster-mother, attaining classic stature through natural stages of growth. The arts of comedy and conversation aside, in which personality is almost obliterated and the social, appreciative, and purely intellectual faculties are most actively engaged, French art does not in general contain enough personal flavor to escape conventionality. To thus escape it depends on its geniuses, its wholly exceptional names. Certainly strenuous personality is sure to *percer* —to come to the surface—and its ability to issue from the mass to which culture gives a conventional uniformity, is excellent test and witness of its quality. A triumph over the Institute affirms an artist's force and fortifies his vitality as nothing else can. And it is equally true that where art is classic and its following popular, more individuals practise it, and the chances of thus developing an exceptional personality are proportionally increased. But these considerations, however obvious, are more or less speculative, and the fact remains that not only the mass of French art, but the portion of it which is at once most characteristic and most cordially appreciated by the French public, is altogether too impersonal to be poetic.

Personality, I take it, is of the essence of poetry. Wherever the note of culture predominates and the individual is subordinated, poetry suffers. The personality may be illusory, and "barbaric yawps" as unaccompanied by poetry as by culture. But there is no poetry without sentiment and feeling, and sentiment and feeling mean individuality accentuated in proportion to their intensity. The intellect is in comparison impersonality itself. Less personal, less concentrated, and less sentimental than any other people's, French expression in every department of art is less poetic also. Wordsworth's objection to Goethe's poetry, that it was not "inevitable enough" is applicable to all French art. "Possession" implies not less, but more personality, since it means an intensification of the sentimental, incommunicable, individual side of the poet's nature, and its proportionate emancipation from control by the definite and rational standards which mankind enjoy in common. "Superiority of intellect," Carlyle notes as Shakespeare's distinguishing characteristic, but his Protean personality is rather what separates Shakespeare from other giants of intellect, and this indeed is what we really mean by calling his art "objective." Just as in the instance of the "objective" Goethe, the "Gedichte" and "Faust" are called immortal works by Goethe's most incisive critic, who says that here only is Goethe "truly original and thoroughly superior," because "they issue from a personal feeling and the spirit of system has not petrified them." Perfectly impersonal art is infallibly marked by convention, and convention is the implacable foe of poetry everywhere. It is, on the other hand, a friend and ally of prose, of what is communicable and rational.

Frenchmen resent being told that their genius for prose is a possession which involves an incapacity for poetry, an insensitiveness to what is intimately poetic. But they must pay in this way for their highly-developed social and rational side. "As civilization advances, poetry almost necessarily declines," says Macaulay; which is perhaps too general a statement, considering the coincidence of civilization and poetry of the very highest order at one moment, at least, in the race's history. But M. Scherer is undoubtedly right, speaking for France alone, in doubting whether "our modern society will continue to have a poetry at all." M. Francisque Sarcey, who is in general good nature itself, becomes almost irritated at an English judgment of Victor Hugo maintaining that Hugo is a great romancer rather than a true poet. Yet in his charming "Souvenirs de Jeunesse," having to confess that he has made verses, he exclaims : "Where is the man who can flatter himself that he knows the language of prose, if he has not assiduously practised that of poetry ?" And he adds, "One learns the happy choice of words, the number of the phrase, and the grace of felicitous expression only in forging his style on the hard anvil of the Alexandrine." *La pénible enclume de l'alexandrin !* Fancy an English or American writer of M. Sarcey's eminence speaking in that way of what a French critic calls "the majestic English iambic." "On n'est trahi que par les siens," according to the French proverb. This statement of M. Sarcey's hits the nail exactly on the head. Poetry is in France an exercise, not an expression. It is to real French expression, to prose, what gymnastics and hygiene are to health. And not only is this true of the verses of

the littérateur forging his prose on the anvil of the
ten-syllable couplet, the littérateur of whom M.
Sarcey may be taken as the type, but of the poets
themselves it is true that poetry is conceived and
handled by them as something external rather than
native, something whose qualities they are felicitously to illustrate rather than to employ sympathetically and spontaneously for illustration of the idea
or emotion seeking expression. Conceived in this
way, it is easy to see how the form became tyrannical, how the despotism of the Alexandrine arose.
And we may certainly say that conceived in this way
it never would have been, but for the national genius
for highly-developed regularity and symmetry of
form, for clearness, compactness, measure, and bal-
ance, for forging its fine prose, in a word, on the
anvil of the Alexandrine.

But for form the French have an unrivalled sense
—a sense which unites them closely to the antique
and to the Italian Renaissance. If they have not the
highest substance, they have the severest expression
of any modern people ; if they are the least poetic,
they are certainly the most artistic. I know that
nowadays the latter epithet is frequently used in
a rigidly esoteric sense. But such terms have a
literary as well as a professional and pedantic value,
and no one will fail to seize the distinction here
hinted at, however he may himself identify artistic
with poetic. The one means keeping one's self
well in hand, and the other *abandon* and exal-

tation ; one is constructive, the other inventive ; one manipulates, the other discovers. In this sense, then, "artistic" may be used to describe the Frenchman's universal attitude. He is disinclined to accept nature in any of her phases or aspects. His passion is to arrange, to modify, to combine. He is ineradicably synthetic. His gardens, parks, farms, the entire surface of France, in fact, are landscape compositions. At Hampton Court you are in the presence of the natural forces ; at Versailles or St. Cloud, of artistic ones. That alliance with nature through the inspiration of sentiment, which gives such repose and delight to every other nationality, the Frenchman takes no satisfaction in. It does not call for that active exercise of his intellectual faculties which is necessary to his enjoyment. And it seems to him rudimentary and formless. He is as intensely human as he is impersonal, and nature outside of man and unmoulded by man's influence interests him only scientifically. She is emphatically not something to be enjoyed in itself, but artistic material rather, lying more or less ready to the artist's hand, but demanding co-ordination and organizing before becoming truly worthy of contemplation. The hap-hazard, the fortuitous, what we call the picturesque, either jar on the French sense or strike it as insufficient and elementary. Naples, Andalusia, London are picturesque. They are formless, full of the unexpected, full of color, physical and moral. They are in these respects in complete contrast to Paris and the provinces, where every aspect is ordered and the *coup-d'œil* on every hand artistically organic. Here nothing is left to itself in any department of possible human activity. "The trouble with the French," said an Italian fellow-traveller to me once, "is that they can leave nothing alone. They charge you more for potatoes *au naturel* than for potatoes served in any other way."

French art is thus naturally characterized more by style than substance. It insists upon what Buffon calls "order and movement" more than upon motive. It addresses itself to the intellect mainly rather than to the sense or the susceptibility. French painting occupies itself more than any art except that of the Dutch masters with subtle values, which give a refined intellectual pleasure. The magic of color or composition which moves and the sensuousness which charms are quite lacking. It is in line and mass, and light and shade, and delicate adjustments of harmonious tones that French painting excels. Baudry passes for grandiose, and Bouguereau for subtile, spite of the eclecticism of the one and the emptiness of the other, fundamentally considered, because, abstractedly and impersonally considered, mass and line respectively are thus handled by them. The excess of a devotion to form is precisely this traditionalism and inanity. The excess of a devotion to color is violence. Violence of any kind is instinctively repugnant to the

17

French sense. It is Ingres, and not Delacroix, that permanently attaches and really interests his countrymen. Delacroix seems to them not merely romantic; he seems violent. Théophile Gautier, himself a thorough romanticist, calls Tintoretto *le roi des fougueux*—quite missing the ineffable sweetness and distinction of Tintoretto's hues and poetic poses. There is very little color at the *Salon*; although there is an immense amount of quality, and of quality very sapiently understood, so that nature's color filtered through the *plein air* process is satisfactorily reproduced. Yet passed through the alembic of the painter's personality, specially observed, insisted on, developed, it rarely is. "Gray," says M. de Biez again, "which is the color of the sky in France, is also the color of truth itself, of that truth which tempers the impetuosity of enthusiasm and restrains the spirit within the middle spheres of precise reason." Nothing could more accurately attest the French feeling in regard to color—the French distrust of its riotous potentialities. And, as when one looks constantly at one side of any thing its other side escapes him, the *Salon* is not only lacking in color, but it frequently illustrates how a constant pre-occupation with its *value* leads to toleration of very disagreeable *character* in color. The light and dark harmony is now and then perfect, while at the same time charm, perfume, purely sensuous quality is quite lacking.

Keats speaks somewhere of "Lord Byron's last

flash poem." Following the lead of the English enervated school which one of its admirers recently described as trying to do for painting what Keats did for poetry, one very frequent notion of an important side of French art is exactly expressed by this epithet. I mean the decorative side—everything in fact in which severity does not noticeably preside. The decorative art of the French does indeed oftener than not lend itself to the rococo, though baroque it has rarely been. The extravagances of the late Italian, Spanish, and German Renaissance were but imperfectly emulated in France, where, with an occasional exception, such as the sculpture of Puget's school, the keynote of all the second-rate art since the days of Goujon's and Delorme's imitators has been the academic quality. Vulgarly sensational, whimsical, eccentric, that is to say " flash," it has never been except in that comparatively inconsiderable part which has always obtained infinitely less consideration than frivolity of the kind does elsewhere. Education and the subordination of idiosyncrasy make it rare and disesteemed. There is nothing in France like the cemetery at Genoa. There is nothing like the interior of the House of Lords, which a recent French writer compares to a " thirty-cent Bohemian-glass bazar." Nor like the spectacle in the same hall during an important sitting, "when the Peeresses' Gallery is adorned with women in blue dresses, yellow flowers, red fans, and apple-green feathers," and when, consequently, he adds, "the Bohemian glass shop seems to have been invaded by an assortment of Brazilian parrots." And we may affirm that, even to M. Charles Garnier himself, who has loaded the Nouvel Opéra at Paris with every mark of luxurious elegance conceivable or collectable by him, the decoration of most American theatres and public buildings which antedate the present era of fastidious and forceless eclecticism would seem "flash" to the last degree. What we call "*Salon* nudities" are not the catch-penny things similar canvases would be with us. Nudity is in no Latin country the sensational thing it is in the world inhabited by the British matron and the American young person, whose cheek it is traditionally so difficult to keep from blushing. In the second place, the *Salon* nudities are studies in the most difficult department of pictorial art, namely, in the painting of flesh; and the appeal of the painter concerns his success in this, and is directed to a trained jury and not at all to people to whom for climatic reasons nudity is a sensational thing. It is indeed doubtful if the Anglo-Saxon notion of his motive and of his accomplishment could be clearly conveyed to a French painter—all that we are apt to regard as "flash" is to him so thoroughly convention.

In fine, so far in general are French painting and sculpture from the extravagant or the wilfully meretricious, that painting and sculpture may be defined as, for the French, the representation of ideas in form. Sometimes the form becomes a mere symbol. Variations of it are esteemed violences. But even when it does not reach this state of petrifaction through system, it is employed mainly to embody ideas rather than images, and though never morally didactic, now and then seems to a true child of nature not a little notional and narrow. "At the Institute," says M. Rodin, contemptuously, "they have recipes for sentiments." As for *character*, style shrinks a little from representing anything so little systematized, so little brought into harmony with itself, so complex, so vague in outline and condensed in essence, so discordant, so tumultuous. Geniuses like Michael Angelo and Tintoretto, who have a special faculty for fusing style and character, form and color, are rare. Generally the artist leans toward one or the other— toward Raphael or Rubens, toward Leonardo or Velasquez. The "School of Athens" is the exemplar of French effort, minus its spirituality, which is as foreign to the French genius, perhaps, as it is sealed to Mr. Ruskin. Where we find the artist preoccupied with character it is apt to be a little factitious, as if he had wandered from, for him, the true path and were engaged in an effort for which he was distinctly not born, a work whose conditions are quite foreign to his capacities. Spontaneity thus is rather stifled than stimulated. All formative influences induce restraint, measure, order, and oppose invention and experiment. Even in conversa-

tion you hear the same expression, the same joke,
indefinitely repeated.   No one seeks to vary them
because they have become classic, because their
form is not to be improved upon, and any attempt
in this direction is foredoomed to failure.   Because,
too, there is such an infinite variety of them.   Excellence in this department of activity depends upon
eclectic taste and cultivation ; not at all upon personal inventiveness.   An American gets tired of "Je
vous le donne en mille," "Il n'y a plus de Pyrénées,"
and the infinitude of such classic combinations and
tradition-enshrouded expressions.   The Frenchman
thinks no more of them than we do of "yes" and
"no" and the ordinary parts of speech taken separ-
ately.   He is interested in further combinations,
and enjoys dealing with the classic ones as simple
elements, so that his result is always far more refined and developed.   But it is, after all, wholly impersonal and artistic ; his originality has nowhere
the chance of penetrating the substance, but exhausts
itself in modifying the form.   The same thing is
true, not only of plastic art and of poetry, but even
of music.   French music is as scientific as Palladian
architecture.   Distinctly it lacks melody.   It is full
of ideas, and its form is full of interest ; but compare not the sentiment of Saint-Saens to that of
Schubert, but the counterpoint of Berlioz to that of
Bach.

On the other hand, the predominance of the element of style rarely results in the insipidity which

elsewhere seems the inevitable fate of the refugee from the rococo. The devotion to form is sometimes tiresome, as in superficial articles and prosy books, where a completeness, not logical and philosophical like the completeness of the Germans, but purely of literary form, is sought. Subject, which is in general made so little of, is occasionally valued in proportion to its hackneyed and lifeless dignity. But insipidity is usually escaped because the artist's work is always positive, and, however conventional, almost never perfunctory. Even if it can be called insipid on occasion, its insipidity is never stupid. The special training of the artist gives at least the interest of competence in execution, and his general culture, the demands of the environment, his familiarity with the best models, ensure that its substance shall not be contemptible. There is nowhere the flatness, the lack of accent, the pallor, the wan, chill, meagre aspect which characterizes much of our Protestant and polemic reaction from the earlier tropicality. We are no longer brutal or boisterous, but candor must compel us to acknowledge that our artistic Puritanism is a trifle bleak. It is possible to avoid the commonplace and still be uninteresting. Round door-knobs and legible inscriptions may make an insufficient appeal to the sensitiveness which demands the soothing stimulus of pleasurable aspect everywhere, but merely to destroy the roundness and the legibility results in nothing positive enough to escape insipidity. Dis-

gust with the painting of panoramas and the sculpture of ideal inanity does little to justify itself by
resorting to equally empty possibilities and reali-
ties. French culture and artificiality save art from
that spontaneity which ends in sterility. M. Ben-
jamin Constant's "seraglio" painting is not truly
rococo, nor is M. Jean Béraud's realism insipid. The
sense for form indeed is equally a safeguard in
either instance.

In every artistic effort, where the poetic note is
not so imperatively needed that its absence is a positive flaw, it would be difficult to attach too much
value to form. Form is the safeguard and quick-
ener of all elevated prose. If it be not itself the
highest of qualities, if free and forceful as it shows
itself in Greek sculpture it is even there subordinate to sentiment and color, it is everywhere and
always the inexorable condition of the highest qualities ; they are useful to it—it is necessary to them.
And how admirable and elevating is the prose
which in every department of art the French sense
for form produces! To talk of French painting as
many of our amateurs and artists do, and as they
would of French sculpture were they familiar
enough with it to perceive that most of it has the
same characteristics, is merely to exhibit blindness
for a number of excellent qualities which, whatever
they fail in, at least save French art from the pure
caprices which many of our artists and amateurs
execute and admire. As the national turn for in-

telligence prevents life in France from being taken
en amateur, so the national sense for form prevents
amateurishness in French art. Our art students go
to Paris for instruction in technic, but it is a pity
that they so universally content themselves with
that, and so rarely acquire there the general artistic
cultivation which is there as much a mark of professional excellence as is excellence of technic. Very
seldom is a painter like Mr. Bridgman, let us say,
a painter who understands his capacities as well as
his tastes—a thoroughly professional painter, in a
word—returned to us by Paris itself out of the varied and abundant material we send her. In the
vast majority of cases she sends us back amateurs—
the same amateurs who sought her schools, immensely better equipped in technic, but, in pretty
exact proportion to their individuality, preserving
still the notions, whims, and ambitions with which
they set out—the visions, that is to say, of the in-
curable amateur. Hence our art, spite of the very
great improvement in technic within the past dozen
years, still remains essentially the experimentation
which it has been from the first. Our artists are as
anxious as ever to reconstruct the basis of art, to
give it in their practice a national and personal flavor, to be racial and individual, to display originality, and to do all this fundamentally and radically
quite without regard to the immutable decorum of
evolution, and in defiance rather than through the
aid of culture. Europe has constantly been saying

to us at every international exhibition, "Be less im-
itative. Give us something new, some 'new birth
of your new soil.'" And quite unconscious that
European interest in our art is one mainly of curiosity, and forgetful of the fact that our new soil,
whatever its capacities for producing great natural
triumphs from human character to railroads, from
the very fact that it is new demands careful culture
to produce anything so artificial as fine art, we
have gone about being racial and individual by
pointedly neglecting culture and by breaking definitively with tradition.

Culture has been acutely defined as "the power
of doing easily what you don't like to do." Of culture in this sense our artists, in general, have not,
I think, a sympathetic comprehension. Doing
painfully what they nevertheless like exceedingly
to do, describes rather their practice. What they
like to do, at any rate, not at all what they are
fitted to do, is the rule of their effort. And it
is the unfailing trait of the amateur. No amount
of cleverness can prevent the result from insecu-
rity, from essential triviality, from having that
ephemeral quality characteristic of pure experimentation. Like the cleverness of Walt Whitman's
defiance of culture, only for a time can it conceal
the essential elementariness, the really rudimentary
attitude of mind which conceit leads *naïveté* to mistake for *finesse*. Curious conception of the relations
of means to ends our amateur artists and their

amateur admirers must entertain, in conceiving our formlessness of sufficient substance to revolutionize the judgment of the ages as to form and fitness. Interested as Europe may be in seeing us more "original," we may be sure we shall never compel her obeisance to amateur originality, to "originality" painfully retesting the exclusions which mark the progress of culture and imagining itself inventive. The inexpressible flatness which coexists with our lack of sobriety, of measure, of form is grotesque. We can all nowadays recognize this quality in our yesterday's art—in the architecture which aimed at effects in "frozen music" that would have been the despair of the flamboyant Gothic epoch; in the sculpture which attempted to unite repose and action, the "far off" and the familiar, in a way which Phidias and Donatello were too prudent to essay; in the painting which, despising Nature considered as merely artistic material, surprised her in her own pictorial moods and endeavored to surpass her in intensifications of autumn color, exaggerations of sierras, volcanoes, and cataracts, arrangements of woodland cascades, romantic pools, "coming storms," and sentimental *genre* situations, —endeavored, in fine, to "paint the lily" with an impasto touch, the mere notion of which would have startled Claude and dismayed Rembrandt. But we are quite blind to the same quality in our current art, which displays in its own way the same mental preoccupation with the search for the philosopher's stone and perpetual motion, in complete neglect of the cautious dictates of scientific discovery.

The amateur view of art, of its functions and character, pervades the public as well as the profession, which is thus at once measurably excused for and encouraged in its superficiality. Mr. Howells draws up a list of short story writers, embroidered with laudatory comment calculated to make several dozen people imagine themselves the equals of Mérimée and Maupassant. It is followed promptly by a catalogue of poets from an equally friendly hand, which pleads for a more attentive audience for as many as forty-one "poets," few of whom have ever suffered for the want of a meal, a new suit of clothes, or a theatre-ticket, have ever committed a serious moral indiscretion, know either pain, ecstasy, or remorse, have ever experienced any deep emotional perturbation, or enjoyed any unusual spiritual excitement, and whose culture is shown by their product to correspond to their experience. The popular and good-natured criticism which thus rescues our littérateurs and poets from any peril of self-depreciation, and keeps them a little dazed as to the exactness of their equivalence to Boccaccio and Keats, has a similar effect in plastic art, where, as in the matter of prose and poetry, it merely formulates the feeling of the entire public which occupies itself with such subjects. The American attitude in the presence of novelty of any kind has been described as speculation as to "how

to make something just as good for less money."
In art, at all events, this accurately characterizes the
demand of the public upon the artist, who is therefore stimulated to " supply long felt wants " rather
than permitted to produce naturally.   Of an artist
of great taste and refined appreciation, for instance,
we excuse, if we do not exact, parodies of the grandiose effects of Rome and of the large picturesqueness of Flanders.   Of a painter born and trained
evidently for high class periodical illustration, we
greet with effusion *naïf* experimentation in the
sphere of Christs, Venuses, Last Suppers, the acme
of classic subject.   Of a sculptor who has a decorative sense, we persist in calling for the heroic and
statuesque.   And while we thus pervert mere instinct and talent, we afford little scope to the free
and natural exercise of its energy by the conspicuous genius we may legitimately boast.   If in the informal organization some semblance of which in
every civilized country all professions tend inevitably to acquire, our artists did not resemble less an
army than a mob ; if in the exercise of their functions normal conditions were not so sourly disturbed
that " time is lost and no proportion kept ; " does
anyone suppose that Mr. Eidlitz would build an
ecclesiastical savings-bank, Mr. La Farge set a
Theocritan idyl in a church casement, or Mr. Eakins
choose the Crucifixion for his masterpiece ?

Of course, in all these respects artistic France
presents the completest possible contrast to our-

selves. The French art public does not demand
mediæval cathedrals and Titians, early Renaissance
low relief and pre-Raphaelite intensity, the Floren-
tine line and the Venetian palette. It demands instead M. Gérôme. M. Gérôme is by no means a
favorite of mine. His work, largely considered,
lacks just that element of reality which apparently
its author and his public conceive to be its *raison
d'être*. But the evolution of such a painter and his
popularity witness strikingly the culture of the environment, where all serious effort is soberly and
sanely made, where every artist seems occupied with
what he was born to do, and where that crying disproportion between ambition and accomplishment
characteristic of the amateur stage of progress is reduced to a minimum. M. Gérôme's work is in this
sense admirably professional, and the almost universal honor in which it is held is admirable recognition of this aspect of it—its excellence, that is to say,
in form, in restraint, in a certain felicity of style,
often, which raises it far above almost any contemporary work of the kind, and occasionally (as in the
"Ave, Cæsar! Morituri te salutant") achieves for it
a dramatic distinction bordering on grandeur. Compare it for these qualities with any work produced
among us by fellow-craftsmen who find Gérôme
terribly deficient in charm, who have the true interests of art so much at heart as to fear compromis-
ing them should they admit the value of education,
even in the absence of afflatus. And observe the

prodigious difference between the *milieu* whose admiration fosters these qualities and our own, which expiates its ignorance of their importance by attaching itself to the experimental and the ephemeral, and which by its ingenuous exaction of stimulating and contempt for sustaining viands is condemned oftenest to a Barmecide banquet in the halls of art.

Compare, on the other hand, such a work as the "Ave, Cæsar!" with the historical painting of Piloty, or Wagner, or Kaulbach, or even Hans Makart. How wide is the interval by which it escapes their touch of commonness—that clement which in art as in life we know best as the exact opposite of distinction, the *Gemeinheit* which Goethe was always reprehending, and before which Heine fled into exile. Gérôme, Meissonier, Boulanger, Baudry, Laurens, Dubufe, Henner, Detaille, Mercié, Dubois, Lefebvre, Barrias, Luminais, Cabanel, Bouguereau, Chaplin, and a score of others placed in the front rank by their compatriots' esteem, testify, in a word, to the success of the national sense for form in developing the fine qualities of distinction and elegance, as well as the solid ones of special competence and general culture. Distinction is a trait as proper to prose as to poetry. It is perhaps even more necessary to prose, and hence apt to be therein more generally developed. It is at any rate a native and penetrating quality, which shows itself in every effort of the artist who possesses it. It implies that his point of view is always special and fastidious, that he does not look at things in a preoccupied and matter-of-course way, permitting their grosser traits to impress him, and inertly accepting the actual impression on the retina as equalling the artistic suggestion of the object. Such a painter as M. Alfred Stevens, for example, and such a sculptor as M. Moreau-Vautier, evince in the highest degree the French feeling for distinction, for what is fastidious in its correctness, for refinement, polish, artistic decorum. The patrician element is as characteristic in plastic art as in character or manners, and the French have an instinctive affinity for it. M. Moreau-Vautier stoops to trifles and M. Stevens sometimes suffers his art to exhale in mere millinery; but in each instance, and in a host of others of which these are simply typical, there is a highbred, cultivated dignity which confers on the most frivolous work a certain amount of unmistakable distinction.

We come finally, thus, to recognize elegance as the characteristic quality of French art in its widest scope, and to perceive that the divinity which presides over every æsthetic shrine is Taste. In everything plastic, taste is universally the French test of excellence. Offences against taste are the sins most shocking to the French sense; obedience to its dictates is the attitude most cordially approved by the French mind. One can see how distinctly national the trait is by observing, not merely how quickly elegance became the dominant note in all artistic importation at the Renaissance epoch—how even Primaticcio at Fontainebleau, for example, shows the effect of the new environment upon the Italian inspiration—but also how it struggles with the grandiose severity of Gothic at Rouen and Beauvais ; as indeed, centuries before, the instinctive feeling for it developed Gothic line and movement out of the sombre massiveness of Romanesque. The quality is as noticeable in every department of effort as in formal art. From landscape gardening to needlework, from bookbindings to placards, from the carefully-considered proportions of a Neo-grec palace to the mouldings on a block of builder's buildings, from the decoration of a theatre to the arrangement of a kitchen-garden, in dress, in amusements, in household furnishings, in carriages, chandeliers, clocks, mirrors, table services—in fine, in every object produced by the hand of man—is visible the working of the art instinct under the direction of taste to the end of elegance. In Paris every vista is an artistic spectacle. From the point of view of art nothing in the world equals the picture one sees in looking toward the Louvre from the Arc de l'Étoile—unless it be the line of the boulevards, where the buildings, the terraces, the shop-windows, the people combine in the production of a scene from which every natural element except the sky above it has been eliminated, and which would therefore be dazing and depressing if its harmony, its taste, its elegance did not render it beyond all expression stimulating and

18

delightful. The entire city is a composition, the principle of fitness in whose lines and masses, tones, and local tints secures elegance in the *ensemble*. Elegance is embodied by Paris as perfectly as, according to Victor Hugo, majesty is by Rome, beauty by Venice, grace by Naples, and wealth by London.

Naturally the rule of taste results in the tyranny of the mode. Nowhere, perhaps, is fashion so exacting, not only in dress and demeanor, but in plastic art itself. Hence the development of schools, the erection of methods into systems, the succession of romanticists to classicists and of realists to both, the sequence of academic, pre-Raphaelite, *plein air*, impressionist notions. So that if the mass of French art is too conventional, too little spiritual, too far separated from nature, too material in a word, to be constantly renewed by fresh impulses operating in the work of original geniuses continually springing up, it nevertheless always makes the most of a novel view, a fresh position by developing, systematizing, and finally imposing it as the mode. And however extraordinary the germ of the mode, so severe is French taste and so acute is the French sense for harmony, that in its full flower any fashion is sure to be distinguished more by unity and measure than by caprice. Women's bonnets and dress, and certain accompanying accoutrements, for example, of a most *bizarre* character in themselves, are wholly transmuted in the laboratory of the French *modiste* and *couturière*. In this way the inventions of English eccentricity actually acquire, when transplanted to France, the quality of elegance in which they are most conspicuously lacking, and French taste and constructive art have done for the ulster and the Gainsborough hat what the Fontainebleau landscape school did for the germ transmitted to it by Constable. Taste, too, is endued with that sanative property which purges French art of the dross of positively ridiculous and extravagant fashions. A fashion is not in France the mere "fad" it is in England and with us. The mode is tyrannical, but it is intelligent as well. There was a method and a measure in the costume of the *Incroyables* of the Revolution and the Greek and Roman fantasies of the Empire, which give them dignity in retrospect and must have saved them from that contemporary ridicule of which every Frenchman stands in terror. Good or bad, they were *styles*. They were not the ridiculous results of personal feeling, of whim and freak, intruding themselves in Maudle and Postlethwaite fashion into a realm where reason and convention legitimately reign.

Taste, moreover, is universal in France. It pervades all ranks. It dictates the blouse of the *ouvrier,* the blue and white composure of the *blanchisseuse,* the furnishing of a *concierge's* lodge as explicitly as it does the apparel of the *élégante* or the etiquette of a *salon.* It banishes everywhere raggedness, dirt, slovenliness, disorder. Having classified people, so far as possible it uniforms them ; and by uniforming the classes it unifies the whole which the classes compose. Thus everyone is a critic, everyone instinctively feels, as to any specific thing, whether or no it comes up to the general standard. The first-comer is a judge of art, as in Italy he is of beauty. Everyone's instinct is trained under the influence of taste all the time ; whichever way one turns he receives some imperceptible education. Nature, wilfulness, untrammelled self-expression, and spontaneity are lacking. An English friend of mine complained in disgust of the placidity and *tenue* of the immense crowd at Gambetta's funeral, and of its blue, white, gray, and black monotone of color. An Italian prince or pauper, *raffiné* or rustic, throws the concentrated charm of an absolute unconsciousness into a look, a gesture, an attitude, which the happiest art can never hope to rival. Perhaps we may maintain that there is a subtle order and harmony in the fortuitous, the accidental, which escapes the ordinary eye, and which the ordinary artist does not catch. But whereas this kind of harmony is somewhat insubstantial, and one's feeling for it speculative and fanciful, France presents the stimulating spectacle of an entire people convinced with Sénancour that the tendency to order should form " an essential part of our inclinations, of our instinct, like the tendency to self-preservation and to reproduction," and illustrating its conviction consciously and unremittently in every sphere of life and art—making indeed an art of life itself.

With this feeling impregnating the moral atmosphere, with the architectonic spirit informing all activities, the trifling as well as the serious, it is no wonder that Paris is the world's art clearing-house whither every one goes to perfect, or at least to "consecrate" his talent, and the centre of artistic production whence art objects as well as art ideas are disseminated throughout civilization. Nor is it surprising that even in music—for which the French have certainly no special gift, owing to their lack of sentiment, to the absence of rhythm and the predominance of the *saccadé* note in the French language and character—Paris should have reached its indisputable eminence. What is curious, however, an 1 what constitutes a singular criticism of our century as the "heir of all the ages," is that the least poetic should be the most artistic of modern peoples ; that France, in fact, which "in art cares more for the true than even for the beautiful," should be the only country comparable with the Italy of the Renaissance and the Greece of antiquity, not only for the prodigious amount, but for the general excellence of her artistic activity.

VIII

THE PROVINCIAL SPIRIT

THE PROVINCIAL SPIRIT

As the French social instinct culminates in the French religion of patriotism, French individual vanity becomes conceit whenever the Frenchman contemplates France or the foreigner. The egotism which he personally lacks is conspicuously characteristic of himself and his fellows considered as a nation. Nationally considered, the people composed of the most cosmopolitan and conformable individuals in the world distinctly displays the provincial spirit. Other peoples have their doubts, their misgivings. They take refuge in vagueness, in emotional exaggeration, in commonplaces, in pure brag. We have, ourselves, a certain invincibility of expectation that transfigures our present and reconciles us to our lack of a past. Or, when we are confronted with evidence of specific inferiority, we adduce counterbalancing considerations, of which it need not be said we enjoy a greater abundance even than most of us are prepared on the instant to recall —" comfort and oysters " were all a certain compatriot could think of in one emergency, according to a recent anecdote. But France is to the mind, rather than exclusively to the feeling, of every

Frenchman, as distinctly *la grande nation* to-day as
she was in the reign of *le grand monarque*, when
she had fewer rivals. The rise of these has made
little impression on her. M. Victor Duruy begins
his history by citing from "some great foreign
poet," of whose name he is characteristically ignorant, the statement that France is "the Soldier of
God." Every Frenchman echoes the words of
Stendhal, who, nevertheless, in general strikingly
illustrates what Mr. Spencer calls the "bias of anti-
patriotism :" "We, the greatest people that has
ever existed—yes, even after 1815 !" The "mission" of France is in every Frenchman's mind.
Her many Cassandras spring from the universal
consciousness of it, and are, besides, more articulate
than convinced. Antiquity itself, to which it is a
tendency of much modern culture to revert for
many of its ideals, seems in a way rudimentary to
the French, who, even during the First Empire,
deemed themselves engaged in developing rather
than copying, classic models, from administration
to attire. More than any other people with whom
comparison could fitly be made, they seem ignorant
of what is thought and done outside the borders of
their own territory. It is probable that not only
the Germans, a large class of whom know everything and whose rapacity of acquisition nothing escapes, and the English and ourselves, who are great
travellers, but persons of almost any nationality to
be encountered anywhere abroad, are far more fa-

miliar with French books, French history, French
topography, French ways, than the average intelligent Frenchman is with those of any country but
his own.

The French travel less than any other people.
Less than any people do they savor what is distinctly national abroad. Not only do they emigrate
less; France is so agreeable to Frenchmen, and to
Frenchmen of every station, that it is small wonder
they are such pilgrims and strangers abroad, and
tarry there so short a time unless necessity compel
them. But, as one travels to become civilized, and
as in French eyes civilization reaches perfection
only in France, the chief motive for travel is lacking
to them. "We need to study, not to travel. A
travelled Frenchman is no more civilized than his
stay-at-home compatriots—which is not the case
elsewhere. Besides, nowadays, you know, we have
photographs"—*naïveté* like this it is not uncommon
to hear in Paris. "Le Temps," probably on the
whole the best journal in the world, rarely has occasion to refer to the United States without falling
into some error of fact, such as its American analogue would be incapable of making in regard to
France, though the latter shows considerably less
sympathetic disposition to appreciate French currents of feeling and thought than "Le Temps" does
in the converse case. Every American traveller has
encountered the Frenchman who believed that the
Civil War was a contest between North and South

America, and has been astonished by his general intelligence, which is wholly superior to that of our
people of an analogous ignorance.   The entire
French attitude toward foreigners strikes us as curiously conscious and sensitive.   In Paris, certainly,
the foreigner, hospitably as he is invariably treated,
is invariably treated as the foreigner that he is.
His observations about French politics, manners,
art, are received with what slight impatience civility
permits ; and often, indeed, they are of an exasperating absurdity.   He is made to perceive that all
these things are distinctly matters of French concern.   The Frenchman feels too acutely the privilege of being a Frenchman to extend the favor, even
by courtesy, to the stranger within his gates.   He
has laws which authorize him to expel from French
territory foreigners who displease him.   When
the little American daily, "The Morning News,"
treated the Parisians to some American "journalis-
tic enterprise" about the healthfulness of Nice,
some years ago, there was an amusing outcry for
its immediate exile as a foreign publication.   When
the late King Alfonso passed through Paris after
accepting in Germany a colonelcy of Uhlans, President Grévy was obliged to apologize for the conduct
of the Paris mob, which hissed and hooted him as
if there were no such thing as French civility,
which, nevertheless, is proof against everything but
chauvinism.   Accurately estimated as Wagner is by
the leading French musicians, and avid as are the

Parisians of whatever is new in art, Paris is so distinctly an entity and as such takes itself so seriously, that it would not listen to "Lohengrin" because the author of "Lohengrin" had, nearly twenty years before, insulted it after a manner which, one would say, Paris would be glad to condone as natural to German *grossierté*, and therefore as unworthy of remembrance. The artists of the *Salon* lose a similar opportunity of showing themselves superior to provincialism of a particularly gross kind, in visiting the æsthetic primitiveness of our Congressmen on the individual American painter, who is already only too impotently ashamed of it.

The provincial spirit born of an exaggerated sense of nationality has nowhere else proved so fatal to France, perhaps, as in closing her perceptions to one of the very greatest forces of the century. The modern spirit is illustrated in many ways more signally and splendidly by the French than by any other people, but they have notably missed its industrial side. Industrialism may almost be said to play the chief part in the modern world, to be one of those influences which contribute the most to national grandeur and individual importance. Beside its triumphs, those of the military spirit are surely beginning to seem fleeting and ineffective. Standing armies were never so colossal and never cost so much, but, despite the fact that no one can foresee the manner of their decline, it is already plain that the system which they support must ally itself with industrialism, or perish before it; which is only an extended way of putting Napoleon's remark that "an army travels on its belly." Democracy may have as much use for force as feudalism had, but it is only the more clear for this that the heaviest battalions are to be on the side of the particular democracy which best apprehends and applies the principles of peaceful industry in their widest scope and exactest precision. If there be anything in these inconsistent with eminence in literature, art, natural science, diplomacy, philosophy, with the ideal, in short, so much the worse for the ideal. It is the *fittest* to survive that does survive. But it is far more probable that what is generally called materialism is often only so called because the science of it has not yet been discovered. The future will certainly account nationality a puissant and beneficent force measurably in proportion as the nationality of the future imbues itself with the spirit of industrialism, which at the present time appears, superficially at least, so unnational, so cosmopolitan. Witness already not only the wealth of Anglo-Saxondom, but the way in which this wealth serves to promulgate the Anglo Saxon ideals, imperfect as these are.

Now, at a time when the foundations of modern society were being laid, France was neglecting the practice, if not the philosophy, of industrialism. Only in a philosophical and speculative way—and, indeed, one may add an amateur way—did she concern herself with it. She was wholly given over to the things of the mind, of the heart, of the soul, examining the sanctions of every creed, every conception, every virtue even, and so preoccupied with encyclopædism that she forgot colonization entirely. She threw away Canada, which she had administered with a sagacity wholly surpassing that of the English administration of the then loyal America. She allowed herself to be driven from India. She made only a desultory effort to develop her possessions in South America. While Turgot was studying his reforms, writing political economy, discovering that needless wages were in reality but alms, meditating and administering with a brilliance and power that place him at the very head of French statesmanship, the English Turgot was plundering India. While the French were pondering and discussing the *Contrat Social*, the English were putting money in their purse, with which to fight the Napoleonic wars and restore the ancient régime at the Congress of Vienna. By force of intelligence, of impatience with sophisms, of passion for pure reason, by detestation of privilege and love for humanity, feudality in France was being undermined ; while by force of energy, of strenuous, steadfast, and heroic determination, Hastings was enabling England, by condoning infamy, to substitute wealth for institutional reform.

The result is very visible at the present day, and complicates the French outlook not a little. French

credit is still high, but French finances give the
wisest French economists melancholy forebodings.
France's commerce and manufactures are very considerable, but, unlike her agriculture, they are so in
spite of, rather than because of, French institutions.
The settlement of the land question followed naturally upon the adoption of the Rights of Man, whereas
the Revolution left the questions of trade and finance
untouched in their provincial seventeenth-century
status. Immigration and geographical situation go
far to atone for the un-American stupidity of our
tariff, but the same provincial spirit works much
greater provincial results in France, where no good
luck in the industrial field counterbalances the effects
of subsidies and protection. The nation is at once
the most industrious and the least industrial of the
great nations. Notable exceptions there are ; but
not only do these thrive at the expense of the mass,
but, these included, the business of the nation
seems, by comparison with that of England and ourselves, exaggeratedly retail, where indeed traces of
its activity are not altogether lacking. An Englishman notes at once the tremendous depleting cost of
consuming only native manufactures. An American
remarks a surprising absence of business of all kinds,
except in the luxuries and decorations of life. The
smallness of the scale, the universal two prices for
everything, the restriction of speculation to a small
army of professed speculators, the way in which the
trade in *articles de Paris* and *nouveautés* dominates

in importance that in grain, cotton, groceries, and provisions, the outnumbering of drays and trucks by handcarts and cabs, the immense preponderance of little shops over what we are really etymological in calling " stores"—these things seem provincial not to our philistinism so much as to our ideality.

. It is very well to be at the head of civilization, to represent most perfectly of all nations " the humanization of man in society," but you must manage to live, to endure ; and to endure you must take note of the forces at work around you, you must see the way the world is going. You must not at the present day be so exclusively devoted to *Geist,* however justifiably Mr. Arnold might sing its praises to his own countrymen, as to let your commercial instincts atrophy. Such costly fiascos as the Tonquin expedition are the price paid by France for that uncommercial character betrayed in the use of the term *" article d'export "* for whatever is cheap and poor. At a time when every European nation is colonizing in search of markets, success is not to be won by exporting brummagem. Curiously enough, even in the domain of art, where the French are, one would say, thoroughly commercial (as well as, of course, admirable executants), a critic in "L'Art" rebukes the provincial French disregard of foreign art, by begging his countrymen to be at least lenient enough to examine before disapproving, and asking them how they would like to be judged solely on the art products they themselves send abroad. The French

19

belief that foreigners can be made to buy an article in art or industry that Frenchmen would reject is, indeed, directly associated with their conviction that in all activities you can only be amusing to them, never instructive. Although they welcome the mere strangeness which other peoples resent and which they find curious and intellectually interesting, practically they find no more utility in exchanging ideas than dry goods with you. And not only do they lose in national consideration in this way, but, to note a by no means unimportant detail, they miss the development of character that a national genius for industrialism in its large aspects stimulates in individual citizens. The amassing of money is apt to make misers of Frenchmen. There is little amassing on a large scale that is not known and described as avarice. There are no Vanderbilts. Their laws securing the distribution of wealth stimulate sordidness instead of speculation. For speculation the mass of the people substitute the lottery, which is certainly a provincial form of business risk. Holders of successful tickets almost never dissipate their winnings, but employ them sensibly and economically. Petty gambling is nearly universal, but its scale is usually parochial. The gambling at the Paris Bourse is, of course, colossal in amount, but in its area of influence it is restricted. There are comparatively few "lambs shorn" there, and the temptation to take a "flyer" in the market does not assail the average citizen.

Moreover, the necessity for an immense army keeps the military spirit in fashion. Every citizen passes through the *caserne*, and retains something of its feeling. Duels, fine uniforms, contempt of civilians, superciliousness toward "trades-people" survive from the middle-age predominance of the *noblesse*, through this necessity, with a persistence that strikes our industrialized sense as puerile. Democratic as France is, she is still as feudal, as provincial in these respects, as oligarchical or despotic societies are in others. Material as the community is in many ways, in these it is still steeped in the antiquated ideal of that age of chivalry whose very existence we have arrived at doubting. The truculence of Richelieu's time has been softened, but a statesman is still at the mercy of a *spadassin*, if the latter conceives his "honor" wounded in the course of parliamentary polemics. The sentiment which sustains the soldier against the *avocat* is widespread, and does not differ greatly, except in refinement, from the similar provincialism of our Southern fire-eaters.

French provincialism, however, is exhibited rather in a restricted field of knowledge than in a narrow attitude of mind. It proceeds from ignorance rather than prejudice. Unlike the provincialism of any other people, it is thoroughly open-minded. It is traditional rather than perverse. It is not arrogant but limited—not so much sceptical of foreign merit as conscious of its own. Its development has taken place amid competitive, rather than isolated, conditions, and it shows the mark of the continental struggle instead of insular evolution ; its conceit is derived from a too exclusive contemplation of French accomplishments, not from that vague and sentimental exaggeration with which unchecked emotion accentuates self-respect. Its view of the universe is conspicuously incomplete, but so far as it goes its vision is admirably undistorted. In a word, even French provincialism is remarkably candid and rational. It seems for this reason particularly crass to us, because its exhibition is marked by so much sense and so little sentiment, because a lack of emotional delicacy leads to bald and, so to speak, scientific statement of French merits and attainments. We could sympathize much more readily with pure brag. The absence of buncombe is distinctly disagreeable to us. The palpable sincerity of its air of placid exactitude we find difficult to support. We could forgive it anything more readily than its frank composure. The story of the London cockney who found the French a singular people because they called "bread" *pain,* and replied to a comrade, who observed that calling *pain* " bread " was just as singular, " Oh, well, you know it *is* bread," illustrates rather the French than the Anglo-Saxon order of provincialism. The Englishman would be preoccupied with the contemptible character of the bread itself. The reason why the Germans are such good linguists, says the French Calino, is because "they already know one foreign language." His English correlative esteems foreign languages "lingo." A young and observant Methodist clergyman whom I once saw in Rome, whither he had been sent by his Connecticut congregation in search of health and recreation, was evidently getting none of either because, in the presence of Raphael and Michael Angelo, he was perpetually and painfully reminding himself, as well as others, that "a fine action is finer than a fine picture," and that the Italians were so contemptible a people as to make it natural to infer from their distinction in them something particularly debasing in the influence of the fine arts. It would be hard to find a French priest in our day thus perplexed and tormented by the fascination of pure oppugnation, and well-nigh impossible to encounter a Frenchman of any kind so persuaded that to differ morally from himself was *ipso facto* witness of degradation.

The travelling Frenchman rarely exhibits this pedantic order of contempt for the foreign phenomena with which he comes in contact. He often misconceives and misinterprets them most absurdly, and the serenity of his superiority on such occasions has, first and last, afforded a good deal of amusement. The newspaper letters of the French correspondents are sometimes as good reading on account of the picturesqueness of their blunders as for any other reason. The conceit is colossal. But it arises from ignorance and misconception, from a certain helplessness in the presence of what is unfamiliar that fairly paralyzes even Gallic curiosity, and throws the victim back on his own nation's eminence, with whose justification he is much more at home. It is never combined with feeling, and generally contents itself with such comparisons as observation suggests. Our pedants, on the other hand, are constantly occupied with inferences of the most fundamental nature drawn from the most trivial circumstances. In the case of the travelling Briton, the view of novel objects seems actually to distil dislike. Encountering abroad, for example, a strange costume, the Frenchman finds it in bad taste, the Englishman conceives a contempt for the wearer. Both positions are equally unwarrantable, very likely, but it is clear that the provincialism of the latter only is pedantic. We are all familiar with the budget of opinions about foreigners with which our kindest and gentlest travellers return from Europe : the filth of Italy, the stupidity of the Germans, the insincerity of the French, the ridiculousness of the English, the atrocity of the Spanish *cuisine*, their ultra-radical conviction of American superiority in all these instances being based on the simple fact of difference. No French traveller looks at foreign phenomena in this way, and though his conviction of French superiority may be as unsound at bottom, yet, so far as he is concerned, it is more intelligent, less exclusively sentimental, as well as less uncharitable—one is tempted to add, less unchristian.

The explanation is that the French provincial spirit, like other French traits, is thoroughly impersonal. The individual, everywhere subordinated to the state and the community, appears himself curiously unrelated to the very object of his characteristic adoration. Personally speaking, his provincialism is impartial. He does not admire France because she is his country. His complacence with himself proceeds from the circumstance that he is a Frenchman; which is distinctly what he is first, being a man afterward. And his pride in France by no means proceeds from her production of such men as he and his fellows, but from what France, composed of his fellows and himself, accomplishes and represents. One never hears the Frenchman boast of the character and quality of his compatriots, as Englishmen and ourselves do. He is thinking about France, about her different *gloires,* about her position at the head of civilization. His country is to him an entity, a concrete and organic force, with whose work in the world he is extremely proud to be natively associated, without at the same time being very acutely conscious of contributing thereto or sharing the responsibility therefor. He is, accordingly, a marvel of candor in discussions relating to France, of which in detail he is an unsparing and acute critic. One wonders often at his admissions, which seem drastic, not to say fundamental. We forget that he always has France in reserve —that organic conception which every Frenchman holds so firmly, owing to the closeness of texture in the national life since the nation's birth. In discussions of this kind his attitude is very well expressed by a fine *mot* of the Duc d'Aumale, who, during the Bazaine trial, when the inculpated marshal exclaimed, in justification of his treason, that there was no longer any government left, any order, any authority to obey, said, "*Il y avait encore la France, monsieur!*" The national life of England has been nearly as long and no doubt as glorious as that of France; but, owing to its looseness of texture, to the incomplete way in which it has absorbed the individual, the individual himself seems to make its dignity and eminence subjects of constant concern. And so much personal emotion is in his case associated with this preoccupation, that nowhere more conspicuously than in his chauvinism does he illustrate the disposition of Dr. Johnson, "who," says Emerson, "a doctor in the schools, would jump out of his syllogism the instant his major proposition was in danger, to save that at all hazards." Similarly with ourselves.

In national criticism the Frenchman, on the other hand, never thinks his major proposition in the least danger. This perhaps argues an intenser national conceit, a more explicit provincialism, but it permits a certain syllogistic freedom which an Anglo-Saxon can only envy. Mr. Arnold notes this characteristic as common to the continentals generally in his inimitable essay entitled "My Country-

men." "It makes me blush," he says, "to think
how I winced under what the foreigners said of
England; how I longed to be able to answer it;
how I rejoiced at hearing from the English press
that there was nothing at all in it, when I see the
noble frankness with which these foreigners judge
themselves." But I think this frankness is especially characteristic of the French, and it is, from our
point of view, not a little singular that it should be
accompanied by the most intense chauvinism.
"Modesty is doubt," says Balzac, and the French
thus judge themselves so frankly, very likely, because they are lacking in that modesty which the
screaming of our eagle and the roar of the British
lion attest as an Anglo-Saxon trait. At all events,
the French, with their excessively rational way of
looking at things, esteem modesty a defect rather
than a quality, both in nations and individuals, and
rarely use the word except in the enumeration of
feminine charms, or in the extended sense of "un-
pretentiousness"—as, for example, a modest *savant*.

And it is to be remarked that the French have a
particular justification for their ignorance of foreign
national worth and accomplishment which people of
other countries are without. On principles which
they comprehend, that is to say, such principles as
state action, organic development, scientific study
of special problems, co-operation, and centralization
—every principle, in fact, in accordance with which
the common activities of an entire nation are to be

directed—France presents as a nation a far more
definite and concrete figure than any other. Englishmen, Italians, Americans may excel in a hundred ways, but they are not excellences to which
England, Italy, America concretely contribute as
nations. In the way of direct national accomplishment, the work of France is certainly more palpable than that of other nations. We build for example, an astonishing number of miles of railway
every year, but what we mean by "America" is no
more associated with it than it is with the levying of a
thirty per cent. duty on foreign art. M. de Lesseps's
success or failure is, on the other hand, intimately
and directly French. It is by no means altogether
because French national accomplishment is almost
always a government affair, whereas we make "private enterprise" the great protagonist of our national drama. It is because in France the government is in all matters of this kind so thoroughly
representative, so wholly a popular agent. The result is that "France" is far more real to a Frenchman's intelligence than "America" is to ours, however much our subjective sentiment may atone for
the lack of national palpability. Of "private enterprise," of the attainment of magnificent results
through pure sentiment, through a loose social
organization, through a consistent inconsistency,
the Frenchman has no notion. These are principles
of which he does not comprehend the workings.
But, as I say, the results of those principles whose

workings he does comprehend are far more considerable in France than elsewhere. In the line of social
and political problems whose solution depends upon
the conscious and precise regulation, ordering, and
development of an entire society, French experimentation has, in variety, scope, and thorough going
audacity, been so far in excess of that of other modern peoples that it seems to him idle to examine the
history of the latter. Since the Revolution and the
adoption of the Code Napoléon, for instance, the
phenomena marking the gradual rise of the English
democracy naturally seem to him interesting mainly
from a humanitarian point of view, and only indirectly instructive. And as for studying the details
of our social system, to take another popular example, whereby American relations between men
and women are secured, he necessarily feels that
this would be rather curious than profitable to him,
because of his conviction that these relations, if they
are what our admirers maintain, are owing more to
the favor of Heaven than to that human ordering
upon which his own society must inevitably and exclusively continue to depend.

This justification for French provincialism appears
especially clear in the matter of French ignorance
of foreign languages. Such ignorance is nearly universal in France, and the French have greatly suffered from it both in peace and war. They are now
making a heroic, but probably not very systematic
or successful effort, to remedy the evil. It is one of

the "lessons" of the late conflict with Prussia, like
the lesson of mobilization and full rosters. But certainly one reason of their linguistic limitedness is
the circumstance that for them the acquisition of
foreign languages is in the nature of a pure accomplishment; and for accomplishments as such the
French care very little. In this respect their attitude is far less provincial than our polyglot passion for, in Mr. Arnold's happy phrase, "fighting
the battle of life with the waiters in foreign hotels."
They view language as a distinct expression of definite thought and for this, rightly or wrongly, they
think French suffices—chronicles what of that has
been expressed. Had they the sentimental, the
poetic, the religious temperament, they would be
drawn toward an effort to appreciate English poetry, which is of course absolutely untranslatable.
But not to possess the poetic temperament is not of
itself to be provincial; and, lacking it, an acquaintance with English would teach the French less than
we are apt—provincially—to imagine that would be
new to them. Even of English poetry, there has
been no happier general eulogy than that of Voltaire, and despite the provinciality of the recent
French rendering of "Hamlet" (where, beside the
distortion of ideas, M. Dumas's authority lends itself
to such ludicrous errors as the confusion of "canon"
and "cannon") no one has characterized Shakespeare
more discriminatingly than M. Henry Cochin, whose
commentary is worth a volume of Ulrician profun-

dity. But, poetry aside, all those *problèmes de la vie*, which are so much more definitely treated in prose, are treated in French so copiously as in a measure to justify French preoccupation with French literature, which, indeed, is familiar to and studied by Frenchmen as English rarely is among ourselves. It is impossible to conceive of even Goethe, the incarnation of the cosmopolitan spirit, except as in part the product of French influences ; and the fact that the French can show no one who used German as Heine used French, is not so much witness of their provincial attitude, as of the unprovincial spirit of the French language. French has more concrete and crystallized things to tell us than any other modern tongue and the majority of people can get only distinct things from a language that is not their own. That is why to our average man French is more profitable than English is to the majority of Frenchmen. Only subtle and delicate minds, such as are in any country the rare exceptions, catch the characteristic aroma, the peculiar perfume, the racial point of view of a foreign literature. No one has more discriminatingly expressed the value of studying foreign literatures than Doudan in calling it a means of awakening one's own national genius ; "it is" says he, "like the sound of the trumpet which gave Saunderson the notion of scarlet." For the cosmopolitanism evinced in studying Ollendorf, Doudan would certainly entertain a very slight esteem.

In fine, the peculiarity of the French provincial

spirit is that, for the most part, its manifestations
are national and not individual. Toward other nations abstractly, and toward the people of other nations in the concrete, it is exhibited in very nearly
the proportion in which it is aroused by the exclusive contemplation and knowledge of France itself.
But its reaction upon the individual in his own environment is scarcely apparent. Where neither
France nor the foreigner is directly in question, *un*-
provincial is precisely the epithet for the Frenchman's mental attitude and processes. The Frenchman makes so much of his position as a member of
a society whose texture is extremely close, he employs his relations to his surroundings in such constant and salutary fashion, that personally he avoids
nearly every mark of the provincial spirit. He has
little of its narrowness, its self-concentration, its unremittent experimentation, its confusion of relative
with absolute values. It is, for example, especially
a mark of the provincial spirit to take one's self too
seriously. To take one's self too seriously is the
distinguishing trait at once of the pedant and the
amateur—the person who attaches an excessive importance to trifles, and the person who attacks lightly
matters of great dignity and difficulty ; two arche-
types, one may say, of the provincialism illustrated
by Anglo-Saxons. At home, certainly, however he
may appear abroad, the Frenchman takes himself
far less seriously than the Englishman or the American is apt to do under sufficient provocation, unre-

strained as both are by either the dread or the danger of that ridicule which operates with such salutary universality in France. Beside the pedant and the amateur, the *fat* is conspicuously a cosmopolitan, or, at least, a cockney product. The *badaud* himself is a very catholic-minded character; he sinks himself in his surroundings. Note the essential difference, from the point of view of provincialism, between him and the prig—especially that latest and least attractive variety of the species by which at present our own society is infested, and from which France is free—the prig bent on self-improvement. An environment whose cosmopolitanism is a pervasive force, instead of mainly a mere lack of positive nationality, cannot develop a being of whom it is the cardinal characteristic that his constant discipline and effort are exercised uniformly at the expense of others. So perfectly are the amateur and the pedant fused in him that the most trivial conversation is in his eyes an opportunity; he takes notes for self-education on the most sacred and solemn occasions; at dinner-parties he is studying etiquette, at the whist-table he is improving his game, at church he is exercising his memory, in a neighbor's house or a picture gallery, his taste; he has no intimacy too great for him to employ in practising his voice, his gestures, his carriage, his demeanor—his whole environment, in fact, animate and inanimate, friend and foe, he remorselessly sacrifices to his implacable purpose of educating

himself, whatever may happen. And that he may
advance in virtue as in wisdom he lets slip no opportunity of educating others. No description, indeed,
of a society which lacks him, can be more vivid and
positive to a society which possesses him, than the
mention of his absence. One infers at once in such
a society a free and effortless play of the faculties,
a large, humorous, and tolerant view of one's self
and others, leisure, calm, healthful and rational vivacity, a tranquil confidence in one's own perceptions
and in the intelligence of one's neighbors—characteristics which, very likely, have in turn their weak
side, but which indicate the urban, the metropolitan, the mundane attitude of a community wherein
men rub against and polish each other, and exclude
the village or conventual ideal of laborious effort,
careless of the present, forgetful of the past, its ar-
dent gaze fixed on a vague recompense, in an indefinite future, to the successful contestant in a rigorous
competitive examination.

Religion, too, has contributed as largely in France
to the absence of the provincial spirit as it has fur-
thered the social instinct by tending to social concert and social expansion. Not only, that is to say,
has religion in France exercised the influence peculiar to Catholicism, but Catholicism has there been
without a rival. Protestantism exists. The Re-
formed Church is indeed supported by the state on
a perfectly proportionate equality with Catholicism,
but the blood of the martyrs has not been its seed,

and it does not really count. The leading Paris newspaper is Protestant ; many of the leading men are of Huguenot descent and cherish Protestant traditions. But these themselves discuss every question from a Catholic stand-point, and it never occurs to them that society is not homogeneously Catholic. Catharine de' Medici is in this respect as much the creator of modern France as Henry VIII. is of modern England or Philip II. of modern Spain. It is so far from easy to be content with her work that the Massacre of St. Bartholomew seems to me the greatest misfortune that has ever befallen France. Compared with it the Prussian invasion of 1870 and the loss of Alsace-Lorraine seem insignificant ; when we think of the France of Coligny's time and its potentialities, the France of to-day, even post-revolutionary France, is, in certain directions, a disappointment. But it is not to be denied that to the Massacre of St. Bartholomew and the Revocation of the Edict of Nantes are attributable the religious homogeneousness of French society, and, consequently, its composure, its serenity, its absence of the provincial spirit in one of the profoundest, and most sacred, and most influential of human concerns.

The humanizing effect of unity in religion is one of those phenomena which have only to be mentioned to be immediately appreciated. The attitude of superstition itself is really far less provincial than the attitude of scepticism. The one is traditional and social in its nature, the other of necessity soli-

20

tary and personal. Even superstition implies a placid and serene sympathy between its victim and his environment. Sophocles, Virgil, Raphael, Shakespeare, Erasmus, Goethe—how distinct is the urbanity, the felicity of rounded and complete harmony which the mere mention of these names reminds us they illustrate in common! How different it is from the notion called up by the mention of Luther, Calvin, Bunyan, Knox, Byron, Carlyle! Apollo is one type and Achilles is quite another. To fight it out for one's self in the sphere of religion; to forge one's own *credo* out of materials painfully selected from the workshops of the ages; not to feel one's self sustained and supported by human sympathy in the supreme human concern; to assume the objector's attitude, to place one's self at the sceptic's view-point, to particularize laboriously and sift evidence with scrupulous care in a matter so positive, so attractive, and so universal—how can this fail to stimulate in one the provincial temper, the provincial spirit? The social instinct recoils in the face of such a prospect.

The tendency of unity is to magnify the worship, of diversity to magnify the philosophy, of religion. How many scores of conscientious and piously-disposed young men at the moment when "choice is brief and yet endless" cut themselves off entirely from the former because they cannot make up their minds clearly as to the latter! Everyone's experience has acquainted him with the phenomenon of

"truly religious souls" debarred from the commun-
ion of saints, not to say impelled toward the com-
munion of sinners, by what Renan calls "the narrow
judgments of the frivolous man." The kindred phenomenon resulting from the narrow and frivolous
judgments of the truly religious soul itself, is scarcely less frequent. In New England, at any rate,
where the old Arian heresy *redivivus* has produced
such luxuriant intellectual fruit, it is not an infrequent occurrence to find the anxious seat filled with
candidates carefully conning the different "confes-
sions," the mind concentrated on the importance of
an intelligent and impartial selection, preliminary to
the satisfaction of the soul's highest need. "The
experience of many opinions gives to the mind great
flexibility and fortifies it in those it believes the
best," says Joubert. Nothing can be truer and
nothing more just than the high praise that has
been given to this remark. But it is surely applicable to philosophy rather than to religion, and if applied to religious philosophy it should be read in
conjunction with that other and profoundly spiritual
saying of Joubert : "It is not hard to know God,
provided one will not force one's self to define him ;"
or this : "Make truth lovely, and do not try to
arm her."

The great word of religion is peace, and controversy
here, however practical it may be, is indisputably
provincial. Controversy has become so characteristic of our sectarianism, it is believed in so sincerely,

it is, in effect, so necessary as a protection against the insidiousness of superstition, that one distrusts its universal efficacy at his peril. No one, failing to see how this must be so, can fail to observe that it is in fact so when he contemplates many of the manifestations of the controversial spirit in which our society abounds. A not infrequent spiritual experience, for example, is this : a person of inbred piety, infinitely attracted by the beauty of holiness, comes in contact with the scientific and scrutinizing spirit of the age. The unity of nature, the universal identity of her undertakings, which, as Thoreau says, are "sure and never fail," make a profound impression on him. He is unable to credit or conceive of their overruling to the end that spiritual truth may be attested by thaumaturgy. He pays dearly for his inability. It excludes him from fellowship with spirits a thousand times more akin to his own than he can find outside the doors guarded by the flaming sword of an inflexible *credo*. He begins, nevertheless, to adjust himself to his position. Soon he proceeds to vaunt it, out of sheer self-respect. His heart becomes hardened ; his intellect freezes ; finally he finds a haven in a society for ethical culture, whose cardinal tenet it is that the Sermon on the Mount is too simple for application to the immensely diversified needs of our complex modern society. He may not have lost his own soul, but he has certainly not gained the whole world, nor any considerable part of it. The world stamps him and his society as essentially provincial, and turns with relief to the fellowship of quarters wherein the beautiful and the good stand in no terror of the tyranny of truth. From this variety of provincialism, at least, the Massacre of St. Bartholomew and the Revocation of the Edict of Nantes have done much to spare France, both in her religion and her irreligion.

It would, indeed, be very difficult to persuade a Frenchman visiting America of our good faith in charging him with provincialism in any regard. Every contrast with things French which meets his eye must enforce his sense of our rudimentary and undeveloped condition. He could not fail to find our theatres, some of our churches, our conception of his interest in cemeteries and penal institutions, the transparent dresses of our women on undress, and their high-necked "gowns" on dress, occasions, our diversified tastes in the matter of feminine bonnets and masculine beards, our bathing costumes and manners, our lack of police efficiency, our *cuisine*, the attire and conduct of that immense class among us in whom gentility is uneasily nascent, and our categorical and serious defence of these and scores of other peculiarities, exactly to be characterized by the epithet provincial. He would probably be unabashed even by our "men of general information"—a product in which, perhaps, we may defy competition. He would certainly maintain that in France there are more people who have an academic and critical knowledge of "life" and character, people whose judgments of the innumerable and immensely varied phenomena of life and character, of art and science, are independent without being capricious. "The range within which these judgments are restricted seems limited to you," he would assert, "mainly, perhaps, because yours is extended into the region of triviality. Prices of every sort from pictures to mess pork, railway time-tables, tinkering, horse and dog lore, stitches, sports, the mysteries of plumbing, old furniture, pottery marks, in fact, all that desultory and fragmentary 'information' with which your as yet unsystematized struggle with nature seems to encrust so many among you, is what, on the contrary, we regard as really limited and limiting. And, in general, a crystallized and highly developed community seems provincial to the nomad and the adventurer, whether he be a Bedouin or a Wall Street broker, because it has traditions, local pride, public spirit, and organic relations ; because, great or small, it is and stands for something at once definite and complex, and is not merely a part of the amorphous universe where nothing is settled, where there is no code to systematize the general scramble, and where industry and enterprise thrive at a tremendous cost to the *ensemble*, and substitute a startling social *chiaro-oscuro* for the just pictorial values of civilization. Paris is 'provincial' in the same way as your oldest and maturest city is. Like Boston, it seems 'pro-

vincial ' to the New Yorker and the Chicagoan because it is so completely organic, because it is so
distinctly a community instead of being merely a
piece broken off the wide, wide world.   The desert
of Sahara is not ' provincial ; ' as Balzac said, ' It is
nothing and yet everything, for God is there and
man is not ! ' You Americans strike us as unprovincial, I may observe, mainly in this Sahara sense."

At the same time—we may, I think, legitimately
rejoin—the catholic and cosmopolitan spirit which
leads Emerson to find not provincialism but "characteristic nationality " in Madame de Staël's peremptory "Conversation, like talent, exists only in
France," is probably rarer in France than in an environment where there is, if not more of God, at any
rate less of man.

IX

DEMOCRACY

DEMOCRACY

"HORACE tells us," says Gouverneur Morris, in a letter from Paris to the Comte de Moustier, French Ambassador to the United States, "that in crossing the seas we change our climate, not our souls. But I can say what he could not, that I find on this side of the Atlantic a strong resemblance to what I left on the other—a nation which exists in hopes, prospects, and expectations." This was in 1789, and though of course each country has to-day fewer expectations to realize than it had then, an American in France must still be impressed by the same correspondence of national attitude—by the vivacious and confident way of looking forward to the future which the French people, and, perhaps, the French people alone, share with ourselves. Our own animation is partly due, no doubt, to the fact which Carlyle pointed out, namely, that we have "a great deal of land for a very few people." It is due also to our belief in the American character. But it resembles the analogous French elation in being also based on confidence in democratic institutions. Democratic institutions, however, may differ widely, and it is undoubtedly the very considerable difference between our democracy and that of the French that is responsible for our very popular error, which assumes that their institutions are not really, and in so far as they work easily and with promise of permanence, democratic institutions at all. That this error is a little ridiculous does not, of course, prevent it from being very widespread and very deeply rooted. There is probably no country in which the French Revolution is less understood than it is in America.

Its ideality first of all, I think, distinguishes French democracy from our own. Democracy is a creed, that is to say, with the French—a positive cult rather than a working principle, a standard, general test of particular measures. It is held consciously and with conviction. It provokes enthusiasm. Its devotees have had to die for it. It is not merely accepted as a matter of course, due originally to the triumph of circumstances over national characteristics, as was measurably the case with us. Our government, it is true, was, as General Collins aptly says, "the child of revolution nurtured on philosophy." But it is perfectly certain that, but for Jefferson's French philosophy, called then as now, demagogic Quixotism, we should have had as short-lived a democratic republic as Hamilton prophesied and endeavored to compass. Our next epoch made a nation of us, and crystallized the spirit of nationality in democratic form. But nothing is more significant of the discredit into which democracy, as an ideal, has fallen among us than the way in which this formative period of the nation's growth has been obscured by the struggle with slavery which immediately followed it, and during which democracy, as an ideal, almost wholly disap-appeared. Their interest in the preservation of the rights of States allied the slaveholding aristoc-racy with democratic philosophy, and the alliance was disastrous. Democratic philosophy nearly per-ished. It ceased to be propagated among "the best people," as they are called. It lost its hold on the mass of intelligence, on the newspapers, on the college graduates, on all those who had not an espe-cial capacity for keeping their heads in the midst of the excitement of a great national crisis, the right set-tlement of which was infinitely more important than the keeping of one's head. *Inter arma silent* political principles as well as laws. And though the laws may resume their sway and supreme courts reverse their decisions after the clash of arms has definitely died away, political principles that have once lost cur-rency have irretrievably lost credit also. Great men may restore to them their popular validity. Had Abraham Lincoln lived, perhaps the entire political feeling of the country might have been different. But crises, only, produce great men, and now-a-days Lincoln's lofty maxim has really become transformed into "government of the people, for the people, by 'the best people,'" as the political ideal of many of our purest patriots; though it may be questioned if in this form it will "make the tour of the world."

We have in large measure forgotten our heroic philosophical genealogy. Our English character has come to the surface again, and necessarily philosophy gives place to casuistry.

Our democracy, indeed, was not, to begin with, anything like "the child of revolution nurtured by philosophy," which the French democracy is. We only suffered from political tyranny. We did not rise also from social subjection. Mainly we had at the outset merely the independent spirit, the native Anglo-Saxon instinct for freedom—not the sentiment of equality and a philosophical belief in the essential worthiness of man as man. Gouverneur Morris, in 1790, prefers the English constitution to the French, and one has only to think what the English constitution, in 1790, was, to perceive the significance of such a preference. And Morris was by no means an unrepresentative American. And the French constitution of 1790 was made by the upper classes. It was through self-assertion that we triumphed, whereas the French won their autonomy through the universal appeal of principle. And they came thus to love the abstraction through which they conquered—at first fanatically, and now for a long time rationally; whereas the democratic creed never had the universal validity of an abstraction to us, except to our philosophic minds, like Jefferson, for example, and through them to our Democratic party. Neither Federalist nor Whig ever thought of it as universal at all.

Nor have their successors since. The great mass of our people undoubtedly believe in democratic institutions for Americans, though undoubtedly an important portion of our " wealth and intelligence" thinks our own altogether too democratic. But many even of those whose politics are not merely traditionary, would probably echo the general Anglo-Saxon conviction, that institutions in themselves, democratic or other, are unimportant, compared with national character; that there is no abstractly good kind of government, and that every people should have the kind its own racial constitution and its degree of development call for. We did, to be sure, make one of the very boldest democratic experiments that any society ever made during the Reconstruction period, but it hardly proceeded from our faith in universal suffrage as a civilizing agent ; it was due rather, to use an extenuating epithet, to political diplomacy, and it was really undemocratically imposed on an unwilling section by an imperious one. Probably the most popular cry now audible in strictly American political circles, is for the regulation of immigration and naturalization, in order that " ignorance and poverty " may be fitted for the suffrage, to the end that property may be more secure, and " hidden and forbidden forces " less powerful. Sound as this may be, it is a long way from the democratic ideal as held and illustrated by France. It is not consistent with an enthusiastic subscription to the gospel of Liberty, Equality, Fra-

ternity.   Its tendency is rather in the direction of
such a democracy as that of slaveholding Athens (so
far as a parallel may be drawn between a nation of
sixty millions of people and a community " at most
a subprefecture "), in which the democratic ideal
found expression mainly in an equality of the *élite*.

In fine, it must be evident to all close observers
that the ideal of government by " the best people "
is growing with us.   It is by no means yet
triumphant, and in many instances it is so closely
associated with a pharisaical habit of mind, that
very likely our many publicans and sinners, who believe in democratic institutions at least for themselves, and as satisfying their individual instincts
of independence, will contrive to keep it permanently under.   The " masses " are solidifying, perhaps, as fast as the " classes " crystallize, and
whereas it used to be our boast that our cities had
no " populace," and our country districts no " peas-
antry," we shall possibly have enough of both to
prevent the · establishment of the ideal of government by " the best people "—by the people, that is
to say, who are doing their reckless utmost toward
the production of the American proletariat they so
abjectly dread.   Of course in America, by " the best
people," we do not yet mean the richest ; we mean
very generally the most intelligent.   Mr. Lowell,
for example, who courageously patronizes democracy
in England, and with equal courage castigates it at
home, affirms that " the duty of the more intelligent

is to govern the less intelligent." It is a matter
mainly of color, perhaps, but I own to a feeling that
when Mr. Lowell, and indeed most of our publicists
who have cut themselves adrift from the aristocratic
party on questions of morals and taste rather than
of political principles, praise the democratic creed,
what they are really thinking of is not "Liberty,
Equality, Fraternity," but the New England town-
meeting of earlier and better days. The moment the
milieu becomes heterogeneous and uncolonial, their
democracy seems really to vanish in distrust of that
average man, respect for whom is the corner-stone
of the French democracy. Whenever, as in large
cities, elaborate political machinery with its attendant evils becomes necessary, it is significant how
instinctively their minds turn to disfranchisement
as a remedy. No one has eulogized Lincoln more
sympathetically than Mr. Lowell, exercising his noble poetic faculty. But it is difficult to fancy the
man who said "the Lord must love the common
people, he made so many of them," laying much
stress upon the "duty of the intelligent to govern
the unintelligent." And undoubtedly Mr. Lowell's
crisp prose just now appeals to "the intelligent"
among us far more cogently than the looser democratic feeling of Lincoln. How many of our writers,
whose philosophic utterances have any credit, would
echo La Bruyère's famous " Faut-il opter ? Je veux
être peuple."

Our democracy indeed shows its unideal quality

21

in no wise more clearly than in the exaltation thus
implied of character, national as well as individual, over institutions.   We like our institutions,
in cases where we do not accept them with amused
resignation, because they suit us, because they give
us personal independence, because we can—some
of us—grow rich under them; and not at all because *per se* we admire institutions, are attracted
by them, and believe in their universality.   On the
other hand, it is the French notion that civilization
means the improving of character by institutions.
Mankind tends naturally to inequality.   Inequality tends naturally to establish itself.   Inequality
is undemocratic and uncivilized.   The only bulwark
against it in the long run is the careful, systematic,
and minute formulation of political principles in the
light of reason, aided by experience, and their universal application as institutions to the society subject to their sway.   To use a fanciful, but exact,
figure, whereas, thus, we regard institutions as anti-
septic, the French consider them as therapeutic.
Our democracy is a working hypothesis, establishing
the lines through which national and individual
character may work out their salvation.   French
democracy is a positive and highly differentiated
system, designed for direct and active agency in the
securing of social well-being and political progress.
Each has, of course, its peculiar peril.   For the lack
of institutions tending to secure equality—as directly as excise laws tend to promote temperance,

anti-lottery laws to prevent gambling, anti-usury laws to prevent extortion, and strict divorce laws to promote chastity—our democracy is constantly menaced by the growing heterogeneity of our society, the geometrically increasing power of wealth, culture, position. For the lack of the free play of individual expansiveness and independence inherent in systematic and effective organization, the French social democracy is in constant danger of losing its political freedom. And the effect of the loss of political freedom on social democracy is one of constant and subtle attrition.

I must say, however, I think the French are more conscious of their danger than we are of ours. Indeed, this particular one I have mentioned is the only political peril concerning which we seem just now to be displaying no anxiety whatever. Our pessimists are optimistic on this point. But the experience of France, in the difficulties of securing and sustaining democracy, has been considerably greater than our own. And this circumstance has doubtless done much to strengthen, as well as to sober, the ideality with which its mainly philosophic, instead of mainly practical origin, endued it at the outset. And the particular practical form which this ideality takes on, distinguishes French democracy from ours, in even greater measure than does the positive spirit from which it proceeds. Its great practical distinction, in a word, is that it is *at once popular and authoritative*. We are accustomed

to believe the two qualities incompatible. Author·
itative government is inseparable in our minds from
what is called paternal government, and we feel
that if government with us should show any particular authoritativeness, even in the way of greater
efficiency of administration, it would infallibly, to
just that extent, lose its popular character. But
when the popular character of a government is
secured, not by the cordial initiative of independent
individuals inspired by intelligently understood interest, but by a natural enthusiasm for the democratic ideal, rationally interpreted and vigorously imposed, it is easy to see that it may be as authoritative,
or even as intolerant, as it finds it effective to be,
without really sacrificing anything of its essentially
popular nature. No one can have lived in France,
at all events, since the establishment of the present
Republic, without observing how *popular* the government is. Everyone talks politics. People everywhere are politically alive, however remiss they
may be about voting. One perceives a general interest in active self-government. The difference between the political atmosphere in this respect and
that of England, for example, is very noticeable to
an American sense, and, so far as its influence
operates, makes an American feel far more at home
than in English society, where the political talk is
almost exclusively sentimental and apt to be confined to the personal character of Mr. Gladstone,
and the national traits of the Irish. The press is as

fundamentally democratic as the English press is fundamentally contemptuous of popular ideas. It is, moreover, quite as free. Personal privacy is the only ground it may not invade. One notes that, whereas English liberty, up to the Reform bills at any rate, was individual rather than popular, the individual left to do as he liked, even to the point of "going to the devil his own way," with no voice in the control of the society of which, indeed, it was not recognized that he formed a part in the ab sence of substantial titles to recognition ; and, whereas, even now, the voice many individuals have is practically a ludicrously feeble one, and, to their own stolid perceptions, often scarce worth the pains of uttering at all, except for the purpose of "saying ditto" to their respective Mr. Burkes, French liberty, as it exists at present, works in entire and efficient harmony with the social instinct.

The French *canaille* itself enjoys much more consideration than does ours, and the fact contributes powerfully to the democratic homogeneity of society. It is significant that, when such a born aristocrat as M. Jules Simon has occasion to make a contemptuous allusion to the *canaille*, he feels compelled instantly to add : "Don't be alarmed, I mean *la sainte canaille*." Certainly it would occur to no English, and I doubt if to any American, publicist of M. Jules Simon's temperament and convictions, to apologize sarcastically for calling the *canaille* the *canaille*. And the reason is that in France the

canaille has, in common with every other class of
society, received the advantages of long evolutionary
differentiation, so that it has of necessity developed
the qualities which create companionability. Its
coarseness and grossness are accordingly not shocking, whereas, with us, the grossness and coarseness
are so great as to mislead us into a most unchristian
contempt for those who show them, and cause us to
imagine that what is really ignorance of the essential
moral and spiritual similarity of people, is a witness
of a refined nervous organization. The Frenchman's nerves not being thus exasperated, do not
thus lead him to mistake snobbishness for sensitiveness. And being in this way, and for this reason,
less contemned, even the *canaille* in France becomes
inevitably less contemptible than the *canaille* elsewhere. Being—for cause—better liked, it becomes
in turn more likable. It is intelligent and conscious, and alive to its own interests. It has to
be reckoned with politically. It counts as a force.
It is not merely intractable and turbulent. It at-
tempts, at least, to give its rioting an air of revolutionary intention. It has even then a distinctly
political motive, and the idea of expending its force
in mere wanton marauding, after the Trafalgar Square
order, would seem absurd to it. Its demonstrations,
at their worst, are directed against what it believes
a tyrannical government ; those who take part in
them talk about capturing the Hôtel de Ville, or
marching on the Palais Bourbon ; they do not

smash club windows, and attack casual pedestrians, and loot shops. In brief, the *canaille* is serious. It is very likely more dangerous for this reason to the established order, but it certainly is a more healthful social element, from the democratic point of view, than is either the supine and submissive understratum of German, or the "brutalized lower class" of English, civilization.

The attitude toward it, therefore, of that part of the community whose property and position give it contrary interests, is correspondingly different from the attitude of the upper classes elsewhere. Elsewhere the upper classes' endeavor is to keep it down. In France the analogous endeavor is better described, in vulgar phrase, as an attempt to keep it off. In France property and position are simply engaged in the attempt to hold their own amid the social warfare of clashing interests, according to the laws of the struggle for existence. They are not seeking to impose themselves on the less fortunate and less powerful. They merely sustain their cause, their side, in the general democratic parliament. Permanent domination is a dream they certainly have not cherished since the abdication of Charles X. But what is still more important to note is that these extremes apart—the inheritors of the old aristocratic tradition on the one hand, and the *canaille*, so called, on the other—the rest of the nation explicitly objects to a warfare of opposing interests, and cherishes the ideal of serving the interests of the entire people as a people. "Le Temps," for example, is never tired of preaching this doctrine. The burden of its daily message is that it is unpatriotic to legislate in favor of any class, even of the least privileged ; that to be a truly popular government the Republic should avoid espousing the cause of the poor against the rich as strictly as that of the rich against the poor ; that every class of the community has its right to equal consideration, and that the rule of the masses for the masses is as illogical republicanism as that of the classes for the classes would be. This is a lesson which "Le Soleil" on the one hand, and "L'Intransigeant" on the other, no doubt find it hard to learn ; but save in America, certainly nowhere else is it preached with the same general acceptance, and nowhere else is its practice so well secured by thoroughly positive as well as thoroughly popular institutions. We have an immense advantage from the democratic standpoint in having no classes in the European sense, and of a constant and easy passing from one into the other of the two we do have. So far as classes, therefore, are concerned we are more homogeneous, taken in the mass, and politically considered, than any other people in the world ; it is as individuals that we illustrate such prodigious differences. With, therefore, a comparative identity of interest, it is comparatively easy for everyone to mean by "the people" the whole people, rather than the peasant, the *ouvrier* or the *Tiers État* even. How long this will last with us is, of course, problematical. The wise words of Mr. Lincoln's first annual message : "There is no such relation between capital and labor as assumed, nor is there any such thing as a free man being fixed for life in the condition of ., hired laborer. . . . The prudent, penniless beginner in the world labors for wages for a while, saves a surplus with which to buy tools or land for himself, then labors on his own account another while, and at length hires another new beginner to help him " —these words are or were applicable to us, and are little applicable anywhere else. To be exact, they should have read " the prudent, penniless beginner in America," not "in the world." In the world in general the relation between labor and capital is much more fixed. And, as I have already observed, social differences among us are crystallizing and increasing, and social differences mean very quickly a changed political atmosphere. But should our plutocracy establish itself, and the lines between such classes as we have become in consequence more closely drawn and less passable, we should be very fortunate, so far as the preservation of the democratic spirit is concerned, if our well-to-do and our poor, our educated and our ignorant, classes had the same mutual respect and tolerance which exist in France between the upper, middle, and lower classes. For in France, these classes are cemented by the social instinct and the democratic spirit into a whole, which, if not possessed of identical interests, is, at

least, composed of harmoniously balanced and equally recognized constituent elements. There is a certain advantage, indeed, in the comparative permanence of the class situation in France. The *ouvrier*
who is always to be an *ouvrier*, the *bourgeois* or the
peasant who is always to remain such, as his fathers
did before and as his son will after him, is the more
interested in maintaining his dignity and asserting
his importance as *ouvrier*, *bourgeois*, or peasant;
whence a manifest equilibrium in the regulation of
a society composed of necessarily unequal classes,
by the elastic compensating force of democratic
feeling. Personally the *ouvrier* is likely to count
less, of course, than where, as still with us, he may
hope to become a *patron*. But as a class he counts
more ; and as a class our *ouvriers* are, as I said, rapidly tending to become a class dangerously without class self-respect—a class composed rather of
envious individuals soured by the loss of that opportunity which in a simpler situation their sires possessed. We shall then have Mr. Gladstone's democracy with its cry of "the classes vs. the masses"—a
motto subscribed to at present neither by the French
nor ourselves. Class, in France no more than in
America, implies caste.

One hears a good deal about the French government not being really a republic, about its being as
autocratic and as fond of tyrannical traditions as a
monarchy could be. But it must be admitted that
the reasons assigned for this conviction seem a

little literal. Of course, if to have a large party within your borders which is opposed to a republican form of government is, *ipso facto*, to be "a republic only in name," the French Republic is open to that reproach. But this very circumstance is a sufficient justification for a good deal of the so-called arbitrariness of the Republic's action of recent years. Only a pedant would be embarrassed by the logic of the late Louis Veuillot, who remarked in defence of ultramontanism, "When you are in power we demand tolerance, because it is your principle ; when we are in power we refuse it, because it is not ours." It is no party's principle to the extent of tolerating what would, if tolerated, do its utmost to compass the destruction of tolerance. The republican creed, however superficially inconsistent it may seem, must in its first article require subscription to the republican form as the necessary basis of toleration, of liberty. A great deal of criticism of the Republic's action in removing the Orleanist princes from their positions in the army, and in expelling pretenders, found its way at the time into the American and English press. But no country in the world would for a moment tolerate an analogous formal and avowed conspiracy within its borders. Does anyone suppose that if Lord Wolseley should declare his preference for a republic, and should devote himself to a propagandism in the British, equivalent to that of the Orleans princes some years ago in the French, army, he would remain a day in the royal service ? Why, because a republic is professedly more tolerant than any other form of government, it should therefore be the less, rather than the more, entitled to regard self-preservation as its first law, is a mystery. It is, moreover, a mystery we should find it more difficult to explain now than we might have done before the trials of the German, Polish, and English anarchists in Chicago, and of their truculent and ridiculous spokesman, Most, in New York. But, it is said, we are distinguished for our wise and sober capacity to wait for the " overt act," before we punish its incitement. This is no longer quite true ; but, aside from the ridiculousness of such delay when the " overt act " has been shown by experience to be certain to follow its incitement, it really behooves us to acknowledge that recent events have shown our disposition to go quite as far in the way of repression as the French Republic does, if we had the same temptation, rather than to dwell complacently on our superior republican consistency. Really, the difference between ourselves and the French here is only that which proceeds from the excess of their state action over ours. And what is really extraordinary in the case of the present Republic is, that the logic of republican tolerance has so completely counteracted the tendency to tyranny springing naturally from excessive state action. The tyranny of the government has in no instance, I imagine, exceeded, if indeed it has equalled, the party tyranny which our present tariff and our theory of a civil service produce among us.

The danger of democracy is always despotism, it is true ; but it should always be borne in mind that this despotism means popular, not at all oriental, despotism, as pessimists presume. Universal suffrage gets impatient with parliamentarism whenever any political shoe really pinches, and wishes to assert itself directly. We have ourselves passed through at least one such peril, since Hamilton's hope of a limited monarchy to succeed our initial republican institutions perished at the hands of practical pioneer good sense. I mean, of course, the third term movement in favor of that one of our presidents who was most conspicuously a civic failure. Democracy has precisely this practical peril. Publicists who are especially terrified at it do well not to be democrats. And France has seemed often to "need a strong hand to govern her," as political sciolists are so fond of saying, only because she has, since the Revolution, at all events, been so determinedly and persistently democratic. The democratic instinct is in France too imperative and too irreflective to consider consequences when any unpopular *régime* is in power—to consider the results of confounding nominal distinctions, such as Democratic Republic, Constitutional Monarchy, Party Government, etc.

When Morris and others, during the Revolution, prophesied that the first Republic would end in

a despotism, they were arguing from historical precedent, and prophesying an altogether different kind
of despotism from that of Napoleon. It is amusing
to note the complacency with which these prophets
speak afterward of the fulfilment of their predictions
in this regard. What they really predicted was the
rise of an autocrat like the Russian Czar, or the Roman Emperors—of such a tyrant as Napoleon was
contemporarily believed to be in England, where
nurses used his name to frighten children with;
whereas, of course, instead of being essentially reactionary, Napoleon was in many ways what he called
himself, and what the national temper compelled him
to be, "the incarnation of the Revolution," and Emerson's representative democrat. The despot Morris
foretold would hardly have denounced England as an
oligarchy. Nor, in spite of his Corsican vulgarity,
which made him do so much *grosso modo*, did he attempt the rôle of Augustus—who passes with many
of our political philosophers now-a-days for a kind
of excellent and worthy constitutional monarch—
and endeavor to realize in any completeness the
panem et circenses ideal of government. And when
we wonder at the resignation with which France accepted the *coup d'état* of 1851, we forget that it
was in some sense a popular move; that it appealed
to the people for its justification, and that at all
events it was the overthrow of the reactionary,
which had succeeded a visionary, Chamber. Moreover, the *plébiscites* of the latter part of Napoleon

III.'s reign were so one-sided not so much because the voters were terrorized and corrupted as because, in the first place, the *régime* was extremely democratic in almost every respect except that of administrative centralization, and because, in the second place (and this is too often lost sight of), there was nothing positive and definite for those who did not wish to vote "yes" to vote for; voting "no," under the circumstances, was like voting in the air. In other words, the *régime* was less tyrannical, and France less inert and ductile, than is usually assumed to have been the case.

One of the commonest of errors is to confuse state action with centralization. The two are sufficiently distinct, however practically they may be related and reciprocally imply each other. It is a commonplace that state action—which is another name for authoritative government—is, as a social principle, a question of degree. Matthew Arnold —whose political and social observations will certainly some day obtain the recognition hitherto denied them by our Anglo-Saxon inability to conceive of sound social and political criticism as emanating from the Nazareth of mere culture—has very well expressed the gist of the matter in his remark: "Some things the state had better leave alone, others it had better not." Even in America we acknowledge the efficacy of police. And we are beginning to speculate as to whether railroads and telegraph lines would not be better managed on the principle

which governs postal arrangements than if left in
their present oppressive anarchy. We are, in fact,
approaching a stage of development which makes it
possible for us to recognize that the principle of
state action has something to say for itself. The
late Mr. Washburne, Minister to France in 1870–71,
mentions in his "Recollections" that Napoleon III.
expressed to him—and one can easily fancy the
solemnity with which that potentate made the con-
fession—"his regret that the French people were
not better fitted for more liberal institutions, and
for the concessions he desired to make to them.
The great trouble with the French, he said, was
that they always looked to the government for
everything, instead of depending upon themselves."
Our philanthropists who are anxious to reduce the
Treasury surplus by preventing the people of the
Southern States from depending upon themselves
for popular education, would doubtless object to
the Emperor's implication here ; but most Americans, probably, would be only too ready to admit
the demoralizing effects of state action on the initiative and self-respect of a democracy. And we may
be very right in the main and still, so far as purely
independent criticism is concerned, err in looking
too exclusively at one side of the shield of state action, especially as regards its working in France.
Napoleon III. was certainly very right, as well as
very courteous, in uttering his commonplace ; but
at the same time it might have been replied to him,

in the first place, that one reason for the French being "unfitted for more liberal institutions" was their necessity for an army, and the use to which an army could be put by unscrupulous usurpers in depriving them of such liberal institutions as they *were* fitted for ; and, secondly, that there is no real contradiction between fitness for liberal institutions and the habit of "looking to the government" for many things which "the government" can best compass and supply.

The fact is that we are as likely to underestimate the salutary efficiency of official action as the French are that of private enterprise ; *government*, of course, is a constant quantity and, as has often been suggested, there is as much of it, on the hither side of anarchy, when it is hap-hazard and irresponsible as when it is organized. From the democratic point of view, one of the best effects of state action in a society hampered, like that of France, by the remains of feudalism, is the abolition of privilege by law. The relations between absence of state action and privilege are closer and more direct than we imagine. In England, for example, where the privileges of the privileged classes form a part of that Constitution so greatly extolled as a growth and not a device, minute state regulations, codes, etc., are easily dispensed with, because the strong can readily get along without them, and because only the strong are accounted worthy—and by a natural consequence alone are so in reality, perhaps

22

With us opportunity has hitherto rendered privilege less important than it is anywhere else ; but
where competition is at all close, privilege—which
is no more an artificial product than original sin—
flourishes with a luxuriance as natural and logical
as it is excessive. In France, where such opportunity as ours is necessarily lacking, the democratic
instinct requires that its absence be supplied in a
thousand ways and details by law, by regulations,
by a minute explicitness of administration. The
fact that in France it costs a tenant three cents to
drive a defacing nail into a landlord's wood-work is,
it is easy to see, a democratic provision in a highly
organized society where nail-driving is important.
What is liberty, exclaims M. Scherer, but a regulation and adjustment of warring interests. Tennyson would reply that it is a result arrived at merely
by permitting a man to "speak the thing he will."
But this is, if not fustian, clearly elementary ; and so
are statements of ours like : "The measure of every
man's rights is another's wrongs." What is gained
from the social and democratic point of view if, in the
former case, social tyranny (which is really a political result) is so exaggerated as to make political liberty (which is really a political agent) futile ; and if,
in the latter, a man's rights receive a merely negative authorization for exercise in *vacuo*, so to speak,
or else another's wrongs are measured by traditionary standards which fail to note the degree of wrong
apparent to the instinctive sense of reason and jus-

tice? In spite of these commonplaces, we are obliged to acknowledge that, however good political economy the principle of *laisser faire* may be, in the matter of political and social organization it is a principle very speedily transformed into the principle of *laisser aller*. And in a democracy like that of France which is not rendered elastic by opportunity this means anarchy. Where an active and intelligent proletariat is comparatively permanent on the one hand, and takes the place of a "brutalized lower class" on the other, the feeling that society needs protection against the individual rather than the converse is quickly developed. The proletariat comes quickly to share it, and tends in consequence to socialism. The feeling is carried so far in France that it sometimes seems, for example, as if French jurisprudence itself contemplated the punishment of the innocent with more resignation than the escape of the guilty. And even in this excess it is not an autocratic, but a democratic, feeling. The sense that you are protected is much greater in France than either in England or among ourselves.

Centralization is so much another thing that one may indeed ascribe to it, rather than to authoritative and elaborate state action, the lack of individual initiative and dependence on one's self which so deeply distressed Napoleon III. in the French. When elaborate state action is democratic rather than paternal, when it means simply systematic attention to social administrative needs; when, that is to say, it is not Prussian, but French, it tends, perhaps we may say, to develop rather than counteract individual activities of a high, by preventing the necessity for those of a low, order. For example, a man who is restrained by "officialism" from jumping for ferry-boats, or crossing railway-tracks in front of coming trains, can release for more positive uses some of the alertness he would otherwise be forced to keep under tension to the mere end of continued existence. However, the privilege of looking out for one's self in all such instances—and they are more numerous and varied than we are apt to remember—forms so precious a part of an American's personal liberty, that it would very likely be unwise to insist on this point. As to the effect of centralization on individual initiative, there can, I think, at any rate, be no doubt. Its warmest advocates agree in this with its severest critics. Even under democratic auspices, and when it is of the most loyally representative character, it means inevitably government "for" but not "by" the people, and its liability to abuse is self-evident. It is advocated by French democrats mainly because "it is a condition and not a theory" that confronts them, to quote the admirable expression of President Cleveland. The cardinal necessity for France, in view of this condition, is to be strong. It is as true now as it was during the Revolution—not as true materially, but as true morally—that, as Gouverneur Morris said, "France has an enemy in every prince." It is

this enmity—betrayed every week in the Liberal
London "Spectator," even, which long ago wrote a
famous article entitled "The Fall of the French Republic "—that makes it necessary for France, so far
as her attitude toward Europe is concerned, to be a
unit and a powerful one. This was the reason why
Gambetta permitted the first serious breach in the
Republican ranks, and suffered the schism of the Clémenceau Radicals. He contested M. Clémenceau's
statesman-like contention that the time had come to
consider internal politics, and that decentralization
within certain limits would immensely stimulate, in
modern France, the moral qualities which built the
cathedrals and made the communes of the Middle
Ages what they were. He believed that centralization alone could so weld together politically the various peoples that compose the French nation—the
Norman with the Gascon, the Breton with the Tour-
angeau, the Provençal with the Lorrain—as to keep
the traditional French position in Europe, menaced
as this was by the anti-democratic European forces
marshalled against it, from the reactionary hostility
of united Germany to the traditional Tory distrust
of Great Britain. We may be pleased that his residence in the United States, perhaps, confirmed M.
Clémenceau in his radical belief in the panacea of
local self-government, without presuming to decide
between two such political philosophers and practical statesmen as Gambetta and himself. And we
may wish that the condition of Europe—aggravated

by the barbarous seton which Prince Bismarck, in
taking from France her eastern frontier, inserted in
the European flank—did not so terribly complicate
the problem of French internal progress, without
failing to recognize that if centralization has marred
the welfare, it has largely achieved the greatness, of
that France which finds it impossible to conceive of
welfare apart from greatness. But we may be sure, at
all events, that decentralization would not mean abandonment of state action in France, and that local,
would not imply individual, self-government there.

In a very noteworthy passage of what are curiously
called his theological writings, Matthew Arnold characterizes France as a brilliant and attractive Ishmael,
and exclaims in his happiest scriptural vein : "How
often for France has gone up the cry, 'Oh that Ishmael might live before the Lord,'" maintaining that
just at the moment when the French Ishmael seems
succeeding he breaks down notably, and the homely
Isaac gets the succession. I dare say this is so, with
certain reservations. But what must strike one most
in the history of this brilliant Ishmael is his prodigious success, and not his breakings down at all.
Even his occasional utter collapses such as I suppose Mr. Arnold considered the disasters of Louis
XIV.'s later days, of 1815, of *L'année terrible*, fail,
I think, to impress the imagination as vividly as
his astonishing recuperative power ; and, indeed,
the most terrible of his " disasters " seems hardly

to outweigh the corresponding benefit accompanying or soon succeeding it. So that the average of success resulting from Ishmael's amazing activity seems still high. What experiences he has of sickness and health, of heroic treatment for obstinate ills, of long periods of vigorous activity, of extremes of all sorts, of sensations of all kinds! Beside his varied and full existence, the peaceful and placid hibernation of "the homely Isaac" across the Channel, dreaming of the victory of the hedgehog over the hare, presents certainly a less striking object to the imagination. But Ishmael's admitted success so far predominates over his failures and his "breakings down!" I am perfectly willing to agree with Mr. Arnold that "a little more Biblism would do him no harm." But how he triumphs over this lack, I say, is the striking thing about him, and the explanation of his doing so is one of the most interesting facts in connection with him. If, in spite of his lack of Biblism, he is so successful, it must be either that we overestimate the importance of Biblism, or else that his *institutions* are particularly adapted to bring him success. Either character counts less than ordinarily we think it does, or institutions count more.

And if we examine into the matter closely we shall find that just in so far as institutions affect a people, the French are eminently successful, and that just in those qualities which no institutions can touch in people to affect them in any way, the

French fail. Institutions may be taken by extension to mean all the formulated instincts which the people of a nation possess in common. They have a great, a prodigious, direct effect in determining the national expression, the national character. They have only an indirect association with individual character and expression. Hence we find the French nationally very strong, very conspicuously successful. In individual character the homely Isaac may have charms for us of an enduring attractiveness, to which no Ishmaelite brilliancy and vivacity can pretend. But to anyone who has really seen their working, any doubt of the essential wisdom of French institutions, or any query as to whether the national expression which they embody is not far in advance of any national expression elsewhere illustrated in Europe, is impossible. From nearly every point of view, certainly, France strikes an American sense as successful. There is by general admission more happiness enjoyed by more people in France than in any other European country. Well-being is more evenly distributed there. Henry IV.'s measure of national success, namely, a fowl in every man's pot, is more nearly attained there than anywhere else. In France there is nothing analogous to the famous East End of London; even Paris has no "slums." The people, from top to bottom, is far more perfectly humanized than elsewhere. Equality has been such a practical educator for them that even the ignorant have attained that intelligence which is the end of formal

education in greater measure than the corresponding classes of the most highly educated portions
of Prussia itself. Fewer emigrants leave the most
overcrowded regions, and these almost never without hope of return. The attraction France has for
Frenchmen is something of which we can form no
adequate notion. Everything French suits exactly
every Frenchman. Life is a larger thing, or, at any
rate, people in general are more alive—not nervously
and feverishly, as we are apt to fancy from the nov-
els, but freely and expansively. As to French literature, art, and science, the elegant side of social life,
the characteristics which go to make a nation admired and envied abroad, there is clearly no need to
insist on this element of the contemporary success
of France. She is no longer *la grande nation* to any
but her own citizens, but that is not because she has
diminished, as one is constantly hearing from superficial foreign critics as well as from French fatuity
itself, but because her preponderance has disap-
peared with the rise in the modern world of other
nations. She has herself contributed so much to
this result that she can hardly realize that it has actually taken place. But because there are now a
united Germany, and a united Italy, and the United
States of America in the world, and a Radical party
in England, and so on, it is only a frivolous notion
to suppose that France has stood still any more than
ever these last fifteen years in national development,
or has become internationally a figure of any less

real and serious attractiveness and importance. She
is no longer the arbiter of Europe, but that was a factitious success which was in many ways a drawback
to her real hold on foreign minds; she is much
more attractive to serious strangers when bearing
Victor Hugo from the Arc de Triomphe to the Panthéon than when confiscating his books at the Belgian
frontier. Her internal development since the Republic has been far greater than most persons who
are strangers to any close study of contemporary
politics are apt to suppose; we all know about M.
Ferry's Tonquin failure, for example, but very few
of us know anything of his work for popular education.

French democracy does not practically date from
the Revolution. The Revolution awakened it into
consciousness, imbued it with ideality, saturated it
with sentiment, and endued it with efficient force.
But democracy, in the form of the social instinct indirectly but powerfully shaping political action, is
in France nearly as old as the nation itself. But
for it the despotism of Louis XIV. never would have
been prepared by Richelieu and Mazarin; but for
it indeed, Louis XI. would never have checkmated
his vassals. The democratic spirit sapped the
strength of the Fronde as surely as the autocratic
turbulence of the English barons won Magna Charta
from King John, who was a tyrant of the Byzantine
rather than the Greek order and had no representative character whatever. In estimating the natural

independence of spirit as regards government exhibited by different peoples, persistency in the face of discouragement affords as good a measure of intensity, indeed, as the actual gain in specific liberties, which is more generally taken as the standard. In fact, it may be a better measure of the natural tendency toward independence, for success in achieving liberty increases the love of it, and so the original force which secures it is increased by its attainment in a way almost to be described as mechanical. Now, the French in their communal revolts of the twelfth century demanded for their separate cities very much the reforms which in the Revolution they demanded for the whole of France. Against full success then the nobles were arrayed ; against the retention of what gains were accorded by the crown stood the lack of unity of law and of a jurisdiction to which all should be alike subject, as had been the more favorable condition of England from the time of the Conquest, when the Conqueror brought the Norman talent for administration to bear on Saxon anarchy. A still more hostile element was the very sense of solidarity in the people, a sense greatly quickened by the influence of the crown and the church in conjunction—the crown working to combat the disintegrating and German spirit of separatism and the independence of the nobles, the church contending against the tendency to relapse into barbarism and the decay of faith. This joint effort of church and crown indeed is definitely traceable from the time of Charlemagne, and in germ even from the invasion of the barbarians; and it found its culmination under Louis XIV., when the nobles were definitively conquered by the crown and the Reformation by the church. Meantime the French people, in helping to overcome the nationally disintegrating movement which the Reformation in effect was, erected the church into a tyrant such as it had never been before, and lost their civil liberties to the crown before the tyrannizing nobles, against whom the crown was fighting their fight, were entirely subdued. The attachment to liberty of a people thus cheated of it by circumstances of a fatal perversity—circumstances which but for the Conqueror's earlier and consequently less rigorous centralization, might have triumphed over English energy as well—naturally became fanatical in its intensity when the burden of despotism became at once intolerable and absurd. Nothing so well as its evolution explains the very extravagances of the Revolution—the utopia of '89, the Terror of '93. Only by forgetting their history is it possible to talk glibly of the French as unfitted by nature for self-government. And, indeed, one would think sometimes that the works of Augustin Thierry, instead of being as accessible in English as in French, had never been written at all.

> Nus sumes homes cum il sunt ;
> Tex membres avum cum il unt,

Et altresi granz cors avum,
Et altretant sofrir poüm ;
Ne nus faut fors cuer sulement,

sings the Roman de Rou in the twelfth century.
When the Déclaration des Droits de l'Homme, which
has the same inspiration, was written, the "cuer"
was supplied.

It is, moreover, important to remember that when
we speak of self-government and democracy as
identical, and of self-government as a peculiarly
Anglo-Saxon institution, we lose an essential distinction in vagueness. The only sense in which
self-government is exclusively Anglo-Saxon, in the
view of continental critics—both those who extol
and those who distrust it—is the sense of private
rather than official government. Its maxims are
"the state had better leave things alone," and "the
best government is that which governs least." But
manifestly, when we think of self-government as
government by trusts, corporations, and newspapers,
or by what Professor Huxley calls a "beadleocracy,"
the term appears euphemistic. What we really
mean by self-government, when we praise it intelligently, is either representative government or else
local self-government.— "home-rule," as we say.
Local self-government is, as every American must
believe, an admirable institution as it works with
us ; but clearly it has not the universality of a principle, and if, when we say that self-government is a
lofty ideal, we really mean that it is a good thing

for a village community to elect its own selectmen, or for a city to be independent of a State legislature, we shall certainly say it with less emotion. Representative government is also a splendid piece of political machinery, but in itself it is machinery. Nor is it by any means necessarily democratic. Everything depends on the degree and character of representation.

Of recent years especially, "representative government" has become one of the hardest worked elements of our inveterate Anglo-Saxon self-laudation. Glimmerings of it are discovered in the twilight of the Teutonic genesis, with an assiduity curiously oblivious of the fact that it gains its practical significance only from its application to a Third Estate then in the womb of time and since developed by the rise and decay of feudalism with its result of social differentiation. And yet if the East End of London could read, it would no doubt be as proud of the pre-Norman Witenagemote as Mr. Freeman. But here again history shows how easy it is to mistake names for things. History shows that representative government properly so-called has been no more the ally of democracy than it has been of national unity. It was really born in Europe in the twelfth and thirteenth centuries in consequence of the great popular movement of the communes. The circumstance that the Third Estate was first represented (for special reasons and through special causes) in Ara-

gon, next in France, and last of all in England and
Germany—the matter of precedence, that is to say
—is comparatively trivial, though the small amount
of disturbance it created in France indicates how
slight was the change there which it involved, and
therefore how thoroughly in accord with the spirit
of the whole nation was the movement it stands
for. The important consideration is that the movement was general, European, and popular. It declined in France and Spain and increased in England, so that it died under Philip IV. and Louis
XIII., just as it reached a splendid climax in the English struggle against the Stuarts. But it declined
in France because the foe which destiny, in the way
I have already recalled, raised up to the *noblesse*
was despotism—because the king made himself
the leader of the popular party and the personifica-
tion of national unity, just as the tyrants of the
Greek cities did in the contest between the people
and their oligarchies. No despot was ever more
"representative" than Louis XIV. declared himself
in the famous phrase, "L'État, c'est moi." It resumed its sway, sanctioned, secured, and modified
by the Revolution, after the monarchy ceased to
represent its cause under Louis XV., and the
"deluge" issued in constitutional government of a
real, that is to say, a written kind fortified and
guaranteed by a code. In England, on the other
hand, owing its popularity to its sympathy with the
feudal caste notion of contract, it developed because

the Third Estate, never concerned about associating
political power to political freedom, passed into the
control of a powerful set of allied nobles ; and the
politics of the country speedily became a contest
between a Tory and a Whig aristocracy—representative government being the weapon of each,
and used as the instrument of popular oppression
to this day, when it gives Lord Lonsdale forty liv-
ings and the Duke of Westminster half the West
End of London.

In a word, history shows that representative government is, in the first place, not in itself a talisman, and, in the second, that though it tends in
great measure to promote liberty, it easily may be,
and in England has been, used to subvert equality
and fraternity. Hence the wisest eulogists of England refrain from extolling it as a talisman, affect
to disregard "institutions" of all kinds as anything
other than the outward signs of progress really accomplished through force of character, preferring
1640 to 1688, for example, and rightly attributing
every English political step ahead to moral causes.
But this is not at all the case with the French,
whose turn for ideas and intelligence naturally leads
them to invent civilizing agencies instead of relying
on the hap-hazard in this field. An important element in the French character, indeed, is precisely
this confidence in the virtue of philosophic organization—in what we are apt to stigmatize as "paper
constitutions," scientific pedantry, and "revolution-

ary methods" generally. It is just as paradoxical to accuse the French of leaving out of the account the complexity and perversity of human nature in their mathematical and rule and compass political philosophy, as it is superficial to assert that their national character unfits them for self-government— for the democratic institutions which history proves they have won in the face of difficulties that would infallibly have discouraged a less determined and inveterate democratic national instinct. It is all very well to talk about the advantages of personal liberty sanctioned by character and the capacity for self-government (meaning by self-government either the absence of institutions or what we call "home-rule"), but how irrational is it to reproach a people whose character is such that they are disinclined to dispense with institutions and centralization, whose society is so highly developed, so organic and *solidaire* that the limitation of one man's rights by another man's wrongs occurs far more quickly than elsewhere—how irrational is it, I say, to reproach such a people with failing to consider "man's nature as modified by his habits," when their habits have no special sanction for them and, so far as they are inveterate, are in harmony with nature—whose habit it is, in a word, to consider reason rather than habit! If it is the French nature to believe in theories, theories rather than the anomalies and systems of checks in which they do not believe should predominate in their institutions.

23

How idle is it to commiserate them for their instability, when not stability but flux is their ideal!
With us instability would doubtless be very disastrous (though we can easily see how a little of it
would benefit our English kin), because we ourselves
look upon it as a destructive and disintegrating
agent, not as a condition of progress—quite aside
from the additional reason arising from the fact that
we were born in the butterfly state, so to speak,
whereas the French still are, to a degree, enmeshed
in the filaments of their ecclesiastical and civil chrys-
alis of feudality.

This is why we quite misconceive the revolutionary spirit, as exemplified in French history. The
revolutionary spirit, as thus exemplified, is as different from the rebellious and turbulent spirit as it is
from the spirit of submission and servility. It is
the reforming and revising instinct. It delights in
making over everything, in carrying out new ideas,
in taking a new point of view. It has invariably a
programme. It disbelieves in the sanctity of the
status quo because its instinct is to press forward.
It believes, for the same reason, in experiment, in
essay, effort, intention. It is restlessly constructive.
It is scientific rather than sentimental. It aims at
administering rather than governing. When in
reply to Louis XVIth's "C'est donc une révolte?"
the Duc de Liancourt answered: "Non, Sire, c'est
une révolution," he meant something very different
from a revolt on a very large scale, and likely for

that reason to be successful. He was prophesying an organic change, the disappearance of the old order before the rise of the new. Revolution, in fine, with the French, means largely change of administration, not the subversion of order which we fancy it to mean with them, and which it would mean with any people who regard not social (or civil) but political law as the basis of the established order and the condition of civilization. The two points of view are very different, and spring respectively from the individual spirit anxious for freedom from constraint, and the social instinct concerned about effective organization, and therefore bent on changing the organic, rather than disobeying the statutory, law. The state being regarded as the most important instrument of civilization, a truly democratic people like the French is naturally predisposed to revolutions whereby it may get possession of an administration which it believes either tyrannical or ineffective—which is, for any reason, unpopular; whereas, trusting solely to individual initiative for civilizing agencies, it is far easier for Anglo-Saxondom quietly to await a revolution of the Duke of Wellington's kind—that is to say, a revolution which is no revolution at all, and which involves a delay that has undoubtedly caused untold misery to the *people* of England, however serenely Tennyson may celebrate the slow broadening down from precedent to precedent, and however comfortably "The Saturday Review" may sneer at the

searching and lofty criticism of such works as Mr.
Whiteing's "The Island." To "hold a fretful
realm in awe" is not, in a word, considered in
France the only or the main function of "the common sense of most."

Nor does the French revolutionary spirit conflict
with what we ordinarily mean by respect for law,
and it is quite erroneous to imagine, from their political tumultuousness, that in general the French
have less of this than ourselves. On the contrary,
they have considerably more of it, as, inconsistently,
we frequently attest when we have an opportunity to
accuse them of being "slavish" in this regard. The
deference for authority shown in conduct is as great
as that witnessed for public opinion in the matter
of individual ideals of all sorts. Demeanor which
we describe as outrageous is with the French not
permis. There is nothing corresponding to the lynch
law established *en permanence* in some of our communities that are by no means to be called
"pioneer sections." Purely social disturbances
never reach the degree of violence indicated in the
existence of White Caps and similar organizations.
No one carries a revolver. No individual—no cor-
poration even—ever "defies the law." Such riots
as the Cincinnati outburst some years ago over
the continued miscarriage of justice, do not occur.
Labor troubles, however marked by turbulence and
even bloodshed on occasion, do not result in such
subversion of order as the Pittsburgh riots of 1877.

The confidence one feels in freedom from the perils of darkness and unsavory neighborhoods, from molestation or annoyance, is quite sensible to the American in Paris, and is certainly attributable rather to the ingrained law-abidingness of the people than to the perfection of the Paris police system. It need hardly be added that this respect and regard spring rather from the sense of conformity than that of subjection. During the Commune of 1871, which we always think of as a "Saturnalian" riot, private property, if it was not perfectly safe, went at all events extraordinarily unmolested. The very cry that "the people" should be permitted to be their own police was as ideal as it was absurd. The license that reigned in many respects was by no means brigandish and disorderly. It was the inevitable concomitant of attempting to execute the wild notion that order could be preserved by good will as well as by organization. The "government" still administered and directed the Théâtre Français, for example. And in fine, theoretically speaking and except for the inevitable laxity accompanying the overturning of the established order, respect for law was essentially undiminished. The burning of the Tuileries was the work of despair and an incident of the Commune's death agony ; but the overthrow of the Vendôme column was a very decorous and solemn—solemn in the sense of *solennel*—proceeding.

A good deal of the turbulence of the Revolution

we misunderstand in the same way, from mistaking
the proper point of view.   Even as hostile a critic
of the Revolution as Gouverneur Morris, totally
out of sympathy with every effort for reform that
did not imply the adoption of English institutions,
whose " Diary " hardly mentions any of the great
popular leaders except Mirabeau, and testifies to a
curious unconsciousness of the great movement going on about him outside of boudoirs and *salons*, is
less impressed by the popular violence than we are
apt to be, because he was inevitably better oriented.
He enjoyed the truth of impressionism, and was at all
events not misled by a factitious perspective.   "Freedom and tranquillity are seldom companions," he
observes with characteristic sententiousness, and he
considers the capture of the Bastille "an instance of
great intrepidity "—which is valuable testimony to
contemporary feeling.   Much of the violence of the
Revolution was animated by a certain loftiness of
political purpose, even when exasperated by a situation typified in the spectacular contrast of starving
Paris and feasting Versailles.   Excess loses a certain element of its viciousness when it is indulged
in by temperaments ordinarily responsive only to
the intelligence.   The intelligence guided only by
what metaphysicians call "the logical understanding," and unaffected by the sentiment surrounding the *status quo*, inevitably leads to uncompromising conduct, which to instinctive dependence
on precedent seems more like excess than it really

is. In other words, excess is wholesomely and essentially modified when those who are guilty of it do not regard it as excess at all. During all the tumult of the Revolution, society subsisted with a completeness we should find it difficult to imagine, and such as certainly could not exist during an anarchy as absolute as that which we fancy existed during the Terror. Not only was the amount of beneficent legislation accomplished prodigious, as Mr. John Morley points out, but art, letters, society flourished as gaily as they had done under the *ancien régime*. The galleries of the Louvre were opened with *éclat* October 10, 1793. The Revolution in fact produced a school of painting of its own. Every sign of civilization subsisted; the political turmoil was, in fact, universally accepted by its authors as in the interest of civilization.

It is easy indeed to look at even the cruelty and savagery of the Terror, often instanced as an evidence of racial bloodthirstiness, from a more impartial point of view than we usually take, without in any sense assuming an apologetic attitude. It was not at all the cruelty and savagery of the last Valois days, any more than it partook of the *bouffe* character so significantly pointed out by Voltaire in the conduct of the Fronde tumults. The cruelty of the Revolution proceeded from individual rather than national character. The Catholic Church and administrative centralization had modified individual character greatly in the direction of greatly lessening the

individual sense of responsibility—to the point indicated by Michelet in calling France "a nation of sav-
ages civilized by the conscription." By this extravagant remark Michelet did not at all mean that
before the conscription Frenchmen were brutal, but
simply that they were uncivilized ; that individually
they needed self-control, and as a nation social organization. But the sense of the dignity of human
nature is an even more civilized feeling than the
sense of the sanctity of human life, and many of the
atrocities, even, of the Revolution were committed in
ostensible vindication of the former principle. One
is the maxim of a live-and-let-live individualism, the
other that of a society penetrated by the feeling that
life is not worth considering, except in accordance
with principles which make it worth living. Compare, for example, the "blood-thirsty clinging to
life" of Matthew Arnold's famous portly Cheapside
jeweller, with the sentiment animating the proscribed
Condorcet writing a eulogy of the Revolution at the
moment its excesses were forcing him to suicide—an
event which he regarded as a passing and comparatively trifling incident. A certain recklessness of
one's own life and the contempt for that of others
go together. Condorcet's heroic indifference to
death was not at the time extraordinary. Many of
the important victims of the guillotine may almost
be said to have "yielded gracefully." Respect for
human life is undoubtedly, as we are never tired of
preaching to some of our own communities, the first

condition of civilization, but only under ordinary circumstances. In crises of great moment the maxim has a routine and perfunctory ring. In such crises it is only a firmament of brass that echoes harmoniously Wellington's great principle of revolution by due course of law. Given an enthusiasm for ideas which excludes a care for personality, an unqualified belief in reason unmodified by any sentimental conservatism whatever, and a subordination of the sense of individuality and individual dignity and responsibility, and it is easy to see how the cruelty and savagery of the Revolution is to be explained.

Nationally and ideally, even during the Revolution, France was eminently humane. She emancipated her slaves and those of everybody else whom she could control. Whatever the individual failures of her citizens, nationally she essayed the *beau rôle* then, as since. In the recent Tonquin war the French soldiers treated the Annamese " black flags " with great cruelty, according to accepted accounts; but officially the French authorities never blew Sepoys from the mouths of cannon. It was perhaps the Quixotism, but it was at any rate the generous humanity of M. Clémenceau and his fellow-Radicals, which prevented France from joining England in Egyptian interference in the interest of bondholders; and what the sacrifice was, the envious chafing of France under the English Egyptian occupation abundantly witnesses. Nice and Savoy

were perhaps a sufficient reward for French aid to
Victor Emmanuel in 1859, but what fought Solferino
and Magenta was French national enthusiasm for
the unification of Italy. The Mexico scheme had
nothing of the same backing, and would have failed
in consequence, perhaps, without our own determined hostility and admirable attitude. One recalls also the French interest in Greece, and the
French indisposition to join all other powers in
"coercing" her in 1886. The massacre of Jaffa,
again, was savagely inhuman, but the army which
committed it would not have destroyed the canal
of Bruges. Nor is it any more possible to fancy the
contemporary Irish evictions taking place under
French auspices, than it is to imagine the *noy-
ades* of Nantes conducted by Englishmen, unless
the *noyés* had been proved guilty of some offence
against positive legality. As to the Revolution, it is
possible, no doubt, to say much in excuse of its violence, its inhumanity, and its aggression. Mr. John
Morley has pointed out, in reply to M. Taine, what
especial justification the French *Tiers État* had for
its vengeance on the noblesse and the clergy. To
the last the king and his party were conspirators;
there was no opportunity for a revolution like that
of 1688 in England, accomplished only through a
change of dynasties. And in 1649 it was no harder
to dispose of Charles than in 1793 it was of Louis.
Had Charles had a court, had the English crown reduced its feudal chiefs to courtiers, had England

aimed at the transformation instead of the mitiga-
tion of feudalism, had London been Paris in a
word, the taking off of Charles would have been less
decorous and less solitary, though it could not have
been more cynical and brutal. As for aggression,
when it is observed that France, even before Napoleon, had the dream of succeeding the Roman Empire in " assuring to herself the empire of the world,"
as Mr. Arnold asserts, the fact is lost sight of that
the very existence of the French Republic compelled
aggression. Had the wars been carefully defensive,
the great cause would have been lost and the Bourbons restored. The Republic was engaged in a life
and death struggle, and if it had not been defiant it
would have been destroyed.

After all, both historically and essentially, the
French revolutionary spirit means devotion to reason. Of the two great maxims of the modern
creed : no class can legislate for another, and legislation should conform to reason and not to habit,
which is born of unreasoning adjustments, the
French excel us perhaps in believing in the second
as firmly as they do in the first. We may fairly
say in explanation that our conservatism is really
the clinging to a custom and habit essentially radical. Our *status quo* is the Radical hope of Europe.
We have no need of the revolutionary spirit, since
reason rather than tradition presided in the counsels crystallized in our Constitution itself. Content
and unrest mean very different things here and

abroad. Our party of change—called during the war period "Radical" in the etymological sense alone —has really thus far been the one which corresponds to the European Right. Like the European Right it stands for strong government, government by "the best people," centralization, subsidies, state control of education, limitation of the suffrage, opposition to immigration. Should the popular party become largely proletarian, the case may alter ; but at present our popular party is our conservative one, and the fact makes it impossible to institute a parallel between our party relations and development and those of Europe. But this very fact leads us to misconceive the European revolutionary spirit still endeavoring to plant the standard of reason in the citadel held by custom—a citadel we fortified rationally a century ago. It leads us to conceive of it as merely turbulent, lawless, unpractical.

Nevertheless, we are prone to reflect, the revolutionary spirit, whatever its attendant advantages, has inevitably the effect of establishing a crisis *en permanence*. It is a force, we insist, that may be either rigorously repressed or blindly followed, but cannot profitably be utilized. To the conservative Anglo-Saxon political temperament, it seems to mean a degree of instability inconsistent with sound political growth. We cannot help, in consequence, always considering the political situation in France as a spectacle rather than a study. What interests

us in it at present, for example, is solely the pros
pect for continuance of the present parliamentary
régime. But, though it would be idle to hazard predictions in the case of a people which has no regard
for precedent, it is, I think, clear that whatever
changes the French organic law is destined to under-
go, they will not be essentially undemocratic. French
democracy is, as I began by saying, held consciously
as an ideal, and for that reason alone its puissance
has the promise of permanence. "It was never any
part of our creed," says Matthew Arnold, with admirable candor, "that the great right and blessedness of
an Irishman, or indeed of anybody but an Englishman, is to do as he likes, and we have no scruple at all
about abridging if necessary a non-Englishman's as-
sertion of personal liberty." Compare with this a
dozen sentences to be found in the same writer's
"Friendship's Garland;" such as: "They [the
French] were unripe for the task they, in '89, set
themselves to do; and yet . . . they left their trace
in half the beneficial reforms through Europe; and if
you ask how, at Naples, a convent became a school, or
in Ticino an intolerable oligarchy ceased to govern,
or in Prussia Stein was able to carry his land-reforms,
you get one answer: *The French!* Till modern society is finally formed, French democracy will still be
a power in Europe." Besides such pertinence as this,
much of Mr. Lowell's famous Birmingham address
has something of a post-prandial flavor, as of enun-
ciations essentially detached and undirected;—"the

French fallacy that a new system of government could be ordered like a new suit of clothes," "no dithyrambic affirmations or wire-drawn analyses of the Rights of Man would serve," "the British Constitution. . . is essentially democratic," "England, indeed, may be called a monarchy with democratic tendencies," the citation from Lord Sherbrooke, the inevitable allusion to M. Zola, the eloquent conclusion that "our healing is not in the storm or in the whirlwind, it is not in monarchies, or aristocracies, or democracies, but rather in the still small voice that speaks to the conscience and the heart!" This last is doubtless very true, but for an address on "Democracy" it does not, I think, betray that enthusiasm for the democratic ideal which a French orator of anything like Mr. Lowell's eminence would display. It has a very different note, a very different tone and color from M. Goblet, for example, addressing the students of the Sorbonne on the same subject. And democracy such as M. Goblet's is neither extreme nor exceptional in France at the present time : it is, in fact, so general as largely to account for the presence at the head of affairs of men of convictions and competent capacity—men like M. Goblet, that is to say—instead of those saviours of society, those "great men" whose absence in the political life of both France and America Mr. Lowell so deeply regrets.

But these men are greatly divided among themselves, they have not that commanding personal popularity which insures their remaining in power, they are surrounded with difficulties. The Catholic church, which is in its nature hostile to political democracy, is a standing menace. So is its ally the monarchic Right. On the other hand there are the Radical extremists, with their tendency to entrust their fortunes to an individual representative, whose representative character may easily cease when he ceases to need it. Behind all is the constant necessity of being ready for a European war of proportions which the imagination only can prefigure. Meantime internal democratic development indubitably goes on, and it is a mistake to fancy that it would show political wisdom to postpone what we call "changes in the organic law" till the more convenient season which would doubtless have its own difficulties. The present Constitution has never been submitted to the popular judgment, the drift of feeling has distinctly been in favor of its revision for years. The questions of the Concordat and of communal decentralization, for example, are pressing ones, and because they are from the nature of the case "organic" questions, to assume that discussion of them indicates instability is rather superficial. Should the present Constitution be revised in these respects, we should of course hear a good deal of French political fickleness in our own press, and the "Spectator" would have another article on "The Fall of the French Republic." All the same, Frenchmen would still reply just as they do now, that the instability of their documentary constitutions doesn't imply the variation in "the fundamental law" we take it to mean, and that our solemnity in the matter is a little pedantic; that the Code Napoléon would still subsist; that if they are not as much attached to Republican nomenclature as we are, their democracy is at least as deeply rooted; that in France political stability, with its accompanying danger of political stagnation, is by no means the basis of social order and progress; that the state not being a medium but an agent, to change its expression when you wish becomes merely rational; that even a dictatorship would with them be more truly popular than are English institutions; that their very attitude toward "organic" change implies the formulation of grievances and definite propositions for their redress, whereas under an unwritten constitution progress is not only slow, but accompanied by the immense cost involved in drifting at the mercy of now one and now the other of two opposite political temperaments, whose preferences are never formulated with anything like precision; and that the formulation of ideas is one of the greatest safeguards of popular government.

With our comparatively simple national politics, due in great measure to the autonomy of our States, it is difficult for us to appreciate the great complexity of French politics, and the number and variety of French political questions. Speculation concerning them, abundant as it is among us—for

France is a perpetually attractive spectacle to even our sciolists—is for this reason, if for no others, somewhat barren. But there is one clarifying and illuminating consideration which it is especially pertinent to bear in mind. French differences of opinion in regard to French political questions are in the highest degree practical, rather than, as we imagine, irreconcilable antagonisms of sentiment, tradition, temperament, passion. "The internal quarrels which seem so profoundly to disturb and distract us are not, as Europe may assume, the result of an anemic fever," said M. Floquet at Marseilles recently, "but on the contrary, a proof of superabundant vitality, and, so to say, a passing convulsion of political growth." On what a high key of statesmanlike color, of patriotic courage, that is said! The division of French Republicans into not only radicals and conservatives, but into subsidiary groups, is commonly misinterpreted by us in two ways. It is supposed in the first place to indicate an inaptitude for, and restiveness under, democratic institutions—a native, constitutional repugnance to self-government. On the contrary, it attests the French disposition toward democracy, the French belief in it, and fearlessness about its perils. The absence in France of any hearty and instinctive subscription to the ethics of what Anglo-Saxons know and worship as party government, witnesses, if not a remarkable individual independence, at any rate a far livelier interest in, a far greater and more intelli-

gent devotion to principles of political philosophy,
than are illustrated by party sheep following some
masterful personality as a bell-wether, which has
generally been the case in England, or by the
tyranny of the caucus with us. In England, the
rare political independent is apt to be grotesque.
With us the tradition of party fealty has notoriously
been carried by that party which has no political
principles, and is based on interests and sentiment,
to the ridiculous length of assuming the independent to be a negative instead of a positive force, a
passive and temperamental, rather than an active
and philosophic, person. The far larger number of
French independents, their variety, their activity,
their eminence and influence, certainly indicate a
democracy not only ingrained but very highly developed. And indeed, since the Revolution, it has
been developing very constantly, though not always
visibly, until it has now reached a stage of differentiation which makes strict party government seem
very oligarchical in contrast.

In the second place, we misinterpret the existence
of "groups" in the French Chamber as evidence of
a French "lack of political sense." That is a phrase
constantly recurring in those of our journals partially *au courant* with French affairs, that is to say,
our only journals thus *au courant* at all. Whenever
anything happens distinctly traceable to the excess,
or even the exercise, of the democratic instinct, this
phrase appears as if issuing from the lumber-room

of perfunctory political Toryism. French political independence has undoubtedly its weak side. It was certainly one of Gambetta's distinctions that he perceived this so clearly and labored so strenuously to the end of party unity. In crises, manifestly, disunion is, if not fatal, highly dangerous; and though French Republican independence does not contemplate showing itself recalcitrant in crises, it is certainly true that the habits formed and the passions excited by internal dissension in ordinary times of routine legislation, so to speak, have a powerful disintegrating effect, that might easily go so far as to rob a crisis of that crystallizing power which French Republicans ascribe to it, and on which they so confidently rely. It is also true that Republican independence has done something to keep alive that standing menace to the Republic, the conservative and clerical Right. Had radicalism exhibited a discretion such as in no country in the world it has ever shown, the conservative ranks might have become permanently thinned, owing to the disappearance of traditional distrust before the continued absence of any visible reason for its existence. Had M. Clémenceau, for example, not seceded from the Gambettist ranks upon the question of centralization, very likely the French Left would have been better able to-day than it is to give satisfactory guarantees for the continuance of the salutary republican form as well as of democratic substance in the Government of the nation. The monarchists might have been less able to nourish their organization upon the vague hopes derived from the spectacle of Republican differences. They might possibly have become discouraged. But this is surely speculative and, manifestly, for a great party with a large majority to resign itself to purely defensive tactics until Bourbons are driven into learning or forgetting something, contenting itself meanwhile with what many of its members believed to be the shadow without the substance of a Republic; to delay needed and urgent reforms out of a timorous regard for the tactics of parliamentary strategy; to look at every question from an indirect and party, instead of a directly patriotic, point of view—to do this would clearly be to paralyze every beneficent activity belonging to government by discussion. It might be diplomatic, but it would be as little a demonstration of "political sense" as it would be democratic.

But whatever character the further evolution of the French nation may assume, whatever fate may have in store for the most sentient, the most organic, the most civilized, the most socially developed people of the modern world, it is certain that, for a long time to come, " the country of Europe in which the *people* is most alive"—according to Matthew Arnold's acute synthesis of the results of the Revolution—the country of Europe to which we owe it that the Declaration is the definition rather than the source of our national and individual rights, will remain for Americans, if not the most exemplary, at least the most animating figure among the European states.   And however tradition, prejudice, ignorance, and a different language may obscure our vision, we shall never fail to find politically instructive, in proportion to our intelligence and the preservation of our own democratic instincts, that one of the European powers the vast majority of whose citizens —not being "subjects" in either a real or a nominal sense—instinctively echo La Bruyère's sentiment which I have already cited: "Faut-il opter? Je veux être peuple!"

X

NEW YORK AFTER PARIS

NEW YORK AFTER PARIS

No American, not a commercial or otherwise hardened traveller, can have a soul so dead as to be incapable of emotion when, on his return from a long trip abroad, he catches sight of the low-lying and insignificant Long Island coast. One's excitement begins, indeed, with the pilot-boat. The pilot-boat is the first concrete symbol of those native and normal relations with one's fellow-men, which one has so long observed in infinitely varied manifestation abroad, but always as a spectator and a stranger, and which one is now on the eve of sharing himself. As she comes up swiftly, white and graceful, drops her pilot, crosses the steamer's bows, tacks, and picks up her boat in the foaming wake, she presents a spectacle beside which the most picturesque Mediterranean craft, with colored sails and lazy evolutions, appear mistily in the memory as elements of a feeble and conventional ideal. The ununiformed pilot clambers on board, makes his way to the bridge, and takes command with an equal lack of French manner and of English affectation distinctly palpable to the sense, sharpened by long absence into observing native characteristics as closely as foreign ones.

If the season be right the afternoon is bright, the range of vision apparently limitless, the sky nearly cloudless and, by contrast with the European firmament, almost colorless, the July sun such as no Parisian or Londoner ever saw. The French reproach us for having no word for "patrie" as distinct from "pays;" we have the thing at all events, and cherish it, and it needs only the proximity of the foreigner, from whom in general we are so widely separated, to give our patriotism a tinge of the veriest chauvinism that exists in France itself.

We fancy the feeling old-fashioned, and imagine ours to be the most cosmopolitan, the least prejudiced temperament in the world. It is reasonable that it should be. The extreme sensitiveness noticed in us by all foreign observers during the antebellum epoch, and ascribed by Tocqueville to our self-distrust, is naturally inconsistent with our position and circumstances to-day. A population greater than that of any of the great nations, isolated by the most enviable geographical felicity in the world from the narrowing influences of international jealousy apparent to every American who travels in Europe, is increasingly less concerned at criticism than a struggling provincial republic of half its size. And along with our self-confidence and our carelessness of "abroad," it is only with the grosser element among us that national conceit has deepened; in general, we are apt to fancy we have become cosmopolitan in proportion as we have lost our provincialism. With us surely the individual has not withered, and if the world has become more and more to him, it is because it is the world at large and not the pent-up confines of his own country's history and extent. "La patrie" in danger would be quickly enough rescued—there is no need to prove that over again, even to our own satisfaction ; but in general "la patrie" not being in any danger, being on the contrary apparently on the very crest of the wave of the world, it is felt not to need much of one's active consideration, and passively indeed is viewed by many people, probably, as a comfortable and gigantic contrivance for securing a free field in which the individual may expand and develop. "America," says Emerson, "America is Opportunity." After all, the average American of the present day says, a country stands or falls by the number of properly expanded and developed individuals it possesses. But the happening of any one of a dozen things unexpectedly betrays that all this cosmopolitanism is in great measure, and so far as sentiment is concerned, a veneer and a disguise. Such a happening is the very change from blue water to gray that announces to the returning American the nearness of that country which he sometimes thinks he prizes more for what it stands for than for itself. It is not, he then feels with a sudden flood of emotion, that America is home, but that home is America. America comes suddenly to mean what it never meant before.

Unhappily for this exaltation, ordinary life is not composed of emotional crises. It is ordinary life with a vengeance which one encounters in issuing from the steamer dock and facing again his native city. Paris never looked so lovely, so exquisite to the sense as it now appears in the memory. All that Parisian regularity, order, decorum, and beauty into which, although a stranger, your own activities fitted so perfectly that you were only half-conscious of its existence, was not, then, merely normal, wholly a matter of course. Emerging into West Street, amid the solicitations of hackmen, the tinkling jog-trot of the most ignoble horse-cars you have seen since leaving home, the dry dust blowing into your eyes, the gaping black holes of broken pavements, the unspeakable filth, the line of red brick buildings prematurely decrepit, the sagging multitude of telegraph wires, the clumsy electric lights depending before the beer saloon and the groggery, the curious confusion of spruceness and squalor in the aspect of these latter, which also seem legion— confronting all this for the first time in three years, say, you think with wonder of your disappointment at not finding the Tuileries Gardens a mass of flowers, and with a blush of the times you have told Frenchmen that New York was very much like Paris. New York is at this moment the most foreign-looking city you have ever seen ; in going abroad the American discounts the unexpected ; returning after the insensible orientation of Europe, the contrast with things recently familiar is prodigious, because one is so entirely unprepared for it. One thinks to be at home, and finds himself at the spectacle. New York is less like any European city than any European city is like any other. It is distinguished from them all—even from London—by the ignoble character of the *res publicæ*, and the refuge of taste, care, wealth, pride, self-respect even, in private and personal regions. A splendid carriage, liveried servants without and Paris dresses within, rattling over the scandalous paving, splashed by the neglected mud, catching the rusty drippings of the hideous elevated railway, wrenching its axle in the tram-track in avoiding a mountainous wagon load of commerce on this hand and a garbage cart on that, caught in a jam of horse-cars and a blockade of trucks, finally depositing its dainty freight to pick its way across a sidewalk eloquent of official neglect and private contumely, to a shop door or a residence stoop—such a contrast as this sets us off from Europe very definitely and in a very marked degree.

There is no palpable New York in the sense in which there is a Paris, a Vienna, a Milan. You can touch it at no point. It is not even ocular. There is instead a Fifth Avenue, a Broadway, a Central Park, a Chatham Square. How they have dwindled, by the way. Fifth Avenue might be any one of a dozen London streets in the first impression it makes on the retina and leaves on the mind. The opposite side of Madison Square is but a step away. The

spacious hall of the Fifth Avenue Hotel has shrunk
to stifling proportions. Thirty-fourth Street is a
lane ; the City Hall a band-box ; the Central Park
a narrow strip of elegant landscape whose lateral
limitations are constantly forced upon the sense by
the Lenox Library on one side and a monster apartment house on the other. The American fondness
for size—for pure bigness—needs explanation, it appears ; we care for size, but inartistically ; we care
nothing for proportion, which is what makes size
count. Everything is on the same scale ; there is
no play, no movement. An exception should be
made in favor of the big business building and the
apartment house which have arisen within a few
years, and which have greatly accentuated the gro-
tesqueness of the city's sky-line as seen from either
the New Jersey or the Long Island shore. They
are perhaps rather high than big ; many of them were
built before the authorities noticed them and followed unequally in the steps of other civilized muni-
cipal governments, from that of ancient Rome down,
in prohibiting the passing of a fixed limit. But bigness has also evidently been one of their architectonic
motives, and it is to be remarked that they are so
far out of scale with the surrounding buildings as to
avoid the usual commonplace, only by creating a
positively disagreeable effect. The aspect of Fifty-
seventh Street between Broadway and Seventh
Avenue, for example, is certainly that of the world
upside down : a Gothic church utterly concealed, not

to say crushed, by contiguous flats, and confronted
by the overwhelming "Osborne," which towers
above anything in the neighborhood, and perhaps
makes the most powerful impression that the returned traveller receives during his first week or two
of strange sensations.   Yet the "Osborne's" dimen-
sions are not very different from those of the Arc
de l'Étoile.   It is true it does not face an avenue of
majestic buildings a mile and a half long and two
hundred and thirty feet wide, but the association
of these two structures, one a private enterprise and
the other a public monument, together with the obvious suggestions of each, furnish a not misleading
illustration of both the spectacular and the moral
contrast between New York and Paris, as it appears
unduly magnified no doubt to the sense surprised
to notice it at all.

Still another reason for the foreign aspect of the
New Yorker's native city is the gradual withdrawing
of the American element into certain quarters, its
transformation or essential modification in others,
and in the rest the presence of the lees of Europe.
At every step you are forced to realize that New
York is the second Irish and the third or fourth
German city in the world.   However great our success in drilling this foreign contingent of our social
army into order and reason and self-respect—and it
is not to be doubted that this success gives us a distinction wholly new in history—nevertheless our effect upon its members has been in the direction of

development rather than of assimilation. We have given them our opportunity, permitted them the expansion denied them in their own several feudalities, made men of serfs, demonstrated the utility of self-government under the most trying conditions, proved the efficacy of our elastic institutions on a scale truly grandiose ; but evidently, so far as New York is concerned, we have done this at the sacrifice of a distinct and obvious nationality. To an observant sense New York is nearly as little national as Port Said. It contrasts absolutely in this respect with Paris, whose assimilating power is prodigious ; every foreigner in Paris eagerly seeks Parisianization.

Ocularly, therefore, the "note" of New York seems that of characterless individualism. The monotony of the chaotic composition and movement is, paradoxically, its most abiding impression. And as the whole is destitute of definiteness, of distinction, the parts are, correspondingly, individually insignificant. Where in the world are all the types? one asks one's self in renewing his old walks and desultory wanderings. Where is the New York counterpart of that astonishing variety of types which makes Paris what it is morally and pictorially, the Paris of Balzac as well as the Paris of M. Jean Béraud. Of a sudden the lack of nationality in our familiar literature and art becomes luminously explicable. One perceives why Mr. Howells is so successful in confining himself to the simplest, broadest, most representative representatives, why Mr. James goes abroad invariably for his *mise-en-scène*, and often for his characters, why Mr. Reinhart lives in Paris, and Mr. Abbey in London. New York is this and that, it is incontestably unlike any other great city, but compared with Paris, its most impressive trait is its lack of that organic quality which results from variety of types. Thus compared, it seems to have only the variety of individuals which results in monotony. It is the difference between noise and music. Pictorially, the general aspect of New York is such that the mind speedily takes refuge in insensitiveness. Its expansiveness seeks exercise in other directions—business, dissipation, study, æstheticism, politics. The life of the senses is no longer possible. This is why one's sense for art is so stimulated by going abroad, and one's sense for art in its freest, frankest, most universal and least special, intense and enervated development,is especially exhilarated by going to Paris. It is why, too, on one's return one can note the gradual decline of his sensitiveness, his severity—the progressive atrophy of a sense no longer called into exercise. "I had no conception before," said a Chicago broker to me one day in Paris, with intelligent eloquence, "of a finished city!" Chicago undoubtedly presents a greater contrast to Paris than does New York, and so, perhaps, better prepares one to appreciate the Parisian quality, but the *returned* New Yorker cannot fail to be deeply impressed with the finish, the organic perfection, the elegance, and reserve of the Paris mirrored in his

25

memory. Is it possible that the uniformity, the monotony of Paris architecture, the prose note in Parisian taste, should once have weighed upon his spirit? Riding once on the top of a Paris tramway, betraying an understanding of English by reading an American newspaper, that sub-consciousness of moral isolation which the foreigner feels in Paris as elsewhere, was suddenly and completely destroyed by my next neighbor, who remarked with contemptuous conviction and a Manhattan accent : "When you've seen one block of this infernal town you've seen it all ! " He felt sure of sympathy in advance. Probably few New Yorkers would have differed with him. The universal light stone and brown paint, the wide sidewalks, the asphalt pavement, the indefinitely multiplied kiosks, the prevalence of a few marked kinds of vehicles, the uniformed workmen and work-women, the infinite reduplication, in a word, of easily recognized types, is at first mistaken by the New Yorker for that dead level of uniformity which is, of all things in the world, the most tiresome to him in his own city. After a time, however, he begins to realize three important facts : In the first place these phenomena, which so vividly force themselves on his notice that their reduplication strikes him more than their qualities, are nevertheless of a quality altogether unexampled in his experience for fitness and agreeableness ; in the second place they are details of a whole, members of an organism, and not they, but the city which they compose, the " fin-

ished city " of the acute Chicagoan, is the spectacle ;
in the third place they serve as a background for
the finest group of monuments in the world. On
his return he perceives these things with a melancholy *a non lucendo* luminousness. The dead level of
Murray Hill uniformity he finds the most agreeable
aspect in the city.

And the reason is that Paris has habituated him to
the exquisite, the rational, pleasure to be derived
from that organic spectacle a "finished city," far
more than that Murray Hill is respectable and
appropriate, and that almost any other prospect, except in spots of very limited area which emphasize
the surrounding ugliness, is acutely displeasing.
This latter is certainly very true. We have long
frankly reproached ourselves with having no art commensurate with our distinction in other activities,
resignedly attributing the lack to our hitherto necessary material preoccupation. But what we are
really accounting for in this way is our lack of
Titians and Bramantes. We are for the most part
quite unconscious of the character of the American
æsthetic substratum, so to speak. As a matter of fact,
we do far better in the production of striking artistic personalities than we do in the general medium
of taste and culture. We figure well invariably at
the *Salon*. At home the artist is simply either
driven in upon himself, or else awarded by a *naïve
clientèle*, an eminence so far out of perspective as to
result unfortunately both for him and for the com-

munity. He pleases himself, follows his own bent, and prefers salience to conformability for his work, because his chief aim is to make an effect. This is especially true of those of our architects who have ideas. But these are the exceptions, of course, and the general aspect of the city is characterized by something far less agreeable than mere lack of symmetry; it is characterized mainly by an all-pervading bad taste in every detail into which the element of art enters or should enter—that is to say, nearly everything that meets the eye.

However, on the other hand, Parisian uniformity may depress exuberance, it is the condition and often the cause of the omnipresent good taste. Not only is it true that, as Mr. Hamerton remarks, "in the better quarters of the city a building hardly ever rises from the ground unless it has been designed by some architect who knows what art is, and endeavors to apply it to little things as well as great;" but it is equally true that the national sense of form expresses itself in every appurtenance of life as well as in the masses and details of architecture. In New York our noisy diversity not only prevents any effect of *ensemble* and makes, as I say, the old commonplace brown stone regions the most reposeful and rational prospects of the city, but it precludes also, in a thousand activities and aspects, the operation of that salutary constraint and conformity without which the most acutely sensitive individuality inevitably declines to a lower level of form and taste.

La mode, for example, seems scarcely to exist at all ;
or at any rate to have taken refuge in the chimney-
pot hat and the *tournure.* The dude, it is true, has
been developed within a few years, but his distinguishing trait of personal extinction has had much
less success and is destined to a much shorter life
than his appellation, which has wholly lost its original significance in gaining its present popularity.
Every woman one meets in the street has a different
bonnet. Every street car contains a millinery mu-
seum. And the mass of them may be judged after
the circumstance that one of the most fashionable
Fifth Avenue *modistes* flaunts a sign of enduring
brass announcing " English Round Hats and Bonnets." The enormous establishments of ready-made
men's clothing seem not yet to have made their
destined impression in the direction of uniformity. The contrast in dress of the working classes
with those of Paris is as conspicuously unfortunate
æsthetically, as politically and socially it may be
significant ; ocularly, it is a substitution of a cheap,
faded, and ragged imitation of *bourgeois* costume
for the marvel of neatness and propriety which composes the uniform of the Parisian *ouvrier* and *ou-
vrière.* Broadway below Tenth Street is a forest of
signs which obscure the thoroughfare, conceal the
buildings, overhang the sidewalks, and exhibit sev-
erally and collectively a taste in harmony with the
Teutonic and Semitic enterprise which, almost exclusively, they attest. The shop-windows' show, which is

one of the great spectacles of Paris, is niggard and shabby; that of Philadelphia has considerably more interest, that of London nearly as much. Our clumsy coinage and countrified currency; our eccentric book-bindings; that class of our furniture and interior decoration which may be described as American rococo; that multifariously horrible machinery devised for excluding flies from houses and preventing them from alighting on dishes, for substituting a draught of air for stifling heat, for relieving an entire population from that surplusage of old-fashioned breeding involved in shutting doors, for rolling and rattling change in shops, for enabling you to " put only the exact fare in the box " the racket of pneumatic tubes, of telephones, of aerial trains: the practice of reticulating pretentious façades with fire-escapes in lieu of fire-proof construction; the vast mass of our nickel-plated paraphernalia; our zinc cemetery monuments; our comic valentines and serious Christmas cards, and grocery labels, and " fancy " job-printing and theatre posters; our conspicuous cuspadores and our conspicuous need of more of them; the " tone " of many articles in our most popular journals, their references to each other, their illustrations; the Sunday panorama of shirt-sleeved ease and the week-day fatigue costume of curl papers and " Mother Hubbards " general in some quarters; our sumptuous new bar-rooms, decorated perhaps on the principle that *le mauvais goût mène au crime*—all these phenomena, the list of which might be indefinitely extended, are so many witnesses of a general taste, public and private, which differs cardinally from that prevalent in Paris.

In fine, the material spectacle of New York is such that at last, with some anxiety, one turns from the external vileness of every prospect to seek solace in the pleasure that man affords. But even after the wholesome American reaction has set in, and your appetite for the life of the senses is starved into indifference for what begins to seem to you an unworthy ideal; after you are patriotically readjusted and feel once more the elation of living in the future owing to the dearth of sustenance in the present—you are still at the mercy of perceptions too keenly sharpened by your Paris sojourn to permit blindness to the fact that Paris and New York contrast as strongly in moral atmosphere as in material aspect. You become contemplative, and speculate pensively as to the character and quality of those native and normal conditions, those Relations, which finally you have definitely resumed. What is it—that vague and pervasive moral contrast which the American feels so potently on his return from abroad? How can we define that apparently undefinable difference which is only the more sensible for being so elusive? Book after book has been written about Europe from the American standpoint—about America from the European standpoint. None of them has specified what everyone has experienced. The spectacular and the material contrasts are easily enough characterized, and it is only the unreflecting or the superficial who exaggerate the importance of them. We are by no means at the mercy of our appreciation of Parisian spectacle, of the French machinery of life. We miss or we do not miss the Salon Carré, the view of the south transept of Notre Dame as one descends the rue St. Jacques, the Théâtre Français, the concerts, the Luxembourg Gardens, the excursions to the score of charming suburban places, the library at the corner, the convenient cheap cab, the manners of the people, the quiet, the climate, the constant entertainment of the senses. We have in general too much work to do to waste much time in regretting these things. In general, work is by natural selection so invariable a concomitant of our unrivalled opportunity to work profitably, that it absorbs our energies so far as this palpable sphere is concerned. But what is it that throughout the hours of busiest work and closest application, as well as in the preceding and following moments of leisure and the occasional intervals of relaxation, makes everyone vaguely perceive the vast moral difference between life here at home and life abroad—notably life in France? What is the subtle influence pervading the moral atmosphere in New York, which so markedly distinguishes what we call life here from life in Paris or even in Pennedepie?

It is, I think, distinctly traceable to the intense individualism which prevails among us. Magnificent results have followed our devotion to this force ; incontestably, we have spared ourselves both the acute and the chronic misery for which the tyranny of society over its constituent parts is directly responsible. We have, moreover, in this way not only freed ourselves from the tyranny of despotism, such for example as is exerted socially in England and politically in Russia, but we have undoubtedly developed a larger number of self-reliant and potentially capable social units than even a democratic system like that of France, which sacrifices the unit to the organism, succeeds in producing. We may truly say that, material as we are accused of being, we turn out more *men* than any other nationality. And if some Frenchman points out that we attach an esoteric sense to the term " man," and that at any rate our men are not better adapted than some others to a civilized environment which demands other qualities than honesty, energy, and intelligence, we may be quite content to leave him his objection, and to prefer what seems to us manliness, to civilization itself. At the same time we cannot pretend that individualism has done everything for us that could be desired. In giving us the man it has robbed us of the *milieu*. Morally speaking, the *milieu* with us scarcely exists. Our difference from Europe does not consist in the difference between the European *milieu* and ours ; it consists in the fact that, comparatively speaking of course, we have no *milieu*. If we are individually developed, we are also individually isolated to a degree elsewhere unknown. Politically we have parties who, in Cicero's phrase, "think the same things concerning the republic," but concerning very little else are we agreed in any mass of any moment. The number of our sauces is growing, but there is no corresponding diminution in the number of our religions. We have no communities. Our villages even are apt, rather, to be aggregations. Politics aside, there is hardly an American view of any phenomenon or class of phenomena. Everyone of us likes, reads, sees, does what he chooses. Often dissimilarity is affected as adding piquancy of paradox. The judgment of the ages, the consensus of mankind, exercise no tyranny over the individual will. Do you believe in this or that, do you like this or that, are questions which, concerning the most fundamental matters, nevertheless form the staple of conversation in many circles. We live all of us apparently in a divine state of flux. The question asked at dinner by a lady in a neighboring city of a literary stranger, "What do you think of Shakespeare?" is not exaggeratedly peculiar. We all think differently of Shakespeare, of Cromwell, of Titian, of Browning, of George Washington. Concerning matters as to which we must be fundamentally disinterested, we permit ourselves not only prejudice but passion. At the most we have here and there groups of personal acquaintance only, whose members are in accord in regard to some one thing, and quickly crystallize and precipitate at the mention of something that is really a corollary of the force which unites them. The efforts that have been made in New York, within the past twenty years, to establish various special *milieus*, so to speak, have been pathetic in their number and resultlessness. Efforts of this sort are of course doomed to failure, because the essential trait of the *milieu* is spontaneous existence, but their failure discloses the mutual repulsion which keeps the molecules of our society from uniting. How can it be otherwise when life is so speculative, so experimental, so wholly dependent on the personal force and idiosyncrasies of the individual? How shall we accept any general verdict pronounced by persons of no more authority than ourselves, and arrived at by processes in which we are equally expert? We have so little consensus as to anything, because we dread the loss of personality involved in submitting to conventions, and because personality operates centrifugally alone. We make exceptions in favor of such matters as the Copernican system and the greatness of our own future. There *are* things which we take on the credit of the consensus of authorities, for which we may not have all the proofs at hand. But as to conventions of all sorts, our attitude is apt to be one of suspicion and uncertainty. Mark Twain, for example, first won his way to the popular American heart by exposing the humbugs of the Cinque-cento. Specifically the most teachable of people, nervously eager for information, Americans are nevertheless wholly distrust-

ful of generalizations made by anyone else, and little
disposed to receive blindly formularies and classifi-
cations of phenomena as to which they have had no
experience.   And of experience we have necessarily
had, except politically, less than any civilized people
in the world.

We are infinitely more at home amid universal
mobility.   We want to act, to exert ourselves, to
be, as we imagine, nearer to nature.   We have our
tastes in painting as in confectionery.   Some of us
prefer Tintoretto to Rembrandt, as we do chocolate
to cocoanut.   In respect of taste it would be impossible for the gloomiest sceptic to deny that this is
an exceedingly free country.   "I don't know anything about the subject (whatever the subject may
be), but I know what I like," is a remark which is
heard on every hand, and which witnesses the sturdi-
ness of our struggle against the tyranny of conventions and the indomitable nature of our independent spirit.   In criticism the individual spirit fairly
runs a-muck; it takes its lack of concurrence as
credentials of impartiality often.   In constructive
art everyone is occupied less with nature than with
the point of view.   Mr. Howells himself displays
more delight in his naturalistic attitude than zest
in his execution, which, compared with that of the
French naturalists, is in general faint-hearted
enough.   Everyone writes, paints, models, exclusively the point of view.   Fidelity in following out
nature's suggestions, in depicting the emotions nat-

ure arouses, a sympathetic submission to nature's sentiment, absorption into nature's moods and subtle enfoldings, are extremely rare. The artist's eye is fixed on the treatment. He is "creative" by main strength. He is penetrated with a desire to get away from "the same old thing," to "take it" in a new way, to draw attention to himself, to shine. One would say that every American nowadays who handles a brush or designs a building, was stimulated by the secret ambition of founding a school. We have in art thus, with a vengeance, that personal element which is indeed its savor, but which it is fatal to make its substance. We have it still more conspicuously in life. What do you think of him, or her? is the first question asked after every introduction. Of every new individual we meet we form instantly some personal impression. The criticism of character is nearly the one disinterested activity in which we have become expert. We have for this a peculiar gift, apparently, which we share with gypsies and money-lenders, and other people in whom the social instinct is chiefly latent. Our gossip takes on the character of personal judgments rather than of tittle-tattle. It concerns not what So-and-So has done, but what kind of a person So-and-So is. It would hardly be too much to say that So-and-So never leaves a group of which he is not an intimate without being immediately, impartially but fundamentally, discussed. To a degree not at all suspected by the author of the phrase, he "leaves his character" with them on quitting any assemblage of his acquaintance.

The great difficulty with our individuality and independence is that differentiation begins so soon and stops so far short of real importance. In no department of life has the law of the survival of the fittest, that principle in virtue of whose operation societies become distinguished and admirable, had time to work. Our social characteristics are inventions, discoveries, not survival. Nothing with us has passed into the stage of instinct. And for this reason some of our " best people," some of the most "thoughtful" among us, have less of that quality best characterized as social maturity than a Parisian washerwoman or *concierge*. Centuries of sifting, ages of gravitation toward harmony and homogeneity, have resulted for the French in a delightful immunity from the necessity of "proving all things" remorselessly laid on every individual of our society. Very many matters, at any rate, which to the French are matters of course, our self-respect pledges us to a personal examination of. The idea of sparing ourselves trouble in thinking occurs to us far more rarely than to other peoples. We have certainly an insufficient notion of the superior results reached by economy and system in this respect.

In one of Mr. Henry James's cleverest sketches, "Lady Barberina," the English heroine marries an American and comes to live in New York. She finds it dull. She is homesick without quite knowing why. Mr. James is at his best in exhibiting at once the intensity of her disgust and the intangibility of its provocation. We are not all like "Lady Barb." We do not all like London, whose materialism is only more splendid, not less uncompromising than our own ; but we cannot help perceiving that what that unfortunate lady missed in New York was the *milieu*—an environment sufficiently developed to permit spontaneity and free play of thought and feeling, and a certain domination of shifting merit by fixed relations which keeps one's mind off that disagreeable subject of contemplation, one's self. Everyone seems acutely self-conscious ; and the self-consciousness of the unit is fatal, of course, to the composure of the *ensemble*. The number of people intently minding their P's and Q's, reforming their orthoepy, practising new discoveries in etiquette, making over their names, and in general exhibiting that activity of the amateur known as "going through the motions" to the end of bringing themselves up, as it were, is very noticeable in contrast with French oblivion to this kind of personal exertion. Even our simplicity is apt to be *simplesse*. And the conscientiousness in educating others displayed by those who are so fortunate as to have reached perfection nearly enough to permit relaxation in self-improvement, is only equalled by the avidity in acquisitiveness displayed by the learners themselves. Meantime the composure born of equality, as well as that springing from unconsciousness, suffers. Our society is a kind of Jacob's ladder, to maintain equilibrium upon which requires an amount of effort on the part of the personally estimable gymnasts perpetually ascending and descending, in the highest degree hostile to spontaneity, to serenity, and stability.

Naturally, thus, everyone is personally preoccupied to a degree unknown in France. And it is not necessary that this preoccupation should concern any side of that multifarious monster we know as "business." It may relate strictly to the paradox of seeking employment for leisure. Even the latter is a terribly conscious proceeding. We go about it with a mental deliberateness singularly in contrast with our physical precipitancy. But it is mainly "business," perhaps, that accentuates our individualism. The condition of *désœuvrement* is positively disreputable. It arouses the suspicion of acquaintance and the anxiety of friends. Occupation to the end of money-getting is our normal condition, any variation from which demands explanation, as little likely to be entirely honorable. Such occupation is, as I said, the inevitable sequence of the opportunity for it, and is the wiser and more dignified because of its necessity to the end of securing independence. What the Frenchman can secure merely by the exercise of economy is with us only the reward of energy and enterprise in acquisition—so comparatively speculative and hazardous is the condition of our business. And whereas with us money is far harder to keep, and is moreover something which it is far harder to be without than is the case in France, the ends of self-respect, freedom from mortification, and getting the most out of life, demand that we should take constant advantage of the fact that it is easier to get. Consequently everyone who is, as we say, worth anything, is with us adjusted to the prodigious dynamic condition which characterizes our existence. And such occupation is tremendously absorbing. Our opportunity is fatally handicapped by this remorseless necessity of embracing it. It yields us fruit after its kind, but it rigorously excludes us from tasting any other. Everyone is engaged in preparing the working drawings of his own fortune. There is no co-operation possible, because competition is the life of enterprise.

In the resultant manners the city illustrates Carlyle's "anarchy plus the constable." Never was the struggle for existence more palpable, more naked, and more unpictorial. "It is the art of mankind to polish the world," says Thoreau somewhere, "and everyone who works is scrubbing in some part." Everyone certainly is here at work, yet was there ever such scrubbing with so little resultant polish? The disproportion would be tragic if it were not grotesque. Amid all "the hurry and rush of life along the sidewalks," as the newspapers say, one might surely expect to find the unexpected. The spec-

26

tacle ought certainly to have the interest of picturesqueness which is inherent in the fortuitous.
Unhappily, though there is hurry and rush enough,
it is the bustle of business, not the dynamics of
what is properly to be called life. The elements of
the picture lack dignity—so completely as to leave
the *ensemble* quite without accent. More incidents
in the drama of real life will happen before midnight
to the individuals who compose the orderly Boulevard procession in Paris than those of its chaotic
Broadway counterpart will experience in a month.
The latter are not really more impressive because
they are apparently all running errands and include
no *flâneurs*. The *flâneur* would fare ill should anything draw him into the stream. Everything being
adjusted to the motive of looking out for one's self,
any of the sidewalk civility and mutual interest which
obtain in Paris would throw the entire machine out
of gear. Whoever is not in a hurry is in the way.
A man running after an omnibus at the Madeleine
would come into collision with fewer people and
cause less disturbance than one who should stop on
Fourteenth Street to apologize for an inadvertent
jostle, or to give a lady any surplusage of passing
room. He would be less ridiculous. A friend recently returned from Paris told me that, on several
street occasions, his involuntary "Excuse me!" had
been mistaken for a salutation and answered by a
"How do you do?" and a stare of speculation.
Apologies of this class sound to us, perhaps, like a

subtle and deprecatory impeachment of our large tolerance and universal good nature.

In this way our undoubted self-respect undoubtedly loses something of its bloom. We may prefer being jammed into street-cars and pressed against the platform rails of the elevated road to the tedious waiting at Paris 'bus stations—to mention one of the perennial and principal points of contrast which monopolize the thoughts of the average American sojourner in the French capital. But it is terribly vulgarizing. The contact and pressure are abominable. To a Parisian the daily experience in this respect of those of our women who have no carriages of their own, would seem as singular as the latter would find the Oriental habit of regarding the face as more important than other portions of the female person to keep concealed. But neither men nor women can persist in blushing at the intimacy of rudeness to which our crowding subjects them in common. The only resource is in blunted sensibility. And the manners thus negatively produced we do not quite appreciate in their enormity because the edge of our appreciation is thus necessarily dulled. The conductor scarcely ceases whistling to poke you for your fare. Other whistlers apparently go on forever. Loud talking follows naturally from the impossibility of personal seclusion in the presence of others. Our Sundays have lost secular decorum very much in proportion as they have lost Puritan observance. If we have

nothing quite comparable with a London bank holi-
day, or with the conduct of the popular cohorts of
the Epsom army; if only in "political picnics"
and the excursions of "gangs" of "toughs" we illustrate absolute barbarism, it is nevertheless true
that, from Central Park to Coney Island, our people exhibit a conception of the fitting employment of
periodical leisure which would seem indecorous to a
crowd of Belleville *ouvriers*. If we have not the cad,
we certainly possess in abundance the species "hoodlum," which, though morally far more refreshing,
is yet æsthetically intolerable ; and the hoodlum is
nearly as rare in Paris as the cad. Owing to his
presence and to the atmosphere in which he thrives,
we find ourselves, in spite of the most determined
democratic convictions, shunning crowds whenever
it is possible to shun them. The most robust of us
easily get into the frame of mind of a Boston young
woman, to whom the Champs-Élysées looked like a
railway station, and who wished the people would get
up from the benches and go home. Our life becomes
a life of the interior ; wherefore, in spite of a climate
that permits walks abroad, we confine out-door existence to Newport lawns and camps in the Adiron-
dacks ; and whence proceeds that carelessness of the
exterior which subordinates architecture to "household art," and makes of our streets such mere thor-
oughfares lined with "homes."

The manners one encounters in street and shop
in Paris are, it is well known, very different from

our own.   But no praise of them ever quite prepares
an American for their agreeableness and simplicity.
We are always agreeably surprised at the absence of
elaborate manner which eulogists of French manners
in general omit to note ; and indeed it is an extremely elusive quality.   Nothing is further removed
from that intrusion of the national *gemüthlichkeit* into
so impersonal a matter as affairs, large or small,
which to an occasional sense makes the occasional
German manner enjoyable.   Nothing is farther from
the obsequiousness of the London shopman, which
rather dazes the American than pleases him.   Nothing, on the other hand, is farther from our own bald
despatch.   With us every shopper expects, or at
any rate is prepared for, obstruction rather than fa-
cilitation on the seller's side.   The drygoods counter, especially when the attendant is of the gentler
sex, is a kind of *chevaux-de-frise*.   The retail atmosphere is charged with an affectation of unconsciousness ; not only is every transaction impersonal, it is
mechanical ; ere long it must become automatic.   In
many cases there is to be encountered a certain defiant attitude to the last degree unhappy in its effects on the manners involved—a certain self-assertion which begs the question, else unmooted, of social equality, with the result for the time being of
the most unsocial relation probably existing among
men.   Perfect personal equality for the time being
invariably exists between customer and tradesman
in France ; the man or woman who serves you is first

of all a fellow-creature ; a shop, to be sure, is not a *conversazione*, but if you are in a loquacious or inquisitive mood you will be deemed neither frivolous nor familiar—nor yet an inanimate obstacle to the flow of the most important as well as the most impetuous of the currents of life.

Certainly, in New York, we are too vain of our bustle to realize how mannerless and motiveless it is. The essence of life is movement, but so is the essence of epilepsy. Moreover the life of the New Yorker who chases street-cars, eats at a lunch counter, drinks what will " take hold " quickly at a bar he can quit instantly, reads only the head-lines of his newspaper, keeps abreast of the intellectual movement by inspecting the display of the Elevated Railway news-stands while he fumes at having to wait two minutes for his train, hastily buys his tardy ticket of sidewalk speculators, and leaves the theatre as if it were on fire—the life of such a man is, notwithstanding all its futile activity, varied by long spaces of absolute mental stagnation, of moral coma. Not only is our hurry not decorous, not decent ; it is not real activity, it is as little as possible like the animated existence of Paris, where the moral nature is kept in constant operation, intense or not as the case may be, in spite of the external and material tranquillity. Owing to this lack of a real, a rational activity, our individual civilization, which seems when successful a scramble, and when unlucky a *sauve qui peut*, is, morally as well as spectacularly, not ill de-

scribed in so far as its external aspect is concerned
by the epithet *flat*.   Enervation seems to menace
those whom hyperæsthesia spares.

" We go to Europe to become Americanized,"
says Emerson, but France Americanizes us less in
this sense than any other country of Europe, and
perhaps Emerson was not thinking so much of her
democratic development into social order and efficiency as of the less American and more feudal
European influences, which do indeed, while we are
subject to them, intensify our affection for our own
institutions, our confidence in our own outlook.   One
must admit that in France (which nowadays follows
our ideal of liberty perhaps as closely as we do hers
of equality and fraternity, and where consequently
our political notions receive few shocks) not only is
the life of the senses more agreeable than it is with
us, but the mutual relations of men are more felicitous also.   And alas !   Americans who have savored
these sweets cannot avail themselves of the implication contained in Emerson's further words—words
which approach nearer to petulance than anything
in his urbane and placid utterances—" those who
prefer London or Paris to America may be spared
to return to those capitals."   " Il faut vivre, com-
battre, et finir avec les siens," says Doudan, and no
law is more inexorable.   The fruits of foreign gardens are, however delectable, enchanted for us ;
we may not touch them ; and to pass our lives in

covetous inspection of them is as barren a performance as may be imagined. For this reason the question "Should you like better to live here or abroad?"
is as little practical as it is frequent. The empty
life of the "foreign colonies" in Paris is its sufficient
answer. Not only do most of us *have* to stay at
home, but for everyone except the inconsiderable
few who can better do abroad the work they have to
do, and except those essentially un-American waifs
who can contrive no work for themselves, life abroad
is not only less profitable but less pleasant. The
American endeavoring to acclimatize himself in Paris
hardly needs to have cited to him the words of
Epictetus : "Man, thou hast forgotten thine object ;
thy journey was not *to* this, but *through* this"—he is
sure before long to become dismally persuaded of
their truth. More speedily than elsewhere perhaps,
he finds out in Paris the truth of Carlyle's assur-
ance : "It is, after all, the one unhappiness of a man.
That he cannot work ; that he cannot get his destiny
as a man fulfilled." For the work which insures the
felicity of the French life of the senses and of
French human relations he cannot share ; and, thus,
the question of the relative attractiveness of French
and American life—of Paris and New York—becomes the idle and purely speculative question as
to whether one would like to change his personal
and national identity.

And this an American may permit himself the
chauvinism of believing a less rational contradiction

of instinct in himself than it would be in the case of anyone else. And for this reason : that in those elements of life which tend to the development and perfection of the individual soul in the work of fulfilling its mysterious destiny, American character and American conditions are especially rich. Bunyan's genius exhibits its characteristic felicity in giving the name of Hopeful to the successor of that Faithful who perished in the town of Vanity. It would be a mark of that loose complacency in which we are too often offenders, to associate the scene of Faithful's martyrdom with the Europe from which definitively we set out afresh a century ago ; but it is impossible not to recognize that on our forward journey to the celestial country of national and individual success, our conspicuous inspiration and constant comforter is that hope whose cheering ministrations the " weary Titans " of Europe enjoy in far narrower measure. Living in the future has an indisputably tonic effect upon the moral sinews, and contributes an exhilaration to the spirit which no sense of attainment and achieved success can give. We are after all the true idealists of the world. Material as are the details of our preoccupation, our sub-consciousness is sustained by a general aspiration that is none the less heroic for being, perhaps, somewhat *naïf* as well. The times and moods when one's energy is excited, when something occurs in the continuous drama of life to bring sharply into relief its vivid interest and one's own intimate share

therein, when nature seems infinitely more real than
the societies she includes, when the missionary,
the pioneer, the constructive spirit is aroused, are
far more frequent with us than with other peoples.
Our intense individualism happily modified by our
equality, our constant, active, multiform struggle
with the environment, do at least, as I said, produce *men ;* and if we use the term in an esoteric
sense we at least know its significance.   Of our
riches in this respect New York alone certainly
gives no exaggerated idea—however it may otherwise epitomize and typify our national traits. A
walk on Pennsylvania Avenue ; a drive among the
" homes " of Buffalo or Detroit—or a dozen other
true centres of communal life which have a concrete
impressiveness that for the most part only great capitals in Europe possess ; a tour of college commence-
ments in scores of spots consecrated to the exaltation of the permanent over the evanescent ; contact
in any wise with the prodigious amount of right
feeling manifested in a hundred ways throughout a
country whose prosperity stimulates generous impulse, or with the number of " good fellows " of large,
shrewd, humorous views of life, critical perhaps
rather than constructive, but at all events untouched
by cynicism, perfectly competent and admirably confident, with a livelier interest in everything within
their range of vision than can be felt by anyone
mainly occupied with sensuous satisfaction, saved
from boredom by a robust imperviousness, ready to

begin life over again after every reverse with unenfeebled spirit, and finding, in the working out of their own personal salvation according to the gospel of necessity and opportunity, that joy which the pursuit of pleasure misses—experiences of every kind, in fine, that familiarize us with what is especially American in our civilization, are agreeable as no foreign experiences can be, because they are above all others animating and sustaining. Life in America has for everyone, in proportion to his seriousness, the zest that accompanies the "advance on Chaos and the Dark." Meantime, one's last word about the America emphasized by contrast with the organic and *solidaire* society of France, is that, for insuring order and efficiency to the lines of this advance, it would be difficult to conceive too gravely the utility of observing attentively the work in the modern world of the only other great nation that follows the democratic standard, and is perennially prepared to make sacrifices for ideas.

171 D